The African-Arab Conflict in the Sudan

THE AFRICAN-ARAB CONFLICT IN THE SUDAN

Dunstan M. Wai

AFRICANA PUBLISHING COMPANY
New York • London

First published in the United States of America 1981 by
Africana Publishing Company, a division of
Holmes & Meier Publishers, Inc.
30 Irving Place
New York, N.Y. 10003

Great Britain:
Holmes & Meier Publishers, Ltd.
131 Trafalgar Road
Greenwich, London SE10 9TX

Library of Congress Cataloging in Publication Data
Wai, Dunstan M
The African-Arab conflict in the Sudan.
Bibliography: p.
Includes index.
1. Sudan—History—Civil War, 1955–1972.
I. Title.
DT157.67.W34 1980 962.4'04 80–15410

ISBN 0–8419–0631–9

Manufactured in the United States of America

To my fellow countrymen
the living and the dead

Contents

ACKNOWLEDGMENTS

SOUTHERN SUDAN POLITICAL MOVEMENTS, 1953–1972

SOME PRINCIPAL ACTORS

CHRONOLOGY OF IMPORTANT EVENTS IN THE AFRICAN-ARAB CONFLICT IN THE SUDAN

INTRODUCTION

Part I.
Society and Historical Context

Chapter I.
THE AFRICAN-ARAB SCHISM
Physical Setting
Communal Cleavages
Conclusion

Chapter II.
PRECOLONIAL PERSPECTIVES
The Sudan: Before and During the Turkish Era
The Mahdiyyah and the Southern Sudan
Conclusion

Chapter III.
THE COLONIAL INTERREGNUM
The Anglo-Egyptian Imperial Occupation of the Sudan
The Southern Policy
The Abandonment of the Southern Policy
Decolonization and Preparation for Self-Government
Elections and Transfer of Power
The Pax Britannica and the Sudan: An Appraisal

Part II.
Praetorian Politics and Civil War

Chapter IV.
PARLIAMENTARY POLITICS AND AFRICAN-ARAB CONFRONTATION
Southern Reactions to the Sudanization Report
Northern Administrators and Politics in the South
The Nzara Riots

The Issue of the Southern Corps and Eruption of the Civil War
Declaration of Independence
The Federal Issue and the Search for a Constitution
The Failure of Parliamentary Politics 1956–58
Conclusion

Chapter V.
THE MILITARY REGIME OF THE GENERALS: BENEVOLENT DICTATORSHIP IN THE NORTH AND ARAB HEGEMONY IN THE SOUTH
Governmental Structure and Divisions Within the Army
The Search for Legitimacy
The Abboud Regime and the Southern Sudan
The Southern Reaction to Arab Hegemony
The Civilian Coup
Conclusion

Chapter VI.
THE SOUTHERN SUDAN QUESTION AND THE FAILURE OF THE POLITICIANS
The Transitional Government
The Khartoum Round Table Conference on the Southern Question
The Transitional Government and the Southern Sudan
The Coalition Government and North-South Relations
Divisions in the Southern Sudan Liberation Movement
The Failure of the Politicians
Conclusion

Part III.
The African-Arab Conflict in the Sudan and the International Community

Chapter VII.
EXTERNAL INVOLVEMENT
The Sudan as a Bearer of Recognized Sovereignty
Africa, the Arab World, and the Sudan War
The Attitude and the Role of the Major Powers
External Aid for the Southern Sudan
Conclusion

Chapter VIII.
FROM CONFRONTATION TO ACCOMMODATION: THE WORLD COUNCIL OF CHURCHES IN CONFLICT MEDIATION
The WCC and the AACC in Mediatory Contacts
The Nimiery Regime and the Policy of Regional Autonomy for the South
Steps Toward a Negotiated Settlement: The WCC and the AACC in an Intermediary Role
The Addis Ababa Agreement on the Problem of South Sudan

Ratification of and International Response to the Addis Ababa Agreement
Conclusion

Part IV.
Vision for the Future

Chapter IX.
TOWARD A NEW POLITICAL SYSTEM
Repatriation, Resettlement, Relief, and Rehabilitation
Military and Political Aspects
Political Integration and Federalism
Conclusion

Chapter X.
CONCLUSION

NOTES

BIBLIOGRAPHY

INDEX

Acknowledgments

I am greatly indebted to two centers of higher learning on opposite sides of the Atlantic Ocean: Oxford and Harvard. As an undergraduate in Oxford, I was introduced to the rigors of critical and logical thinking; and as a graduate student in Harvard, I was introduced to the world of knowledge and scholarship. Both institutions awarded me scholarships and I am deeply grateful to them and to those persons who made the decisions in my favor. Special thanks must also go to Dr. Peter Hacker, my tutor at Oxford, and to Professors Karl W. Deutsch, Martin L. Kilson, and Samuel P. Huntington of the Harvard Faculty, all of whom at various times were a source of insight, stimulation, counsel, and encouragement.

I must also express my deep appreciation to The Rockefeller Foundation for awarding me a Visiting Research Fellowship in the International Relations Division. I benefited tremendously in many ways during my stay with the Foundation and I am grateful to all its officers for launching the Visiting Research Fellowship program of which I was a beneficiary. Particular thanks and gratitude must go to Dr. Mason Willrich, the former Director of the International Relations Division, Dr. Edwin A. Deagle, Jr., and Dr. John J. Stremlau for all their kindness, understanding, intellectual support, encouragement, and friendship. I am also deeply appreciative of the help I received from and the friendship of the support staff of the Division, past and present: Susan Garfield, Pamela Aal, Cecilia Lotse, Karen Noonan, Jackie Bassett, Frances Herwitt, Maurren Gillen, and Maria M. Ramos. Mr. Henry Romney, the Director of the Information Services, developed a keen interest in this book and I am indebted to him for facilitating its publication.

Professors Ali A. Mazrui and Crawford Young read a completed copy of the manuscript and made a number of very valuable suggestions. I am very grateful to both of them. Linda Potter of New York City, who worked for me as a research assistant on a different project, helped me in preparing the final draft of the manuscript. I am thankful to her.

John and Carolyn Stremlau welcomed us to Roosevelt Island, New York City, and provided a companionship and friendship which my family and I deeply appreciate.

I have benefited a lot in discussing the African-Arab conflict in the Sudan with many fellow Southern Sudanese. To mention their names here would take too long, and to mention a few only would be unfairly selective. Suffice to note that without their moral support, encouragement, and commitment to the cause for self-determination, this book could not possibly have been written. The book itself is my humble contribution to human knowledge on the saliency of the conflict along the Nile Valley.

My concentration in writing this book conflicted with my family obligations. My wife, Nyakwea, was extremely understanding and tolerant. Over the years, she has stimulated and sometimes even changed my perspective on a number of issues. My largest personal debts are to her.

Southern Sudan Political Movements, 1953–1972*

Name	*Leader*
Southern Party (SP)	Benjamin Lokwe
Liberal Party (LP)	Fr. Saturnino Lohure
Federal Party (FP)	Ezibon Mondiri
Sudan African Closed Districts National Union (SACDNU)	Joseph Oduho
Sudan African National Union (SANU)	Aggrey Jaden (External Wing) William Deng (Internal Wing)
Southern Front (SP)	Clement Mboro
United Party (UP)	Santino Deng
Azania Liberation Front (ALF)	Joseph Oduho
Sudan African Liberation Front (SALF)	Aggrey Jaden
Southern Sudan Provisional Government (SSPG)	Aggrey Jaden
Nile Provisional Government (NPG)	Gordon Mayen
Sudan Azania (SA)	Ezibon Mondiri
Anyidi Revolutionary Government (ARG)	Emidio Taffeng
Sui River Republic (SRR)	Michael Tawil
Southern Sudan Liberation Movement (SSLM)	Joseph Lagu

*These movements have been listed here according to order of formation.

Some Principal Actors

Lieutenant General Ibrahim Abboud	Commander-in-Chief of the Armed Forces; President and Prime Minister, 1958–1964.
Brigadier Mohammed Idris Abdallah	Military Governor of Kassala Province and leader of Neutral Senior Army Officers who served as mediator between Army and civilian leaders of the United National Front in the people's uprising in October 1964.
Brigadier Mohieddin Ahmed Abdullah	Member, Supreme Military Council during General Abboud's regime. Amassed troops in Khartoum to pressure Abboud to include him in the Supreme Council.
Abel Alier	Lawyer; Secretary General, Southern Front; served in several cabinet posts under General Nimiery, including Ministry of Southern Affairs, Vice-President; and President of the Southern Region, HEC; leader of the Government Delegation to the Addis Ababa peace talks; a very respected Sudanese nationalist and a Southern patriot. Member, Politbureau, Sudan Socialist Union (SSU).
Luigi Adwok	Member, Executive Committee of Southern Front; Member of Parliament; Member, Supreme Council; later served as a Cabinet Minister in the Provisional HEC.
Babiker Awadalla	Chairman, National Constitutional Committee (1956); Speaker, House of Representatives, (1957–58); Chief Justice in the late 1960s; Prime Minister and Vice President under General Nimiery's regime.
Ismael el-Azhari	President, NUP; President, DUP; first Sudanese Prime Minister, 1953–1956; President of the Supreme Council.
El Nazir Dafallah	Vice Chancellor, Khartoum University; Chairman, Round Table Conference, 1965.
Santino Deng	Southern Member of Parliament; the only

	Southerner in General Abboud's Cabinet; later formed his own political party—Unity Party.
William Deng	Administrator, Secretary General, SACDNU; Secretary for Foreign Affairs, SANU under Aggrey Jaden; President, SANU (wing inside the Sudan); Member of Parliament, entered into a coalition with Sadig el-Mahdi Umma group but killed by government forces in the South following the 1968 general elections.
Camillo Dhol	Vice President, SSPG under Aggrey Jaden; Minister of Defense in the Nile Provisional Government. Died in military action in 1971.
Buth Diu	Secretary-General, Liberal Party; veteran politician; and served as Minister in several Khartoum governments.
Fr. Paulino Dogale	Roman Catholic priest in Rumbek, Lakes District. Opposed government law making Sunday a day of work and Friday a day of rest in the South in 1960. Imprisoned for treason with three Rumbek secondary school students.
Joseph Garang	Member, Politbureau of the Sudan Communist Party (the only Southerner in it); Minister of State for Southern Affairs under General Nimiery; hanged in July 1971 for his alleged role in the abortive coup of Major Hashim el-Atta.
Mading de Garang	Journalist, editor, the *Southern Sudan Curtain* based in Britain; Spokesman for the SSLM delegation to the Addis Ababa peace talks.
Imam Abdel Rahman el-Hadi	Head of the Ansars, and patron of the Umma Party. Opposed to self-rule for the South and advocated Islamization of the region. Died in 1970 following a military confrontation with government forces.
Magboul el-Amin el-Haji	Member, Supreme Council of the Armed Forces under General Abboud.
Sir Knox Helm	Last British Governor-General of the Sudan. Authorized British Airforce planes to transport Northern Sudanese Soldiers to the

	South during the uprising of August 1955. Tricked Southern soldiers to surrender, and recognized the Northern military occupation of the South.
Siricio Iro	Southern Member of Parliament; Member of Prime Minister el-Azhari's government (1954–55); Member, Supreme Council (civilian).
Aggrey Jaden	Administrator turned politician; Deputy Secretary-General, SACDNU; President, SANU (wing outside the Sudan); Vice-President, ALF; President, SALF; President, SSPG.
Sir el-Khatim el-Khalifa	Assistant Secretary for Education, South; Deputy Permanent Secretary, Ministry of Education; became Prime Minister after the successful civilian coup against the military regime of General Abboud; later Ambassador to Italy and Britain; and Minister of Higher Education under General Nimiery.
Abdulla Bey Khalil	Brigadier in the Sudan Defense Forces; Secretary-General, Umma Party; Prime Minister, 1956–1958.
Elia Kuze	Liberal Party Member of Parliament for Yambio District, Azandeland (in the Southern Region); collided with first group of Northern Sudanese administrators in his constituency.
George Kwanai	Journalist, Minister for Information, SANU (wing outside the Sudan) Vice-President, ALF.
Joseph Lagu	Colonel/Major-General, Anya-Nya Armed Forces, Supreme Commander, and leader of SSLM. Later Inspector General of the Sudan Armed Forces; Lt. General and Commander, First Battalion, Southern Region; and President of the High Executive Council (HEC) (1978–1979), Southern Region; Member of the Politbureau, SSU.
Hilary Logale	Economist and civil servant turned politician; Secretary General; Vice President, Southern Front; served in several cabinet

	positions in the Central Government; Commissioner, Equatoria Province; Regional Minister of Finance and Economic Planning; Speaker of the People's Regional Assembly; and Assistant Secretary-General (for the South), the Sudan Socialist Union. Commanded wide respect both nationally and as a dedicated Southern patriot. Member, Politbureau, SSU.
Fr. Saturnino Lohure	President, Liberal Party; Patron, SACDNU; killed by Ugandan soldiers near the Sudan-Uganda border.
Elia Lupe	Police Officer turned politician and elected Member of Parliament for Yei in 1957; served in several executive committees of Southern Sudanese movements in exile; became Minister in the Provisional HEC after the Addis Ababa Agreement.
Benjamin Lwoki	President, Liberal Party; Minister in both el-Azhari's and Bey Khalil's governments; Member of the House of Representatives and then was elected a Senator in 1957.
Sadiq el-Mahdi	Grandson of Mohammed Ahmed Mahdi, leader of the Ansars; President of the Umma Party (Sadiq Wing); Prime Minister 1966–1967; leader of the National Front opposed to the Nimiery regime. Following a reconciliation with President Nimiery, Sadiq returned to the Sudan in September 1977, after having organized an abortive coup in July 1976 against Nimiery. Supports Islamization and Arabization of the whole Sudan.
Abdel Khaliq Mahgoub	Secretary-General, Sudan Communist Party; supported regional autonomy for the South; hanged in 1971 for his alleged role in the abortive Hashim el-Atta coup.
Mohammed Ahmed Mahgoub	Umma Party politician; Foreign Minister, Prime Minister, Umma-NUP Coalition. had considerable antipathy toward the South.
Philemon Majok	Southern Member of Parliament; Member, Supreme Council (civilian).
Gordon Mayen	Police Officer turned politician; Member,

	Executive Committee, Southern Front; President, Nile Provisional Government. Refused to return home after Addis Ababa Agreement.
Elijah Mayom	Southern Member of Parliament; President, Liberal Party.
Clement Mboro	Administrator turned politician; President, Southern Front; Minister of Interior under Sir el-Khatim el-Khalifa; Speaker, Peoples Regional Assembly (1978–1979).
Ezibon Mondiri	Southern Member of Parliament; President, Federal Party; jailed by the Abboud regime; Minister of Communications under Sir el-Kahtim el-Khalifa; ALF Secretary for Defense; President, Sudan Azania. Leader of the SSLM delegation to the Addis Ababa peace talks.
Hassan Beshir Nasr	Brigadier/Major-General; Deputy to Lt. Gen. Abboud in the Army Command; Minister of Cabinet Affairs. Opposed to peaceful solution of the Southern problem. He was also opposed to the Army relinquishment of power following the people's uprising in October 1964.
Gaafar Mohammed el-Nimiery	Major-General and Commander-in-Chief of the Sudan Armed Forces; leader of the May coup (1969) and Chairman of the Revolutionary Command Council; President and Chairman of the Sudan Socialist Union; pronounced a policy of regional autonomy for the Southern region and carried it through to its implementation.
Joseph Oduho	Southern Member of Parliament; President SACDNU, ALF and served in The High Executive Council (HEC).
Stanislaus Paysama	Southern Member of Parliament; Vice-President, Liberal Party.
Philip Pedak	Executive Member of SACDNU; Vice-President SANU (outside wing); joined many of the political movements representing the South.
Basai Renzi	Chief of Tembura, Yambio District; sent a letter to the Governor-General protesting

	alleged telegram and way in which signatures supporting the government had been obtained from his area. Supported his Member of Parliament, Elia Kuze who was being harassed by the Arab administration.
Bona Malwal Ring	Journalist by training; Editor, *Vigilant* (a Southern Front [SF] newspaper); Member, Executive, SF; served as Minister of Information and Culture, Central Government Prominent and respected politician.
Marko Rume	Southern Member of Parliament; Vice-President, SACDNU, NPG; Member, Peoples National Assembly.
Emidio Taffeng	Non-commissioned officer in the Southern Command, Sudan Defense Force; imprisoned for his alleged role in the 1955 Southern uprising; joined the Anya-Nya Forces as Commander-in-Chief; President of the "Anyidi Revolutionary Government."
Hassan el-Turabi	Leader of the Islamic Charter Front; supported Islamization and Arabization of the Southern Region.
Ahmed Abdal al-Wahhab	Major-General; son-in-law of Bey Khalil; second in command to General Abboud at the time of their coup; Minister of Defense for a year.
Lawrence Wol Wol	Representative of SSLM in Europe and based in France; Secretary of the SSLM delegation to the Addis Ababa peace talks; and later became a Minister in the Central and Regional Governments.
Ahmad Mohammed Yassin	Judge; Chairman of Inquiry into the Southern Sudan Disturbances, 1955.

Chronology of Important Events in the African-Arab Conflict in the Sudan

1822–	Northern Sudan conquered by Pasha of Egypt. Turko-Egyptian rule firmly established in the North only. Abortive attempts to extend sovereignty over Southern Sudan.
1881–	Successful revolt against foreign rule in the Northern Sudan led by Mohammed Ahmed El Malidi.
1881–1899	Unsuccessful attempts by Mahdists to establish their rule in the South.
1899–	Conquest of Northern and Southern Sudan by Anglo-Egyptian campaign under Lord Kitchener. Joint rule by Britain and Egypt under Condominium Agreement. Britain to appoint Governor-General.
1924–	Abortive uprising in Khartoum by both Northern and Southern Sudanese against Condominium rule.
1930–	Announcement of Southern Sudan Policy by Civil Secretary of the Sudan.
1940–	Almost complete elimination of Arab and Moslem influence in the South.
1945–	Agitation against Southern Policy by Northern Sudanese notables and politicians (particularly members of the Graduate Congress).
1946–	Civil-Secretary decided that North and South were inextricably bound together. Reversal of Southern Policy of 1930. Protests against the new policy by British governors and administrators in the Southern Sudan.
1947–	Juba conference of North and South representatives, chiefs, prominent Arabs and British officials to discuss new Southern policy. The Civil-Secretary wanted to allay the fears of his administrative officers in the South, and to gain support for his

	unilateral decision to reverse the 1930 Southern policy.
1948–	Creation of a Legislative Assembly in Khartoum—thirteen representatives from the South out of a total of ninety-three members. Relaxation of movement between North and South, and unification of educational system.
1951–	Appointment by the Governor-General of a Constitutional Commission composed of thirteen members (only one from the South) with a judge of the British High Court as chairman. The Southern member proposed a federal arrangement between the North and the South. Rejection of any safeguards for the South by Northern representatives.
1952–	Cairo Conference attended by Northern political parties. British and Egyptian representatives to discuss the nature of self-government for the Sudan. No Southern representation in this conference.
1953, February	Anglo-Egyptian Agreement. Recognition by Egypt for the first time of the right of the Sudanese to self-determination. Both Britain and Egypt agreed to liquidate Condominium Agreement.
1954, January	First Sudanese Parliament opened.
February	Sudanization Committee of three Arabs and two Britons set up.
October	Names of Sudanese administrators to replace Britons announced. No Southerners included on claims of none sufficiently qualified.
December	Formation of the Southern Liberal Party.
1955, June	Liberal Party Conference in Juba, preceded by a tour of the South by Southern MPs and some Northern MPs from the Umma opposition party, and a visit to the South by Prime Minister Ismael el-Azhari who was booed wherever he went.
July	The trial of Elia Kuze, the Liberal Party Member of Parliament, opened in Yambio. He was charged with criminal intimidation and was sentenced to twenty years imprisonment. Demonstration against the sentence and riots with the police.

August	Workers strike and riots in Nzara, Yambio District. Uprising in the South against Northern rule.
December	Sudan Parliament voted unanimously for independence. Northern Parties and Government promised to consider federation as a solution to the Southern problem.
1956, January	The Sudan became an independent state.
September	Appointment by Parliament of a National Constitutional Committee (forty-three Northerners and three Southerners). Rejection of a Federal arrangement by Northerners, and withdrawal of Southerners from the Committee.
1957, April	Government take-over of all mission schools in the South.
1958, November	Military coup led by Lt. General Ibrahim Aboud. Suspension of provisional constitution and dismissal of Parliament.
1960, January	Imposition of Friday as day of rest and Sunday of work in the South. Student strikes against the policy throughout the South.
February	Formation in exile of a Southern political organization, the Sudan African Closed Districts National Union (SACDNU).
1962, May	Enactment of "The Missionary Societies Act."
September	Strikes in Rumbek secondary and Juba commercial schools in protest against government policies of Arabization and Islamization in the South.
November	Beginning of expulsion of missionaries from the South, allegedly for interfering in politics.
November/ December	Regrouping of soldiers of the old Southern corps and preparation for attacks against Northern troops.
1963, September	Launching of the Anya-Nya guerrilla movement and declaration of total war against Northern troops in the South.
1964, February	Expulsion of all missionaries from the South.
September	Appointment by General Abboud of a Commission of Inquiry to study the factors which hindered harmony between the North and the South.
1964, October	Public debate in Khartoum University on the

	Southern problem triggered a series of events that led to the fall of Abboud's military dictatorship. Appointment of a Provisional Government headed by Sir el-Khatim el-Khalifa. A Southerner, Clement Mboro was appointed Minister of Interior. Return to party politics.
December	Clash between Northerners and Southerners at Khartoum airport. The riots spread to the city. Confrontation caused by a delay in Clement Mboro's plane return from the South.
1965, March	Round Table Conference on the problem of the Southern Sudan, with representatives of Southern and Northern parties and observers from seven African and Arab countries. Failure of the Conference to produce a settlement.
July	Massacre of innocent civilians by Northern troops in Juba and Wau. Escalation of war in the South.
August	Ultimatum by Prime Minister Mohammed Ahmed Mahgoub to Anya-Nya to lay down arms and surrender. He also appealed to the Pope to tell Southerners to lay down arms.
1965, November	Prime Minister claimed war had ended in Bahr el Ghazal and Upper Nile provinces of the South, and opposed the work of the Twelve-Man Committee appointed by the Round Table Conference to explore areas of constitutional compromise between North and South.
1966, January	Increase in reports on the Sudan war in British press, for example, the *Daily Mail.*
February	Northern Sudanese Minister of Interior warned of imperialist infiltration to South. Warned that Southern "traitors" would be killed. Prime Minister blamed professional "religionists" for trouble in the South, and attacked churches.
May	Prime Minister claimed Anya-Nya did not represent the South. Government in Khartoum rejected recommendations of the Twelve-Man Committee.
1967, January	Massacre of more than four-hundred people in six villages near Torit. Use of Air Force bombing.
March	Failure to hold elections in the South.
1968, April–May	Elections held in Government-secured areas, mainly in towns of the South. Assassination of

	William Deng, a prominent Southern politician by Government troops near Rumbek.
November	Intensification of campaign of destruction in the South by Government forces.
1969, May	A successful coup led by Colonel Gaafar Mohammed el-Nimiery.
June	Declaration of policy of Regional Autonomy for the Southern Provinces. This was immediately followed by creation of a ministry of state for Southern affairs.
September	Visit to the Sudan by a delegation of Southern Sudanese students at Makerere University (Uganda) to ascertain the sincerity and popularity of the policy of Regional Autonomy. The delegation also sought to reopen communication between Southerners inside and outside the Sudan.
December	Visit to Makerere University, Uganda, by Abel Alier on invitation of the Students Guild at the request of the Southern Sudanese Students Union at Makerere. Alier made contacts with Southern politicians in exile.
1970, November	The Southern Student organization in Khartoum University criticized the Nimiery regime in a memorandum to the President for dragging its feet in implementing the policy of Regional Autonomy. The war against the Anya-Nya continued in intensity. Dismissal of three members of the Revolutionary Command Council.
1971, February	Tour of Western Europe by Abel Alier. He met church leaders, Southern exiles, and representatives of the Anya-Nya, and heads of charitable organizations and he also called on the Pope. This trip impressed upon concerned groups the search for peace in the Sudan.
May	A joint delegation of the World Council of Churches (WCC) and the All Africa Conference of Churches (AACC) flew to the Sudan to explore ways toward reconciliation.
June	The WCC began approaches to representatives of the Southern Sudan Liberation Movement (SSLM) in Europe about possibilities of North-South peace talks.

	July	Abortive coup led by leftist officers. General Nimiery lost power for seventy-two hours. Execution of Joseph Garang, a Southern Communist along with his comrades for their role in the abortive coup. Appointment of Abel Alier as Minister of Southern Affairs and Vice President.
	November	Preliminary talks in Addis Ababa, Ethopia, between SSLM and Sudan Government representatives.
1972,	February	Formal peace negotiations began between Sudan and SSLM representatives in Addis Ababa. The successful talks culminated in *The Addis Ababa Agreement on the Problem of the South Sudan*. The Sudan Government delegation was led by Vice-President Abel Alier and the SSLM was headed by Ezibon Mondiri.
	March	Ratification of the Peace Accord.

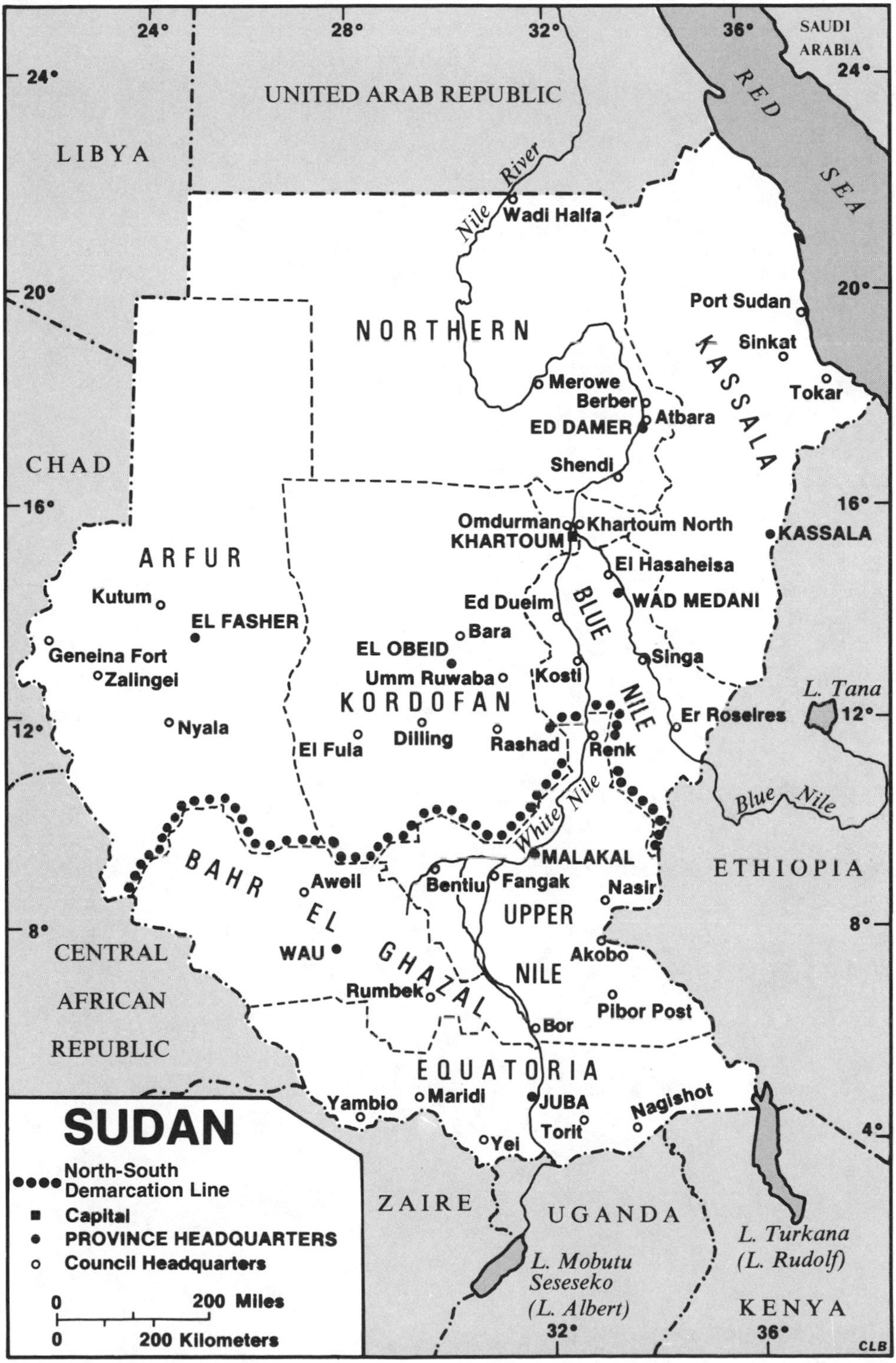

SUDAN
North-South Demarcation Line
Capital
PROVINCE HEADQUARTERS
Council Headquarters
0 200 Miles
0 200 Kilometers
UNITED ARAB REPUBLIC
LIBYA
CHAD
CENTRAL AFRICAN REPUBLIC
ZAIRE
UGANDA
KENYA
ETHIOPIA
SAUDI ARABIA
RED SEA
NORTHERN
KASSALA
ARFUR
KORDOFAN
BLUE NILE
BAHR EL GHAZAL
UPPER NILE
EQUATORIA
Nile River
White Nile
Blue Nile
L. Tana
L. Turkana (L. Rudolf)
L. Mobutu Sesesko (L. Albert)
Wadi Halfa
Port Sudan
Sinkat
Tokar
Merowe
Berber
Atbara
ED DAMER
Shendi
Omdurman
Khartoum North
KHARTOUM
KASSALA
El Hasaheisa
WAD MEDANI
Ed Dueim
Bara
EL OBEID
Umm Ruwaba
Kosti
Singa
Er Roseires
Kutum
EL FASHER
Geneina Fort
Zalingei
Nyala
El Fula
Dilling
Rashad
Renk
MALAKAL
Aweil
Bentiu
Fangak
Nasir
WAU
Akobo
Rumbek
Pibor Post
Bor
Yambio
Maridi
JUBA
Torit
Nagishot
Yei
24°
28°
32°
36°
20°
16°
12°
8°
4°
CLB

Introduction

The prevalence of communal conflicts in Africa, and indeed, in the world at large, is not a revelation. What is lacking is a clear differentiation between such conflicts, and a critical examination of some of those cases which defy comparison.

The African-Arab confrontation along the Nile Valley is a case in point. In essence, it is a conflict of nationalism: One rooted in Africanism and the other in Arabism. It is not a mere case of ethnicity. The Northern Sudanese view themselves as Arabs and whether their Arabness is more by acquisition than heredity is of less importance. Whereas the Southern Sudanese feel themselves to be authentically Negroid Africans in every way. We see here two identities with differing perspectives on the universe.

Imperial Britain recognized the differences between the two collectivities within the area it named the Anglo-Egyptian Sudan: Arab and Muslim in the North, and African and "pagan" in the South.[1] Colonial common sense dictated that two separate administrations must be set up for two regions, which were two distinct worlds culturally, racially, as well as geographically. Such differences were reinforced by historical hostilities and mutual distrust.

The imperial regime decided to keep the South as a human zoo and to concentrate economic and educational development in the North. Subsequently, British interests dictated on the eve of imperial withdrawal that the two regions should be united administratively and that political power should be handed to the Arabs. The Southern Sudanese were deliberately excluded from the constitutional negotiations preceding independence, while the Northern Sudanese were effectively represented. The North pleaded for its right to self-determination and was fully involved in determining the nature of the political arrangement that would sanctify its sovereign rights in the international community of mankind; the South was not considered fit to participate in discussions which were meant to shape its destiny as well.

It was, therefore, not surprising that the South resorted to violence to protest the change of colonial rulers, from the British to the Arabs, which took place without their consent. It took to arms in the transitional period with the hope that imperial Britain would review the situation and allow it to exercise its right to self-determination. The British were not about to retreat from their agreement with the Northern Sudanese and the Egyptians, who were a junior colonial partner in the Sudan. Indeed, they intervened militarily to help the North subdue the South and establish its hegemony over the region.

For the Southern Sudanese, the end of British colonialism in their land meant the beginning of Arab domination and colonialism. That was unacceptable and needed to be challenged in order to preserve Southern Sudanese identity and to gain their self-determination. For the Northern Sudanese, the British withdrawal meant assumption of political power and it also meant gaining of sovereign status by the Sudan which, in their view, included the South as well. Any challenge to the political and constitutional arrangements worked out with the departing imperial power by any group, such as the Southern Sudanese, was viewed by the North as treason.

The Southern Sudanese were willing to compromise in settling for autonomous status within the framework of one Sudan. But the Northern Sudanese political elites of the time were not prepared for such an arrangement, infringing on their ability to dominate the South. Hence, armed conflict continued for seventeen years until the point of a military stalemate was reached, at which time both parties agreed to negotiate. The talks resulted in the granting of self-rule to the South within a united Sudan.

The Sudanese war helps us to make a distinction between political conflicts inherent in the coexistence of diverse racial, ethnic, and cultural groups within a single state in which all of them participated in forming on the eve of the colonial withdrawal, and those conflicts in which one of the parties contests the legitimacy of the sovereignty that it is supposed to enjoy. In both situations the aggrieved group may evoke the right to self-determination, and indeed, the distinction between the two types of conflict may be blurred by the tragedy of violence committed along the structural lines of pluralism and by the cultural biases of propaganda. Nevertheless, in making this distinction here, it is asserted that the sources of motivation for the emergence of cultural loyalty as a medium for political secession can be differentiated along a broad continuum. As I shall show in the following study of the Sudan, the conflict there was not simply a war arising out of hostilities which are generated through the evocation and manipulation of ethnic sentiments by elites competing for power at the national level. It was deeper than that in that it essentially arose from the dynamics of direct interaction between peoples of different cultures and races as experienced through the perceptual prism of their respective heritages and value systems, coupled with the history of antagonism and distrust. The conflict raised questions about the dynamics of secession: its sources, processes and outcome; and about the conventional norms of territorial integrity and the principle of state sovereignty. Specifically, what are the sources of political secession? What kinds of historical, political, economic as well as social issues become translated into secessionist or system rationalizing issues? Why does an African political system, in particular the Sudan, fail to

Empire's glory. The revival of such an anachronistic concept to describe a modern civil war indicates the extent to which historical hostilities have survived, at least at the psychological level, in Nigeria.

In the African context, colonial policies reinforced long-standing historical animosities among some groups. For instance, the British indirect rule philosophy rested on the maintenance and enhancement of native authority. It also meant keeping the components of the colonial territory apart. For instance the situation in the Sudan under the British paralleled that of Nigeria: differential treatment of the various segments of a colonial territorial unit.

Historical hostilities among a culturally diverse people and differential colonial treatment of many components of a presumed territorial entity constitute major obstacles to both horizontal and vertical integration. In the Sudan, such problems of history have not enhanced the formation of a national identity which edifies rather than destroys the natural world views of disparate social elements.[8] But the Sudanese conflict also found its source in the more immediate and overt issues of psychological fears and relative socioeconomic deprivation.

Emphasis on centrality of psychological factors in the causation of civil violence has dominated more contemporary theoretical explanations of communal conflicts. The basic psychological assumption is that wars begin in the minds of man, and that they occur primarily as a response to frustration which is defined as an interference with goal-directed behavior. It is argued that the disposition to respond aggressively when frustrated is part of man's biological make-up, and that there is an innate tendency to attack the frustrating agent. That is, perception of frustration arouses anger, which in turn functions as a drive.

A frustrating situation arises when a group of people is thwarted in attempts to attain, or continue enjoyment of, a value. A group may be identified as being frustrated only when it is aware of interference by another. This awareness is equivalent to the concept of relative deprivation. Concomitantly, the more severe the relative deprivation, the greater the likelihood and intensity of communal violence.

The underlying reality in the African-Arab situation in the Sudan tended to support psychological fear as a cause of civil violence. For in a culturally plural society like the Sudanese one where reciprocal and relentless suspicion permeates all levels of human relations, psychological apprehension by one of the groups will rarely fail to provoke violence.

Nevertheless, the mere existence of fear and hostilities need not give rise to wars. Human beings and societies have a capacity for tolerating a certain level of frustration, fear, and anger. Aggressive actions are often inhibited by a number of factors: for example, in the case of social groups, the expected consequence of aggression on the group members will be weighed, and when the consequences are likely to be adverse, the strength of aroused aggression may be reduced. Judging the expected consequences of aggres-

manage dysfunctional issues and conflicts short of secessionist claims? Is this failure due to the intrinsic nature of a certain system—factionalizing issues in African politics (for instance the large role of ethnicity in the definition of disintegrative issues), or is this failure due to manifestation of a wide range of problems inherent in the development process or practices in African politics and the inability of the governments to provide effective solutions for the problems? Are the secessionist conflicts related to or connected with the political administrative behaviors of African sociopolitical leaders, or are these conflicts externally engineered? What forms do secessionist movements take, and how do challenged regimes attempt to contain them?

Political secession is here defined as the desire of a group of disenchanted people to break away from the state to which they presently belong or are supposed to belong, and who wish to establish a new state or to integrate with another state of their choice. Secessionist demands may not, however, necessarily lead to the independence of the group or its integration with another sovereign state, but they may lead to a redefinition of the association on the basis of equal treatment and respect within the same state. It is systemic frustration with the established order which prompts demands for secession. There are at least four conditions that lead directly to systemic frustration and to subsequent attempts at secession: (1) cultural pluralism and value incompatibilities; (2) historical and mutual distrust; (3) relative social and economic deprivation and psychological fears; and (4) right to self-determination.

Cultural pluralism consists of the coexistence within a single society of groups possessing diverse institutional systems. It differs from mere cultural heterogeneity. Most societies display differences of occupation, stratification, and even ethnicity, but a society is truly culturally plural only when there is "a formal diversity in the basic system of compulsory institutions."[2] Such a society may be dominated by one of the cultural groups. As Smith describes it,

> pluralism is a condition in which members of a common society are internally distinguished by fundamental differences in their institutional practice. Where present, such differences are not distributed at random; they normally cluster, and by their clusters they simultaneously identify institutionally distinct aggregates or groups, and establish deep social divisions between them. The prevalence of such systematic disassociation between the members of institutionally distinct collectivities within a single society constitutes pluralism. Thus pluralism simultaneously connotes a social structure characterized by fundamental discontinuities and cleavages, and a cultural complex based on systematic institutional diversity.[3]

The notion of cultural pluralism as delineated by Smith has three distinct characteristics. First, the differentiated groups tend to form a closed sociocultural unit because any institutional system tends toward internal integration and consistency. Second, "where culturally divergent groups together form a common society, the structural imperative for maintenance of this inclusive unit involves a type of political order in which one of these cultural sections is subordinated to the other. Such a condition derives from the structural requisites of society on the one hand and the condition of wide cultural differences within some populations on the other.''[4] Third, plural societies are defined by dissent and are pregnant with conflict. For there is a high probability that in a situation of fragile social, economic, and political institutions, the greater the degree of cultural pluralism, the greater the competition between the value systems, and hence, the greater the chance for communal conflict and social disintegration.

In the African context, the existence of culturally diverse groups of people in most states is more often than not depicted as the salient destabilizing element in Africa's quest for nation-building. The dysfunctionality of cultural pluralism results from the clear dichotomy between primordial sentiments (ethnicity) and civil ties (territorial national identity). Cultural pluralism expressed in terms of ethnicity is inherently a centrifugal force. The danger of ethnic discontent poses a serious threat to both national unity and nation-building. A sense of ''political dismemberment'' leads to systemic frustration and subsequently to communal violence. Cultural pluralism in Africa, then, is potentially capable of generating an intensity of identification which can eclipse all other issues. Indeed, it can absorb other conflicts and translate them into communal hostility. Racial and ethnic consciousness, facilitated by its extreme visibility, creates its own stereotypes of cultural differentiation. Religion, ''by positing a divine or supernatural imperative for communal identity, removes differentiation from the plane of human rationality or debate. Conflict can become invested with a mandate from heaven and be pursued as a holy duty.''[5] The saliency of racial, or ethnic and cultural distinctiveness, ''assures a daily reinforcement of identity with the group of which one is a member and its uniqueness with regard to other groups.''[6] The desire by public leaders to preserve and protect the values of their respective collectivities poses enormous problems.

Apparently, the European colonial withdrawal marked an important turning point in interracial (as in the case of the Sudan) and interethnic relations (as in the case of Nigeria). It meant that after independence, as the racial and ethnic collectivities struggled for power, they no longer operated within the same limitations as they had in previous times during the colonial period. In other words, the external restraining and cushioning force had now disappeared and such new countervailing factors as central strength, sense of common history and transnational identities and aspirations were all too often incapable of dealing with the new strains. Nigerian experience points up the siginificance of such a change. In Nigeria, imperial Britain prevented a North-South split in the Federal Council of Ministers in 1953 by calling for a redrafting of the constitution. However, in the crisis of 1966, there was no comparable external force to intervene. Post-independence

politics in Africa has increased rather than decreased ir
interethnic conflicts, some of which have now come into the

Cultural pluralism as a disruptive force in nation-buildi
however, be overemphasized. For communal conflict is r
simply by the clashing of differing values. Indeed, race, or etl
may neither be an integrative nor disruptive force, but its ma
individuals or groups for power and privilege leads to these soc
Most of the conflicts generally begin at the elite level among th
the various groups that are ''culturally westernized,'' that i
strata which has engaged in a greater amount of social contact.
sion of traditionality among the elites does not entail the di
ethnicity. Elite competitions for political power and economic
usually translated into ethnic grievances and rivalries:

> The sentiments and emotions associated with ethnic identificatic
> flate the importance of cultural distinctions and, when they surf
> the politico-economic conflict that emerges more profound and
> ethnic issues are often, though not the fundamental cause of
> structural lines on which the struggle is organized and expres
> distinctions can be superimposed upon ethnic labels and thereby c
> initial cause of the conflict. It is not always easy, therefore, to dis
> cause of violent behavior by the context in which it is expressed an
> takes.[7]

Racial or ethnic conflicts generally vary with conditions
cultural differences. Particularly in the Sudanese case, cultural
racial differences between the Arabized and Arab Northerner
African Southerners were not the only factors that led to system
tions of the latter. Other than primordialities, factors such as
hostilities and mutual distrust, psychological elements and the rig
determination deserve more scrutiny and analysis.

Although many racial and ethnic entities survived the colonial
tact, it was clear that many territorial units in Africa housed inhe
tagonistic components. Independence did not succeed in allevi
conflict-laden atmosphere among some groups, but instead ten
high and often exploded. Clearly the most violent internal conflicts
curred in countries where hostile factions have interacted for deca
to colonization. The historical hostility between Northern Arab
and Southern Negroid Africans in the Sudan, for instance, dates
their violent encounters of the precolonial era which fermented ir
year ''cease-fire'' during the period of British colonial rule and re
itself in the form of a modern civil war (1955–1972).

Similarly, in the nineteenth century, Nigeria was an area of religic
between militant and fanatic Moslem empire-builders (including th
and Hausa) and well-entrenched ethnic groups, principally the Yoru
the Ibo. The Nigerian-Biafra conflict was often characterized in
propaganda as another oppressive jihad waged in the memory of the

sion implies a knowledge of the situation, the ability to assess fairly accurately the counterreaction potential of the target of aggression—the out-group—and a careful evaluation of the likelihood of approval or disapproval of aggressive action by other important social groups. Of course, in politics all these are tantamount to political awareness. It is certain that, because of these inhibitory factors, interethnic group hostilities do not always result in civil wars in the majority of African states. Moreover, the cues in all situations do not facilitate the expression of aggression overtly.

Generally, aggression is unleashed only when frustrations truly become intolerable and conditions are not expected to improve in the future without a confrontation with the sources of frustrations. In the case of the Sudan, a series of serious mistakes by the Northern Arab policymakers led to the breakdown of the frustration tolerance of the Southern Sudanese. Their policies, which were seen to thwart the need for protection, self-preservation and economic welfare of the Southern Sudanese were the immediate precipitants of the civil war in August 1955. In other words, psychological apprehension resulting from an unremitting and manifest sense of injustice and victimization can lead to deployment of extraconstitutional means to remedy the situation.

One of the most persistent issues in communal conflicts is the right to self-determination. A demand by an aggrieved group within a polity for such a right may become a source of conflict with the established order. But before a group of people makes the demand for the right to self-determination and to political secession, it must believe in the existence of at least five conditions. First, they must believe that the security of their lives and property cannot be maintained if they are subject to control of a government as it is constituted. Second, they must believe that peaceful and orderly processes of negotiation which aim at the reestablishment of a workable pattern of political relationships between them and the rest of the country have been effectively frustrated and suspended by the government and could not fruitfully be resumed. Third, they must believe that secession is widely recognized throughout the country as a politically legitimate step, and would be acquiesced to, if not actually supported and/or initiated by, the rest of the country. Fourth, they have to believe that the move to independence has overwhelming popular support in their area of domain. Fifth, they must also believe that they did not exercise their rights to self-determination at the time of their country's independence in that they were not involved in the negotiations prior to political independence. The last point was embraced by many Southern Sudanese leaders. The third condition would apply to Biafra, where it was believed that declaration of secession would be supported and followed by other regions, particularly the Western region. The first, second, and fourth conditions would apply to the Biafrans, the Southern Sudanese, the Eritreans, and the Moslem Chadians.

It must, however, be remembered also that the presupposition of strife and communal conflicts within nation-states is not of itself a consequence of the evocation of the principle of self-determination, but the reflection of a desire to resist it. For, indeed, if the states involved are prepared to accept a result based on self-determination, then there is no reason to presuppose that violence will ensue, no more than it did over the British-administered Togoland in 1956 or the Cameroons in 1961. Hence, both the demand for and the denial of the right to self-determination can provoke civil violence.

But the potentially divisive factors of cultural pluralism, hostilities, psychological fears and relative deprivation, and the right to self-determination are not in themselves sufficient to cause eruption of violence. For it is possible to find a community within a polity frustrated and discontented, but it may not engage in violent activities as a means to bring about a change of policies. It is therefore necessary to locate additional determinants that serve to increase or decrease the likelihood of communal conflicts and secessionist movements. The Sudanese experience brings to the open issues of legitimacy of a regime, governmental ineptitude and closed channels for expression of dissent, ideology and external actors, and crisis of leadership.

The Southern Sudanese did not feel that any Khartoum government in the North had a legitimate right to rule them. They resented the manner and the fact of being handed over by the British to their traditional enemies. Moreover, the monopoly of political power by the North confirmed to them the beginning of a second colonial era. On the other hand, the North felt that it had the legitimate right to formulate and carry out policies which would affect the entire country. The failure of the Northern Sudanese politicians to share political power with political elites from the South continually reinforced a feeling of alienation by the South and the belief that the North was, in essence, a colonial successor to Britain. Also, attempts to coerce the South into the Northern fold worsened rather than benefited the perception of Khartoum governments as illegitimate, ultimately leading to armed rebellion.

The resort to extraconstitutional means by the Southern region to challenge the perceived illegitimate rule by what it considered to be a racially and culturally alien group was facilitated by the ineptitude and lack of responsiveness of Khartoum governments. Absence of channels for the legitimate expression of discontent and for the peaceful mediation and settlement of Southern grievances, coupled with application of coercion by successive governments on the disenchanted Southern political elites, led to violent confrontation along the Nile Valley. The frustrated, disaffected, and injured Negroid Africans challenged the Arab hegemony over them.

The intransigence and ineptitude of Northern regimes became the foci of conflict in the Sudan as grievances increasingly became more acute, and as the discrepancies between governmental policy and the Southern conceptions of minimal and adequate welfare increased. The situation was made worse by lack of a unifying ideology between the Southern and Northern Sudanese elites. The Northern ideological orientations were Arab-rooted while those of the Southerners were African-rooted. In other words, whereas the Northerners looked to Cairo and Riyadh, the Southerners were inclined to look to Dar es Salaam and Nairobi for ideological inspiration and empathy. The members of the Arab league saw the Sudan as strategically important for their penetration into black Africa, and therefore continually gave moral as well as material and military support to the North to carry out the war against the Southern Sudan. The potential external support was obvious to the North but less so to the South. However, the Southern political and military elites thought in 1955 that an uprising against the infant Khartoum government would prompt the British to intervene and review the political arrangement it had worked out with the North and Egypt for the Sudan. Indeed, the British did intervene, but to help the North, not the South. Although external actors were not an important factor at the time of the eruption of violence in the Sudan, there are at least two reasons why they would help precipitate or intervene in a communal conflict. They do it either for purely ideological reasons explained in terms of national interest, or to counter the expanding influence of an opponent in the international scene. The two reasons are, of course, related and overlapping.

It is not always the case that conflict-laden situations explode into violence, particularly in situations where there is shrewd and effective leadership. The Sudan in its two decades of independence has unfortunately produced more than its share of squalidly bickering politicians, pervasive corruption of the administrative process, paralysis of the economy by self-interested power groups, floundering of development programs, and general privatization of public purposes. All these negative results, coupled with public divisiveness within the power elites, intolerably strained the fragile unity of the country. Hitherto, the inability of the governments to satisfy expectations which the political elites encouraged led to widespread disaffection and overall frustration. In the North where power rests, the party members became the worst peddlers of sectarianism, and the divisions among them robbed the country of a stable leadership. Their insensitivity to Southern grievances augmented the growing animosity of the South toward the North.

The sources of conflict we have tried to isolate and analyze in the preceding pages do not necessarily form an exhaustive list; they are all overlapping. For instance, social factors are based directly on economic conditions and social and political instability are conversely related (however, it is intellectually profitable to differentiate them here as part of our search for an explanatory typology of communal conflict and political secession).[9] As the African-Arab conflict in the Sudan will reveal in the case study to follow, when differences of race and culture coincide with sharp economic inequalities, and are coupled with historical hostilities, psychological fears and crisis of leadership, they can produce conflict of the most intense sort—civil and/or secessionist war. Lack of viable political institutions also exacerbate rather than reduce the likelihood of communal violence.

There are many reasons why the Southern Sudan has been singled out as the main example of our study of secessionist movements. First, it is my contention that the problems between the African-Arab peoples in the Sudan are not really typical of other African countries, and therefore cannot be compared to other segments of the total African pattern. The conflict in the Sudan was unique by its nature, intensity, and the manner in which it was resolved. Second, the Sudan war has been so far the longest one in independent Africa's experience, going on for a period of seventeen years. Third, to the extent that the Sudanese conflict was in part a secessionist war, it raised questions about African collective policies, and African nation-state systems. To what extent do African states follow a common policy toward the problems of secession? What is the basis of this commonality? Should nation and state approximate more evenly than they sometimes do? Should the principle of state sovereignty remain unchallenged in situations of acute cleavage between different national traditions within a single juridical entity? Was the principle of "non-interference in internal affairs" a bizarre curtain behind which governments could commit atrocities with impunity? To what extent does the Organization of African Unity (OAU) contribute to constructive solutions to the secessionist problems? What problems does the Sudan or African experience in general pose for the international community if it is to play a more active role in seeking to mitigate such conflicts and facilitate their solution through peaceful means? What is it that an international agency or a transnational actor should do in the case of such disputes? Should its primary concern be with the procedures for resolving the issues, or should it be with the substantive character of the solutions? In other words, should it be concerned primarily with promoting peaceful agreement among the competing parties regardless of the particular substantive content which such agreements may have, or should it be concerned with defining certain substantive conditions which solutions must meet? Or perhaps, should it do nothing and leave the competing parties alone to resolve their disputes? Fourth, the African states did not give any support to their fellow black Africans in the Southern Sudan while the Arab states wholly backed the Northern Sudanese Arabs. Fifth, the war in the Sudan was resolved through the mediation of a transnational actor, namely, the World Council of Churches, rather than by the OAU as one would have expected. Sixth, both disputants, the North and the South, made major concessions in the peace agreement. This is unique in that other secessionist movements in Africa were defeated militarily and gained nothing from their struggle.

For independent Africa, the manner in which the African-Arab war in the Sudan ended might be the beginning of a new era in the peaceful settlement of African conflicts in that the significance and the success of the peace agreement lie in the fact that it might serve as an example for other countries experiencing similar problems of territorial unity, to create an order in which racial, ethnic, cultural, and regional identities might coexist in harmony with national interests and needs as a new national entity emerges. On the other hand, both regional and international world organizations might see the Sudanese peace agreement and accommodation as a positive contribution to the principles of peace, security, and order. It is also possible that Africa and the world may learn nothing from it.

The crucial problem in independent Africa is conflict regulation in the quest for nation-building. No regime can endure which does not cope with this problem, for conflict regulation is central to the building and functioning of political institutions. The escalation of cultural or regional conflicts and tensions to the extreme level of crisis is the main cause of secessionist politics in Africa. And whereas political integration and national unity are important, they must not be seen as ends in themselves. They must include a recognition of legitimate human rights which also safeguard the basic rights of ethnic minorities. The growing interdependence of men and nations requires that no political struggle which leads to armed conflict is merely domestic. For "the international community has seen too much of the havoc which the internal politics of a state can inflict on the world beyond its borders, and too much of the inhumanity which may be perpetrated within its borders under the aegis of national sovereignty, to regard all situations of internal conflict as beyond its ken."[10] Hence, our concern in this study will include analysis of the international implications of secessionist politics in Africa.

This study is organized and divided into four parts. In Part I, an attempt is made to describe and analyze the sharp cleavages between Africanism and Arabism, the nature and characteristics of the precolonial relationships between the North and the South, the colonial experiences of the two areas, their differential treatment by the colonial regime; their eventual administrative unification on the eve of decolonization; and the subsequent ugly and agonizing confrontation between them. The praetorian nature of politics in the independent Sudan and the pattern of the Civil War form the basis of Part II. This section discusses in detail the inability of the Khartoum government to respond to the basic grievances of the Southern region, the closure of channels for expression of open dissent, lack of strong and effective political leadership to initiate the development of viable political institutions which would "moderate, refine, and mediate group political action."[11] The pursuit by the Northern Sudanese leaders of policies of Arab cultural imperialism and economic domination in the South that exacerbated the African-Arab dichotomy and led to both systemic frustrations and open violence will be analyzed in detail. An attempt is made in Part III to analyze the form and degree of international involvement in the Sudan conflict and the various stages and steps leading to the Addis Ababa Agreement. Part IV discusses the legitimization of the peace accord, and proposes an institutional arrangement which can mediate and effectively stabilize African-Arab relations in the Sudan.

The purpose of this book is to reveal the saliency of self-determination in post-colonial Africa by offering a comprehensive and specific study of the Southern Sudanese quest for selfhood.

PART I
Society and Historical Context

CHAPTER I

The African-Arab Schism

Physical Setting

The Democratic Republic of the Sudan is a country of diversity and heterogeneity: in its physical and environmental setting, in its racial and ethnic groupings, in its variety of systems of life, and in its competitive religious and ideological relationships. It is the largest geographical territorial unit in the continent of Africa, covering a total area of approximately one million square miles. This represents approximately 8.3 percent of the area of the African continent and 1.7 percent of the land area of the world.[1] To the north, the Sudan is bounded by Egypt; to the west by a small section of Libya, Chad, and the Central African Republic; to the south by Zaire, Uganda, and Kenya; and to the east by Ethiopia and the Red Sea.

There are four fairly distinct geographical regions in the Sudan: (1) The Sudan plain, which consists of desert with rock and undulating sand combined with a clay, to the center of which is a swampy land. (2) In the northwest of the country are flat-topped low hills intersected by steep-sided gullies and occasional sand dunes. (3) The central Sudan is characterized by small clusters of beehive-shaped hills. The largest group makes up the Nuba mountains, and to the west of this plain is the Jebel Marra range, which rises to about 2200 feet and forms the Nile watershed. (4) The Southern Sudan may be broken down into two geographical sectors: a plateau in the western half, and massive mountain ranges and a plain to the east, drained entirely by the Nile River which flows from the southern to the northern boundary, having originated in Lake Victoria, Uganda. Within this huge area of the globe, there are extreme differences and variations in climate, soil, vegetation as well as in ways of life. Yet aside from these specific and complex ecological contrasts, the Sudan may more conveniently be divided into two general zones characterized by desert in the north and tropical savanna grassland in the south.

Communal Cleavages

Corresponding to these natural divisions are two distinct peoples with differing value systems: the Arab in the north and the African Negroid in the south of the Sudan. Ecological differences have played an important part in determining the differences in modes of economic activity: in social, cultural, and political organizations; and in the value orientations of the various collectivities in the country as a whole—but even more remarkably so between the Northern and the Southern regions.[2]

The African-Arab schism is the fundamental problem that besets the Sudan. This sharp cleavage between Africanism and Arabism must not be equated with the issue of ethnic dysfunctionality that is prevalent in other areas of post-colonial Africa.[3] For, although many countries in Africa are struggling with the problem of national integration, few have the pronounced differences of race, culture, religion, or values, which have been reinforced by differences in economic and social conditions and by naked political forces as exist in the Sudan. The depth of the African-Arab schism is portrayed eloquently by Aggrey Jaden:

> The Sudan falls sharply into two distinct areas, both in geographical area, ethnic group, and cultural systems. The Northern Sudan is occupied by a hybrid Arab race who are united by their common language, common culture, and common religion; and they look to the Arab world for their cultural and political inspiration. The people of the Southern Sudan, on the other hand, belong to the African ethnic group of East Africa. They do not only differ from the hybrid Arab race in origin, arrangement and basic systems, but in all conceivable purposes. . . . There is nothing in common between the various sections of the community; no shared beliefs, no identity of interests, no local signs of unity and above all, the Sudan has failed to compose a single community.[4]

Although Jaden's description of the differences between the peoples of the North and the South is somewhat absolute in formulation, it does set out how much each region identifies itself as unique. The historical development of the regional, African-Arab cleavage is well described by Colin Legum:

> The Sudan is a classic example of a divided nation. It is divided by religion, by ethnic kinship, by region, by history. Like most African countries, the modern Sudan was created artificially by a colonial power. But though ruled for a century by a single power as a single country, its two main societies were deliberately encouraged to grow apart—The North developing its largely Islamic traditions and Arab culture; the South emerging as a Christian-based, English-speaking region. The result of this policy was to consolidate and intensify factors making for divisiveness. The great gulf of language, religion, and separate administrative units are easily maintained because of the great distances separating the important centres of the North from the peasant societies of the South, and by poorly developed communications—transport, press, and radio.[5]

Thus "completely isolated from the North until little more than a century ago, embittered by decades of subsequent hostility, and administered separately until the threshold of independence, the Southerner feels himself to be an African, while the ruling Northerner is proud of his Arab consciousness."[6] The underlying reasons for this African-Arab schism in the Sudan must now be uncovered.

The Southern Sudan is a large area of over a quarter of a million square miles, and its inhabitants are exclusively African Negroid peoples, speakers of a wide range of Nilotic, Nilo-Hamitic, and Sudanic languages. The groups within these ethnic categories are shown in Table I. The major Nilotic category includes the Dinka, the Nuer, the Shilluk, and the Anuak. They live predominantly in the provinces of the Bahr el Ghazal and the Upper Nile. Each of these groups is in turn subdivided into tribes. For instance, the Dinka includes the Cic, Bor, Agar, and Ngok tribes. They are the largest single ethnic group in the Southern Sudan, numbering over one million people. The Nilotes are mainly cattle-raisers and have an absorbing interest in their cattle. In Audrey Butt's observation, the Nilotes

> consider their country the best in the world and everyone inferior to themselves. For this reason they scorn European and Arab culture. . . . Their attitude toward any authority that would coerce them is one of touchiness, pride, and reckless hatred of submission, and [each] is ready to defend himself and his property from the inroads of others. They are self-reliant, brave

TABLE I

Ethnic Groups of the African Negroid Peoples of the Southern Sudan

A. The Nilotic Group	*B. The Nilo-Hamitic Group*	*C. The Sudanic Group*
Dinka	Bari	Azande
Nuer	Pojulu	Ndogo
Shilluk	Kakwa	Sere
Anuak	Kuku	Mundo
Acholi	Nyepo	Biri
Bor Belanda	Mundari	Moru
Jur (Jo Luo)	Nyangwara	Madi
Shilluk Luo (Dembo, Shatt)	Lokoya	Bongo
Pari	Luluba	Baka
	Latuko	Fertit (Mandala)
	Logit	Feroge
	Lango	
	Toposa (Topotha)	
	Domjiro	
	Jiye	
	Murle Group—Boma Murle, Beir, Didinga	

fighters, turbulent and aggressive, and are extremely conservative in their aversion from innovation and interference.[7]

Thus there is a strong sense of cultural uniqueness among the Nilotes. Pride in their own identity is so strong that they vehemently resist the assimilation of foreign values and beliefs. They practice exogamy, that is, they do not allow marriages among those who are considered to be related by blood and affinity. Generally, they are opposed to intertribal marriages. Their political society is decentralized, functioning through a complex process of hierarchically balanced opposition.[8] Characteristic of the Dinka in particular, their lineage system is segmentary. According to Middleton and Tait:

> The relations of local groups are seen as a balance of power, maintained by competition between them. Corporate groups may be arranged hierarchically in a series of levels; each group is significant in different circumstances and in connection with different social activities—economic, ritual, and governmental. Relations at one level are competitive in one situation, but in another the formerly competitive groups emerge in mutual alliance against an outside group. A group at any time has competitive relations with others to ensure the maintenance of its own identity and the rights that belong to it as a corporation, and it may have internal administrative relations that ensure cohesion of its constituent elements. The aggregates that emerge as units in one context are merged into larger aggregates in others, so that a segment that in one situation is independent, finds that it and its former competitors are merged together as subordinate segments in the internal administrative organization of a wider overall segment that includes them both. This wider segment is in turn in external competitive relations with other similar segments, and there may be an entire series of such segments. Coordinate groups that are so related are in a state of complementary opposition.[9]

The Nilotes have a long history of cultural continuity, inward-looking tendencies, resistance to assimilation, and a jealous guard over their independence. They view outsiders as "subordinate species of human beings" and, although these aliens may be considered "dignified," they are never quite fully "human beings." According to Francis Deng, "the occasional 'humanization' of the 'animals' . . . and . . . one would assume of the outsider in the bedtime stories, is in line with the religious practice by which Nilotes attempt to tame dangerous creatures by symbolically making them 'relatives' and integrating them into their value-system.[10]

The tribes which make up the Nilo-Hamitic group live mostly in the Equatoria province. They have certain common features and generic linguistic affinities which suggest a shared ethnic origin and a prior geographical propinquity.[11] Their patterns of marriage are exogamous and their inheritance and succession systems are patrilineal. The religious beliefs and practices are only slightly varied from tribe to tribe. These common cultural characteristics, of course, contribute significantly to similarities evidenced in the social, economic, and legal fabric of society. Most of the tribes are both agriculturalists and pastoralists. Some, like the Toposa, practice mixed economy of grain cultivation and cattle-raising. Unity within the Nilo-Hamitic tribes is based on consciousness of similar identity and the ability of the leader to maintain internal order. Thus the village chief is central to the political organization of the tribe. Moreover, he is looked to for spiritual guidance as well.

The Sudanic group of tribes live mostly in the southwestern part of the Sudan where it borders with Zaire and the Central African Empire, in the area of the Ironstone plateau in the provinces of Equatoria and Bahr el Ghazal. These congeries of tribes are agriculturalists; and, with the exception of the Azande, most of them have acephalous patterns of social organization.[12] There is not much interethnic consociation among them.

The political systems of the Southern Sudanese ethnic groups vary considerably.[13] Among the Azande, the apex of political power was formerly occupied by kings, drawn from the Avungara clans, who were constantly struggling among each other. Today it is the chief who holds the highest office. And so too with the Bari-speaking tribes where the chief is both the spiritual and political head of the clan. Among the Shilluk, there is a *Reth* who is generally recognized as supreme head of the people. He, however, no longer exercises as much influence among the lesser chiefs as he did in precolonial Southern Sudan. The Nuer, on the other hand, have "leopard-skin" chiefs who are believed to have certain magic powers but have no authority to settle feuds or to pass judgments. There is, however, a body of elders in each local community which is often called upon for advice and leadership. The Dinka have chiefs as both political and administrative leaders.

Although the peoples of Southern Sudan belong to various ethnic and tribal groups, they are all racially akin to tropical Africa and identify culturally with Africanism. Their value systems preclude the possibility of assimilation into the Arab culture. Their religion is indigenous to Africa while most of the educated elites are Christians. The Southern Sudanese share a history of devastating slave raids into their areas, of the plundering of their natural resources by European and Arab traders, and of foreign opposition and repression. This has served to deepen a consciousness of African identity among them and has brought about a general consensus of accepting and of treating their territory of habitation as a distinctly and exclusively African entity.[14] The point to be grasped here is that the feeling of and identification with Africanism differentiates the South by all criteria from the North where Arabism predominates.

Arabism in the Northern Sudan is rooted in a sense of sharing in the Arab heritage, that is, in the attachment to and reverence for Arab descent, Arab culture, Arab values, Moslem religion, and Islamic law. The great significance of this heritage evidenced by the widespread use of the Arabic language by the great mass of the population and the general adherence to the Islamic religion which permeates the whole of society and provides a background for almost every event of daily life. Thus, among the vast majority of the Northern Sudanese, being an Arab is an article of faith; their claim to Arab descent and identification with the Arab world, racially, culturally, religiously, and ideologically, is an index of distinctness, and exclusiveness from the Negroid Africans of the South. As has been the case, the Northern Sudan may be culturally regarded as a part of the Middle East, whereas the Southern Sudan is culturally a part of tropical sub-Saharan Africa.[15]

In the Northern Sudan, there are two principal groups of inhabitants: the Arabs and the non-Arab tribes who have been Arabized. Arabic and Islamic influences have been felt in the Northern Sudan through three major channels: "the first and the most important Islamic influence came from Egypt as early as the middle of the seventh century; the second came from Arabia (about the same time) across the Red Sea; the third, which assumed importance after the fifteenth century, radiated from the Maghrib and the Central Bilad al-Sudan. The ultimate Islamization and Arabization of the country was achieved primarily through the first two streams where agents of Islamization and Arabization transplanted the frontier into the interior by definite stages."[16]

Intermarriage and other patterns of "racial miscegenation such as concubinage with non-Arab and Negroid slave woman"[17] gradually but surely led to the twin processes of Arabization and Islamization. The Arabic language and culture, and the Moslem religion, which includes certain laws (regarding marriage and property ownership), a code of racial behavior, rituals, and so forth, spread to most parts of Northern Sudan. Now the process of Arab acculturation is so complete that it is virtually impossible to isolate pure "Arabs" from "pure non-Arabs." The resultant synthesis brought about by the interaction between the Arabs and most of the non-Arab groups on the one hand and Islam and other religious beliefs on the other, is Arab and Moslem collectivities which identify themselves genealogically with the Arabs of Arabia. Arabized non-Arabs claim this genealogical ancestry so as to be fully accepted as Arabs.

The main Arab ethnic groups in the Northern Sudan are shown in Table II. These groups regard themselves quite rightly as natural members of the Arab world. Their historical position as conquering invaders and their present concentration in the most highly modernized areas have shown them unmistakably to be a dominant group in the affairs of the country. Positions of status and authority in the realm of business, including industry and commerce, in the military, in the civil service and in politics are almost all held by the Arabs. Their ascendancy and assertiveness have made the Northern Sudan an Arab nation and, in spite of vehement and persistent opposition from the South, have turned the Sudan into a de facto Arab state.

In his historical study of the Sudanic Arab peoples, Sir MacMichael divides the Northern Sudanese Arabs, who came through Egypt, into two main groups according to their genealogies.[18] These groups are the Ja'aliyin and the Danagla groups who are said to be descended from the Ismailite

TABLE II

The Arab Ethnic Groups of Northern Sudan

	A. Ja'aliyin Arabs:	
1. Danagla Arabs	3. Kawahla	5. Husaynat
2. Hassaniya	4. Gima	
	B. Guhayna Arabs:	
1. Jamala: Kababish, Shukriya,		
2. Baggara: Seleim, Hawazma, Mesiriya, Humr, Reizeiqat, Ta'aisha, Beni Rashid, Rashaida, Habaniya		
	C. Gezira Arabs:	
1. Messellimiya	2. Halawin	3. Rufa's
	D. Zebaydiya Arabs:	
	E. Hawawir Arabs (Berber stock)	
1. Hawawir	3. Hawara	
2. Jellaba	4. Korobat	
	F. Mixed Arab-Nubians:	
1. Shaiqiya	3. Rubatab	
2. Manasir	4. Mirifab	

tribes of Northern Arabia, the Yemen and the Hadramut. The Ja'aliyin claim to be descended from the Qurysh tribes, of which the prophet Muhammad was a member (specifically, they claim descent from Ibrahim Jaal, descendant of Al-Abbas, the prophet's uncle). When they first penetrated the Sudan, they occupied the Merowe and Shendi reaches of the Nile, enslaving and mixing with the native population, which consisted of Nubian and Negro Fung elements. The Ja'aliyin now can be found in the Gezira as cultivators and prospering as tenants in irrigation schemes, and in the Kordofan, inhabiting a part of the gum belt around El Obicd and En Nahud (these are the Hamar and Bedeiriya tribes, partly settled and partly nomadic).

The Guhayna Arabs claim descent from Abdullah al-Juhani: they came from Arabia and have retained their nomadic way of life. These are the Kababish of the western Sudan, who are camel owners and who migrate long distances and are wholly nomadic; the Shukriya of eastern Sudan, who keep both cattle and camels in Butana; and the great cattle-owning Baggara of Southern Kordofan and Darfur. Some Guhayna Arabs have settled in the Gezira and these include sedentary tribes such as the Messellimiya, the Halawin, and Rufa's. Another major Arab ethnic group is the Kawahla, who reached the Sudan across the Red Sea and intermarried extensively with the Beja without dominating them to the extent that the Ja'aliyin dominated the Nubians. The Kawahla Arabs are also found in northern Butana, along the White Nile, just south of Khartoum, and in northwest Kordofan.

Among the Arabs, each individual is a member of a household, and in it, he may be either the head or a dependent. Women, as a rule, can only be the latter. Each household is under the control of a sheikh who is responsible for collecting taxes and for the maintenance of law and order. The sheikh is the political leader whether in a settled village or among a group of nomads, and is subordinate to an Omda who may have any number of sheikhs beneath him, ranging from ten to thirty or even more.[19]

The non-Arab ethnic groups in the Northern Sudan are the Nubians, the Beja, the Fur, the Nuba, and the people of southern Funj[20] in the Blue Nile Province (Ingassana, Barta, Burum, and the Uduk). Most of these groups (shown in Table III) have been Arabized and Islamized. They claim as ancestors esteemed Arab tribes for whom they have gathered their fold ideologies. Among the Nubians, local customs of matrilineal descent enabled the invading Arabs to acquire material and political power with remarkable rapidity. The Arab tradition of patrilineal descent induced native Northern Sudanese to claim that they, too, are Arabs. Of no less importance is the fact that conversion of native Africans to Islam, more often than not, tends to establish between them and the Arabs a potent link of spiritual brotherhood and political solidarity.

Characteristic of the Arabization of non-Arab regions of the Sudan is the

TABLE III

The Non-Arab Ethnic Groups of Northern Sudan

A. Beja
1. Beni Amer
2. Amarar
3. Bisharin
4. Hadendowa

B. Darfur
1. Fur (Keira)
2. Daju and Beigo
3. Zaghawa and Berti
4. Masalit, Gimr, and Tama

C. Nuba
1. Jatala and Gubid
2. Koalib
3. Tegali
4. Talodi
5. Tumtum
6. Temein, Keiga-Girru, and Teis-um-Danab
7. Kadugli
8. Heiban

D. Nubians

use of the Arabic language as the medium of communication in education, commerce, and government to a great extent, replacing the indigenous languages and their dialects. Over the years of Arab penetration into their areas, these people (the Beja, the Fur, the Nuba, the Nubians, and the Ingessana tribes) have adopted Arab customs and Arab practices of law in relation to property and inheritance.

Thus in the final analysis, although the North is composed of several ethnic groups with various modes of social, structural, and economic systems, three factors have helped unify the people into a clearly Arab culture and identity: the predominance of Islamic religion, culture, and institutions; the racial and ideological identification with the Arabs of North Africa and the Middle East; and the widespread use of the Arabic language. Islam in the North of the Sudan, as in all Moslem communities, is more than a religion. It is a complete way of life. It regulates every aspect of a Moslem's life by insisting on adherence to the four pillars of faith: witnessing prayer, fasting, charity, and the pilgrimage to Mecca. Besides these, Islam also provides for the governance of every Moslem community. Hence, it embodies a complete culture which must be accepted and adopted in its entirety. After centuries of contact with Arabs, sometimes peaceful and most times violent, infiltrating from Egypt and Arabia, the Northern Sudanese are now very largely Arabic in their culture. They believe they are Arabs, they behave like Arabs, and they think they should, and in fact they do, identify themselves with the Arab world. Therefore, they must be considered as Arabs whether they are so by heredity or acculturation. This deep assimilation of Islam and Arabic culture by the majority of the non-Arab ethnic groups and the measure of unity and cohesion which it generated all over the Northern Sudan has brought about a complete identification with Arabism.

While the physical appearance of the Arabs in the Sudan tends to make them deceptively defy any racial classification, the fact is that visible signs of racial or ethnic identification and differentiation are irrelevant to them. For the Arab Sudanese, their physical appearances do not imply to them a racial stigma and an exclusion. What matters most is their Arab ancestry and their ability to corroborate the claim to it. Hence, though most of them have dark skin pigmentation and not quite straight hair, they feel no less Arab than their brethren in Arabia or Egypt. The vital criterion of identification seems to be in their sociocultural aspects of ethnicity, identity, language, religion, and institutional practices. The question of whether conspicuous racial differences are based on biological heredity or on social and cultural tradition is of no importance and relevance to most of the Arab Sudanese. The so-called synthesis of Arabism and Africanism among them[21] is predominantly of Arab hybrid, and they are dedicated to the defense of Arab culture and Islam against erosion from outside influences, and to Arab interests at the international level.

But even if the Northern Sudan could not be classified as Arab without getting into unnecessary scholarly disputations, what really is the phenomenon of self-conception among influential Arab Sudanese? Invariably most if not all elites in the North have always considered their beliefs, values, and conception of the universe as rooted fundamentally in Arabism. For them, there is little disagreement on the question of what national character the Sudan should adopt and what its national aspirations and loyalties should be. Indeed, as one former Prime Minister, Sayed Sadiq el Mahdi, once described it: "The dominant feature of our nation is an Islamic one and its overwhelming expression is Arab, and this nation will not have its entity identified and its prestige and pride preserved except under an Islamic revival."[22]

While Sadiq's description of the Sudanese identity applies only to the Northern Sudan, it is implicit in the assumption of most influential politicians of the region that in the Southern Sudan there exists a "cultural vacuum," to be filled by Arab culture under an Islamic revival.[23] In their view the Sudan is not part of black Africa, and in their view the south must be assimilated into the Arab fold by all conceivable means. In pursuit of such beliefs and translated into policies, they regard and treat the whole country as an integral part of the Arab world. That is why Arnold Toynbee concluded that: "The Northern Sudan Arabs seem to me to be flagrant colonists trying to impose themselves, their religion, their language and culture on a non-Arab African people that wants to be itself and does not want to be dominated."[24]

The Arab Sudanese politicians would ensure the predominance of the Arab national group by enforcing the ascendency of Islam over politics. Their cultural chauvinism and their "unawareness that other Sudanese might feel for their cultural heritage what they feel for their Arabness"[25] reinforces the African-Arab dichotomy of the Sudan. The idea of building a culturally plural society is repugnant to them because, as they see it, the strong tie between their Islamism and their Arabism is the spearhead leading them toward the future and should be the basis on which to build a Sudanese nation. It is therefore important to recognize the racial element, real or imagined, in the North-South dichotomy in the Sudan. The issue of whether the North is both Arab and African or exclusively either of the two is of less significance. The important point is what those who wield political power, generally the educated elites, think the North is: Arab or African. Their persistent identification with the Arab world and all that it stands for is clear evidence of the fact that they consider the North an Arab nation. Thus, even if biologically they are both Arab and Africans, they have opted in their choice of self-identification for Arabism.

Conclusion

The African-Arab cleavages in the Sudan were further reinforced by the treatment of the Southern Sudanese as a minority group in the postindependent Sudan because of their racial and cultural characteristics and because of their self-conception as Africans. The Arab Sudanese governments singled them out for differential and unequal treatment and excluded them from full participation in the political life of the country. They were debarred from the country's social and economic opportunities, and denied equal access to educational opportunities which further restricted possibilities for their occupational and professional advancement. These deprivations circumscribed their freedom of choice and self-development. Furthermore, the Northerners subjected the Southerners to contempt, hatred, ridicule, and violence. The Southerners reciprocated such treatment with equal zest and vehemence. As is always the case, one cannot discriminate at length against a people without generating in them a sense of isolation and persecution and without giving them a conception of themselves as being more different from others than, in fact, they are.

Finally the sharpening of the African-Arab schism led to armed conflict which has rendered it increasingly difficult to develop a national consensus between the North and the South of the Sudan. With this delineation of the main cleavages between the two regions, we turn to the historical context of their conflict.

CHAPTER II

Precolonial Perspectives

The Sudan: Before and During the Turkish Era

Prior to the Turko-Egyptian conquest of the Sudan, the northern region of the country was ruled by a number of self-contained, independent Christian kingdoms. In A.D. 641 Arabs began to penetrate the North from Egypt, Arabia (across the Red Sea), and the Maghrib. The invading Arabs systematically destroyed the Christian kingdoms and established their hegemony. Thus by the beginning of the sixteenth century, most of the indigenous peoples of the North had been absorbed into Arab culture and fully embraced the Islamic faith. Before the invasions and eventual occupation of the Northern Sudan by the Arabs, the region had been "no more than a geographical area in which many mutually hostile petty kingdoms rose and fell, and which was penetrated from time to time, never very deeply, by the cultural and economic influence, or by the military power of whatever power ruled over Egypt."[1]

Between 1820 and 1822, the north-central areas of the Northern Sudan (Nubia, Sennar, and Kordofan) were conquered by Egyptian armies on behalf of Muhammad Ali, then the Ottoman sultan's viceroy in Egypt. A further campaign in 1840 brought the whole of the Northern Sudan under foreign rule.[2] Governance of these provinces was granted to Muhammad Ali in 1841 by the Sultan of Turkey, whose suzerainty was acknowledged by the rulers of Egypt. Muhammad Ali, who initiated the annexation of the Northern Sudan to his empire, had at least three aims: first, to ensure a constant supply of able-bodied Negro slaves to strengthen his army; second, to search for precious gold, other precious metals, and ivory for his treasury; and, third, to establish his domain in the heart of Africa.[3] In 1821 and for the next decade, Muhammad Ali organized slave raids which were first directed against the Negroid tribes bordering Abyssinia and the Nuba mountains. But as the number of people available for slave raiding in these areas declined, the Turko-Egyptian regime began to look for a fresh market. The Southern Sudan became the target for exploration of new economic possibilities and in particular, for slaves.

While the Northern Sudan was being swollen by the invading Arabs, the Southern Sudan was sheltered and isolated by a series of formidable geographical barriers which rendered communications between the two areas difficult. The South was thus inaccessible to the Arab invaders who occupied the North. Therefore, prior to the Turkish-Egyptian adventures into the South, there had been no communications, no social interaction, and no political alliance or unity between the North and the South of the present Sudan.[4] It was the mission of Muhammad Ali (who coveted the Sudan because of her wealth as well as for reasons of prestige and strategy) which opened the South to the outside world.

In November 1839, an expedition led by Captain Salim left Khartoum on a Turkish frigate to explore the source of the White Nile and the economic potential south of the confluence of the Blue and White Niles. Salim's expedition successfully penentrated the Sudd and reached Gondokoro, a few miles from Juba, the present capital of the Southern region. As the first foreigner to break through the Sudd, Salim opened the way for future expeditions to the South of the Sudan.

The success of Salim's expeditions aroused considerable interest in Europe where his journal was translated into various languages. Thereafter, accounts of travelers and explorers formed "a complement to the more immediate impulses of European commerce and evangelism which seized the initiative in the Southern Sudan in the decade following Salim's expedition."[5] The commercial opportunity in the Southern Sudan seemed great: ivory was the prize which attracted traders. The products manufactured from it, chiefly knife handles, combs, billiard balls, and piano keys, had "an assured and rapidly expanding market in the many western countries which could increasingly afford a wide distribution of such middle-class luxuries."[6] The price of ivory and the quantity exported more than doubled between the 1840s and 1870s, as the trade obtained a recognized and valuable place in the world's economy.

The Southern Sudan became a breeding ground for rapacious slave raids, with clashes between the differing societies and their respective cultures beginning in earnest and reaching unprecedented proportions. European merchants and missionaries as well as Turko-Egyptian soldiers and sailors invaded the South. The aggressiveness of the foreigners met with an equally vehement resistance from the people. The ultimate intentions of the intruders confirmed with all finality the previous intentions of the Southerners by the robbing and hostility evidenced. The Europeans soon decided to undertake direct expeditions into the Southern interior to establish permanent and effective stations. Having realized the degree of insecurity involved in these landlocked expeditions they recruited a large number of armed Arab servants from the Northern Sudan and Egypt.[7]

The European traders and their Arab servants established a network of *zeribas* (frontiers). Although the "search for ivory continued to be the dominant purpose of the foreign activities, it became more closely bound to the extension of violence and capture of slaves.''[8] The armed Arab servants settled as traders and exploited the ''Africans and pre-existing inter-tribal conflicts.''[9] They obtained wives by force from the indigenous people and attempted to ''establish themselves as a ruling caste transcending the barriers of tribal society.''[10]

The goal of the ivory and slave traders was to maximize profits. Thus, they saw no need to set up a government. In the words of Richard Gray:

> The exploitation of tribal hostilities was peculiarly destructive. The political supremacy of the traders was not used to produce an ever-widening sphere of constructive, stabilizing influence in which to establish commercial relationships, instead trading was fused with robbery. The raids on ''hostile'' tribes became an integral, indispensable part of the ivory trade as they produced the two ''commodities,'' cattle and slaves, which began to occupy an essential place in the traders' profits.[11]

The armed Arab servants were not well paid; the average nominal wage was about ten shillings per month. But they were obliged to ''receive a large proportion of their wages in merchandise supplied to them by the trader at a most exorbitant price, and a part of the merchandise so supplied was slaves captured in the raids on the 'hostile' African tribes.''[12] Hence, the traders accrued enormous profits from trade with their own servants. Each slave cost the equivalent of about three months' pay.[13] Many of the captured women became wives of the Arabs and the children they produced became apprenticed to their fathers; other women were sold to traders and taken northward on the Nile to be sold at more than double the price at which they were acquired. By 1884, it was widely believed in Khartoum that all Europeans on the White Nile permitted their agents to ''seize and sell slaves being well aware of the fact and indirectly partners in the profits.''[14]

By 1863, Ismail Pasha, as Viceroy of Egypt, succeeded in establishing full control of trade in the Southern Sudan and eliminated European traders, leaving Arabs in control. Pasha chose Sir Samuel Baker to secure the area up the Nile for his empire and to put an end to slavery. Baker did not receive any cooperation from the people. He was, however, shocked with what he found and saw in the South. He observed:

> It is impossible to describe the change that has taken place since I last visited this country. It was then a perfect garden, thickly populated and producing all that man would desire. The villages were numerous, groves of plantens fringed the steep cliff on the river bank, and the natives were neatly dressed in the bark cloth of the country. The scene has changed. All is wilderness. The population has fled. Not a village is to be seen. This is the certain result of the settlement of Khartoum traders. They kidnap the women and children for slaves and plunder and destroy wherever they set their foot.[15]

Sir Samuel Baker, however, did not succeed either in conquering the South or in suppressing the slave trade. No effective administrative posts were established, and the slave trade continued to flourish unabated. For instance, in the Bahr el Ghazal area, slave traders were very powerful, the most powerful and notorious of them all being Az-Zubair Rahman Mansur, a Ja'ali merchant from Khartoum. Zubair defeated the Egyptian troops in 1872 and was eventually recognized by Pasha as Governor of the Bahr el Ghazal region. Later, however, he was arrested after trying to expand his activities into Darfur in the Northern Sudan. His son Suleiman attempted vigorously to set up a slave-and-Arab army in an effort to conquer all the South. But he was decisively defeated by Romolo Gessi, the leader of the Egyptian troops.[16]

The situation in the Southern Sudan by now had deteriorated into anarchy. Between 1879 and 1881, Gessi, as Governor of Bahr el Ghazal, tried with some limited success to restore order and drove off Arab slave traders on sight. The response of the African people to the rapacious slave raids was characteristic: the Dinka and the Nuer retreated to the swamps while the Avungara of western Equatoria and Bahr el Ghazal resolved not to have any relations with foreigners. The small tribes were the ones who suffered most.

The opening of the White Nile as a commercial avenue became a turning point in the life history of the Southern Sudan. The initial contact with the outside world had far-reaching devastating effects on the social fabric of Southern society. Major Titherington vividly describes the experience of the Dinka:

> There can be no doubt that their social system and personal outlook, as we so lately found it, was in a state of deterioration directly resulting from the continued harrying they received from the Northern slavers, and the demoralizing effects of half a century of subjection to crime at the hands of every stranger before the coming of the present (British) government. That they did not succumb altogether like so many Southern tribes, speaks highly for their stoutheartedness; nor did they take to the vile, but common practice of selling their fellow tribesmen into slavery. They lost hundreds of thousands of cattle; men, women, and children in thousands were slaughtered, carried off into slavery, or died of famine; but the survivors kept alive in the deepest swamps, bravely attacked the raiders when they could, and nursed that loathing and contempt for the stranger and all his ways that even now they are only just losing.[17]

Unfortunately, the slave trade was regarded by the Moslem Arabs as a phenomenon that was fully justified by their religion. Exploitation of the South was seen as an absolute right sanctioned by the Islamic doctrine.[18] The peaceful life of the people of the South consequently was disrupted and there was set forth the beginning of tension, confusion, oppression, and repression—in short, calamities—as a result of the intensive slave raiding and plundering during the period following Captain Salim's successful expedition to the area. For the first time the Negroid Africans of the South and the Arabs of the North of the Sudan were brought face to face. This era also marked the initial stage of British and then Arab Sudanese hegemony over the South. Finally, it was the first time that an attempt was made to certify a geographical entity known as the Sudan.

The Mahdiyyah and the Southern Sudan

In 1881, a certain Mohammad Ahmed ibn Abdullah claimed to be the Mahdi (literally in Arabic: The Guided One), the divine leader chosen by God at the end of time to fill the earth with justice.[19] He was born in 1844 on an island called Labab in the Dongola area, north of Khartoum. Mohammad Ahmed's family claimed "to be Ashraf, descendants of the prophet and one of his ancestors had been noted for his piety." His father was a boat-builder. Right from his childhood Mohammad Ahmed displayed an aptitude for religious studies and later gained a fine reputation for sanctity and learning among his contemporaries.

When Mohammad Ahmed proclaimed himself the Mahdi, he declared that he came to sweep the Egyptians out of the Northern Sudan, to do away with the malpractices of the government seen as repugnant to the Islamic religion, and to establish the right way of life.[20] Thus Mahdism developed from its inception as a fanatical Islamic-revivalist movement cloaked in a political dress. Mohammad Ahmed professed to carry a message telling of the liberation of the Arab Sudanese people from "the yoke of the infidel Turks just as Moses delivered the Jews from the bondage of Egypt."[21] He attracted many followers (called al-Ansars in Arabic, signifying helpers after the first supporters of the Prophet Mohammad) mainly because of tribal discontent with oppressive taxation, grave disruptions caused by the slave trade, and deportation of traders (all these measures were inflicted on the Northern Sudan by the Turkish-Egyptian regime). People flocked to the Mahdi as his ardent disciples, and were known as the Ansars.

In the Southern Sudan, the fight against the Turko-Egyptian agents had by this time intensified. The Mahdist uprising in the North now weakened the Turko-Egyptian forces in the South. In some places the Southerners joined forces with the Mahdists against the Turko-Egyptian forces. But whereas the war against the Turks in the South was essentially a war against a foreign intruder and plunderer, in the North it was both a Moslem religious war (jihad) and a political war. By 1885, the Turko-Egyptians had been driven out of all the Sudan except for small areas in the extreme north and east.

Northern Sudanese enthusiasts for integration of the South into the Northern Arab fold have often cited this instance of the South against the Turko-Egyptian forces as an event that shows some historical solidarity between the two regions.[22] Such an argument tends to overlook the fact that the unity between the North and the South against the Egyptians was only the result of temporary necessity. Nevertheless, as Robert Collins points out:

> Although the tribes of the Southern Sudan were anxious to rid themselves of Egyptian rule, they did not wish simply to exchange the oppressive rule of the Egyptians for that of the Mahdists. Profoundly jealous of their new-found freedom from government and disinterested in the religion of the Mahdists, the tribes resisted attempts by the new invaders to force Mahdist rule and religion upon them. As before, fire and sword were spread throughout the Southern Sudan to force the tribes to submit.[23]

The Mahdists had their own imperial intentions in the Southern Sudan. They invaded the South soon after the Turko-Egyptian forces were successfully driven out of the Sudan. Their military expedition was led by a certain former merchant in Bahr el Ghazal, Karamallah Kurqusawi. He set up ceaseless slave raids and dispatched thousands of Southerners to Omdurman in the North to be sold.

In 1885, the Mahdi died and for the next thirteen years the North was ruled by his lieutenant, the Khalifa Abdullahi. The Mahdist invasion which devastated the Southern Sudan was slowed and eventually abandoned as a result of persistent resistance from the people of the region.

The Mahdist period was no less inhumane than the Turko-Egyptian era: scars of the brutality inflicted on the Southern Sudanese still remain. The Mahdist invasions "upset the traditional pattern of tribal life and left nothing behind but anarchy and fear—strong enough to defeat the Negroids but never sufficiently strong to establish their hegemony over them, the Mahdists were compelled to raid again and again not only to maintain their position but also to secure even the most essential supplies. And the only lasting result of these continual raids was the Southerner's hatred and fear of the Northern Sudanese."[24] These memories of bitterness toward and fear and hatred of the Arabs persisted from generation to generation in the minds of people in the South. A Southern survivor of the period, Chief Giirdit, recounted this sentiment with precision and clarity:

> The Dongolaw (Northern Sudanese) and the Turks were the people who spoiled our country. They were the people who captured our people and sold them. They would go, attack any village, and capture people. . . . They did not bring order. Nor did they unite the country. . . . He would attack and destroy an area and when he conquered them, he would take the people and add them to his army as slaves. And he would use them to attack the next tribe. And when he conquered the next tribe, he would also add them to his group and use them to attack the next. Many sections disappeared. Many Dinkas went into the wilderness and disappeared. . . . In some sections only thirty or forty remained. A section with fifty people was considered a large one. You people have not witnessed destruction. . . . The earlier destruction was one in which people slept in the forest. It was a destruction in which, if you saw a man, you considered yourself dead. Any man at all, even black, if you saw him, you were dead if you had no greater strength of your own. And he would take your things. . . . Great leaders were left without anything.[25]

Thus the fears of the peoples in the Southern Sudan of their Northern neighbors are based on memories of plunder, slave raiding, and suffering caused by the Arab Sudanese and, of course, by other foreigners in the precolonial era. Although slavery flourished universally as a commercial phenomenon, the enslavement of Negroid Africans by Arabs was considered, if not believed, to be both religiously and commercially justifiable. Yet, now there is a strong distaste among Northern Sudanese for the mention of the slave trade. Teaching it in missionary schools during the colonial period was later referred to as "a carefully worked-out, diabolic scheme which has for its aims the fostering of antagonism and alienation between the sons of one country."[26] Nonetheless, Arab participation in slavery explains the deep roots of the Southerners' hostility for the Northerners. One may come to grips with this issue by understanding the precolonial relations between the two regions.

Conclusion

From the previous discussions it should be evident that precolonial relations had an overwhelming and unforgettable impact on the lives and in the minds of the Southern Sudanese. Furthermore, the attitude of Northerners toward Southerners, regarding them as inferior, uncouth, and infidels prevails still today, serving to reinforce the hatred and distrust felt between the North and the South. Anglo-Egyptian colonial rule, an analysis of which follows, did not ameliorate this situation. Although it did not leave the North and the South as the separate territorial entities they had always been, the Anglo-Egyptian administration underscored the deep cleavages embedded in Sudanese society.

CHAPTER III

The Colonial Interregnum

The Anglo-Egyptian Imperial Occupation of the Sudan

In 1898, a joint Anglo-Egyptian military force led by General Kitchener won an easy victory over the fanatical Mahdist army. The Mahdi's lieutenant, Khalifa Abdullahi, surrendered at Omdurman and British hegemony was henceforth ensured. The whole of the Northern Sudan except Darfur came under the control of the Anglo-Egyptian force. In 1899, an Anglo-Egyptian condominium was proclaimed over the entire Sudan.

According to the Condominium Agreement, Britain and Egypt agreed to rule the Sudan jointly.[1] It expressly recognized the authority of the government of Egypt, which had been ousted by the Mahdists. It also referred to the rights which had accrued to the government of the United Kingdom as a result of the conquest. But although both Britain and Egypt agreed to share the governance of the Sudan, the Egyptian presence was nominal, for the British were in actuality the effective rulers.

It became evident that other European countries were also interested in the Sudan, specifically the Southern region which first came under British control in late 1898. King Leopold of Belgium tried unsuccessfully to claim Bahr el Ghazal as part of his Congo colony. The French sent a military expedition as far as Fashoda (now Kodok) in the Upper Nile province. An imminent Anglo-French confrontation was averted, and the British were able to maintain their rule over the region.

However, the Southern Sudanese presented stiff resistance against the imperialist forces. It became necessary to seek a middle ground tactic between ruler and ruled in order to achieve peace. The ethnic groups which suffered most from the Arab invasions—the Sudanese speaking peoples, the Shilluk, and the Bari—easily submitted to the conquerors. But the Nuer and others in the swampy areas south of Malakal held off the British administration until the 1920s despite punitive expeditions against them. In 1901, the Nuer and the Azande waged armed resistance. They were followed by the Anuak who killed forty-seven British soldiers including five officers in 1912. The Aliab Dinka also rebelled and killed the Governor of Bahr el Ghazal,

Chancery Stigand.[3] The Southern Sudanese were not easily willing to accept colonial rule nor the system of taxation that came with it. The Nuer in 1927 were still not completely subdued: they killed the District Commissioner of Bentiu, Vere Ferguson. And as late as 1941, the District Commissioner of Tonj was killed by the Dinka of the area. The pattern of Southern Sudanese resistance was dependent upon the organization of each individual society itself and its relations with the neighboring peoples. But the African resistance in the South had no influence in London. The British in charge were determined to establish firm control over internal as well as external forces. In response to the Belgian invaders from the neighboring Congo they built an army recruited from the indigenous people (later known as Equatorial [Southern] Corps) to help defend the region.[4]

Internally the colonial administration established its authority by enlisting the help of tribal chiefs whenever possible to carry out its policies. It was not interested in and did not introduce a centralized bureaucracy.[5] The powers of the chiefs, however, were limited, and in some areas, those chiefs who did not prove flexible were deposed. Frequently, the legitimacy of the appointed chiefs was questioned by the people. Where this occurred, the British minimized the role these chiefs were to play.

The British District Commissioner had executive as well as judicial powers, which, more often than not, proved burdensome to them. Many clashes took place as a result of the incompatibility of the British criminal laws applied by the colonial administration with the native traditional laws. Eventually, a court system did emerge which served as a basis for native administration.

As far back as in 1902, the colonial administration decided to treat the then six Northern provinces and the three Southern provinces of the Sudan as separate and distinct areas as they had always existed.[6] European Christian missionaries were forbidden to proselytize in the Moslem Arab northern areas of the Sudan. The indigenous African religions were not, however, recognized and respected: the Southern Sudan was divided into spheres of influence among various Christian missionary organizations interested in propagating their faith in the region.[7] In 1918, Sunday became the official day of worship in the South, replacing Friday, which was introduced in some areas by the Moslem Arab slave raiders[8] as the day of rest.

In keeping with this policy of maintaining the distinction between the Northern and Southern regions of the Sudan, the colonial government enacted the Passports and Permits Ordinance in 1922.[9] While giving powers to the Governor General and his representatives to withdraw permits for entry into the Sudan from all non-Sudanese without explanation, this ordinance enabled any part of the Sudan to be declared a "closed district." This served the primary aim of colonial policy by which the Southern Sudan, under the heading of "closed district" became off limits to all non-African Sudanese. Exceptions took place, of course, wherein permission was granted to Northern Arab traders but they were confined essentially to the towns and the established routes. The procurement of cheap labor, specifically by the North from the South, was severely restricted. Thus the Northern Arab Sudanese were, in great part, kept out of the Southern Sudan where feelings of intense hatred still prevailed due to the lingering memories of the Arab slave raids. The ordinance served to protect both peoples who were very sensitive and easily excitable when in contact with one another. Important to add, the Southern Sudanese were restricted, as well, from entering the North, although in fact they had little desire to do so.[10]

The Southern Policy

The colonial administration revealed its understanding of the long divisions between the Northern and Southern regions of the Sudan in the Southern Policy of 1930. This policy was based on two premises: (1) that the Negroid Africans of the South are culturally and, to some extent, racially distinct from the Northern Arab Sudanese; and (2) that the Southern provinces would either develop eventually as a separate territorial and political entity or be integrated into what was then British East Africa. In his directive to the governors of the Southern provinces, the Civil Secretary Sir Harold MacMichael[11] defined in explicit terms what had come to be known as the Colonial Southern Policy:

> His Excellency, the Governor-General directs that the main features of the approved policy of the government for the administration of the Southern Provinces should be restated in simple terms. The Policy of the government in the Southern Sudan is to build up a series of self-contained racial or tribal units with the structure and organization based to whatever extent the requirements of equity and good government permit upon the indigenous customs, traditional usage, and beliefs.[12]

The implementation of the Southern policy required a number of measures that would eliminate all traces of Arab influences in the South and the revitalization of Negroid African customs. The steps instituted by the government to carry out the policy included the encouragement of use of the English language in mission schools and in offices, the prohibition of the use of Arabic language and Arab dress, the replacement of Arab administrators by indigenous ones, the removal of Arab traders from the South and the encouragement of Greek and Syrian traders to come into the area, and the recognition and use of African laws. Specifically, the government's first step was to institute the use of local languages in primary schools. Following a conference held in Rejaf (Southern Sudan), it was recommended that the Dinka, Bari, Moru, Ndogo, Nuer, Shilluk, Madi and Zande languages be recognized and adopted.

The Southern policy was pursued enthusiastically by the British colonial administrators, who were required to be fully informed of the social structures, beliefs, customs, and psychological predispositions of the people. To perpetuate the insulation and separateness of the Southern Sudan:

> . . . education was left in the hands of Christian missionaries whose main objective was the propagation of their faith. Intercourse between the South and North was not encouraged. Northerners were allowed to trade in the South only after very careful screening. Likewise Southerners were prohibited from coming to the North. The use of the Arabic languages was prohibited all over the South, and all manners and manifestations of Northern and Arab culture were studiously eliminated and discouraged. The South was left a huge fertile land for anthropologists, where modernization, social, and economic development were frowned upon by the British Administration.[13]

In some parts of the western Bahr el Ghazal province, where strong Arab influence continued to prevail as a result of the settling and intermarriage of numerous slave traders, it was difficult to eliminate Arab mannerisms completely. Otherwise, there was little difficulty in carrying out the Southern policy. Islam and the Arabic language were excluded from the schools with the result that both were systematically erased throughout the South.

It has been argued that the Anglo-Egyptian colonial administration of the Southern policy erected artificial barriers between the North and South.[14] The colonial regime has also been criticized by some Northern Sudanese for eliminating Arab influence in the South. How valid are these criticisms?

First, the colonial regime did not discover a harmonious relationship between the North and South of the Sudan. On the contrary, tensions and animosities had for a long time characterized their interactions as evidenced by the fact that no previous administrations had achieved political and economic unification in the Sudan. Second, to blame the colonial administration for eliminating Arab influences in the South is to imply that the South needed Arabization. The contention is itself culturally imperialistic; it is an argument against a rival in cultural imperial pursuits. The revitalization of African customs and respect for the cultures of the South was, in general, commendable bearing in mind that previous foreign invaders, the slave raiders for example, tried to destroy the fabric of Southern society. The basic flaw underlying the Southern policy was the encouragement and implementation of Western institutions, Christianity in particular, rather than the discouragement of not only Arab but also European cultural habits. The European missionaries had, of course, condemned the Arab Moslem presence in the South. Viewing the Moslems as rivals, the missionaries argued that since they were not allowed to proselytize the Northern Moslem region, the South should be exclusively their area. Third, whatever the ulterior motives of the colonial administration, there were strong arguments in favor of the Southern policy. From the Southern Sudanese point of view, prohibiting the Northerners from entering the South meant protection of the region from the Arab slave raids:

> Organized raiding continued as long as adjacent parts of the South were unad-

> ministered and therefore unprotected in the late 1920s, and extensive trade in slaves from Ethiopia was unmarked and even today [1946–47] there are occasional kidnappings and the victims are hurried into the hands of the desert nomads of the far North. The Government has therefore been reluctant to throw open the South until its inhabitants could stand on their own feet.[15]

Indeed, at the time of the formulation of the Southern policy secret trade routes of slave traffic were discovered in Bahr el Ghazal province. According to Peter McLoughlin, "Northern Sudanese obtained slaves from non-Moslem and non-Arab groups, some in the Northern Sudan itself, others from Southern Sudan, still others extra-nationally."[16]

Fourth, the Northern Arab Sudanese were ruthless in their dealings with the local people in the South. The point to be emphasized here is that the Southern policy of 1930 did not create hostility between the peoples of the two regions: hatred already had deep roots. The colonial policy attempted to keep the Northerners and Southerners from clashing. Indeed, if the British had attempted to integrate the North and South, they would inevitably have faced enormous resistance, at least from the South.

The most valid criticism of the Southern policy is that it did not strive to bring about social or economic progress in the South as it did in the North. Not only did this two-pronged policy serve to further alienate one region from the other, but after the policy was abandoned, the South was left dangerously vulnerable to the pursuits of the North.

In the South, the government had limited objectives: to establish and maintain law and order while defending its own position in the face of tribal unrest.[17] The British purposefully allowed an increase in the number of missionary societies to gain entry and establish themselves in this region for the purpose of engendering greater support among the peoples for the colonial regime and to serve as a modernizing agent.

While it has been argued that this limited British role was the result of a shortage of money, the magnitude of the resources devoted to development in the North disproves the point. Here, the administration financed social service projects, such as the establishment of schools and hospitals throughout the 1930s, and created an Advisory Council in 1943 in response to the upsurge of nationalism, prevailing in the Third World, but particularly evident in the Northern Sudan. This council was limited to the North on the basis that:

> The general conditions, social, cultural, economic, and linguistic are sharply distinguished from those of the Southern Sudan; and secondly, that the ethnic diversity and comparative backwardness of the Southern tribes preclude the selection of suitable indigenous representatives. In short, the South cannot at present be adequately represented in the North, nor can the North represent the South. The ordinance, however, provides for the possibility of a separate Advisory Council for the whole of Sudan, whenever either of these alternatives may be found desirable and feasible.[18]

The Southern policy continued to function into the 1940s. The restrictions on the Northern Sudanese were maintained. The educational policy, whereby English was actively encouraged to the exclusion of Arabic as the *lingua franca* of the South and the missionaries were entrusted, although not exclusively, with the education of the Southern people, prevailed. The government restricted the deliberations of the Advisory Council to the North as no questions referring to the South were permissible.

However, by this time the British policy came under fire from the Northerners, Egypt, and finally from influential circles at home. It modified and redefined its policy as follows:

> The approved policy of the Government is to act upon the fact that the people of the Southern Sudan are distinctly African and Negroid, and that our obvious duty to them is therefore to push ahead as far as we can with their economic and educational development on African and Negroid lines, and not upon the Middle Eastern Arab lines of progress which are suitable for the Northern Sudan. It is only by economic and educational development that these people can be equipped to stand up for themselves in the future, whether their lot be eventually cast with the Northern Sudan or with Eastern Africa (or partly with each).[19]

Northern Sudanese politicians mounted more pressure on the colonial administration. They accused the British of either intending to "split" the Sudan into two regions or of planning to attach the South or part of it to Uganda. The colonial regime responded that

> . . . the arguments whether such a course could be to the ultimate advantage of the Southern Sudan or to the rest of Africa are many on both sides and the whole question might at some date form a proper subject for consideration by an international commission.[20]

Later it was stated that

> . . . the present government while doing nothing to prejudice the issue, is proposing to associate sympathetic Northern Sudanese with implementation of a policy which aims at giving the South the same chances of ultimate Self-Determination as have been promised to the North.[21]

The British officials in Khartoum became more and more sensitive to continuous criticisms of their Southern policy. Strong pressure was exerted by the Northern Sudanese Graduate Congress in Khartoum for self-rule and eventual independence of the "whole" Sudan, including the South as part of it.[22]

Meanwhile, the partial restoration of Egypt's position in the Sudan in 1936 gave the North more leverage: Egypt pressed Britain not to keep the South as a separate entity from the North in the hope that one day the whole of the Sudan might be united with Egypt. Some British colonial officers began to question the political and economic viability of a Southern Sudan existing on its own and came to view the hostile relationship between the North and South as a colonial creation. Later, it was pointed out that the

British administration in East Africa was not interested in closer links with Southern Sudan: "East Africa's plans regarding better communications with Southern Sudan have been found to be nebulous and contingent on Lake Albert Dam."[23] In addition, there were mounting pressures from the British commercial circles and British supporters of the Mahdi family on the colonial regime to abandon its Southern policy.[24] These forces combined to convince the colonial rulers in the Sudan that the time had come for a reevaluation of the imperial policy in the Sudan.

The Abandonment of the Southern Policy

The crucial decision to change the Southern policy was made following a report of the Sudan Administration Conference held in Khartoum in April 1946. The conference reported that:

> We are fully aware of the relative backwardness of the peoples of the Southern Provinces and the advances which they must make therefore before they can reach the height of civilization attained by many peoples in the North. But at the same time a *decision must be made, and made now, that the Sudan be administered as one country* [emphasis mine]. Though parts may lag beyond, yet the aim of the whole is the same and there is no reason why the peoples of the Southern Provinces in the relatively near future should not reach a degree of civilization which will enable them to play their full part in the progressive development of the Sudan.[25]

The report of the Administration Conference prompted quick and incisive criticisms from the senior British officials working in the Southern Sudan. The governor of Bahr el Ghazal rebutted the report bitterly:

> The South's future is being advised upon and is even likely to be decided by wrong men in the wrong place, i.e., by a body of people capable and conscientious but without any direct understanding of the South; preoccupied with the political ferment of the North and seeing everything through Omdurman spectacles. . . . No Southerner was present. No serious effort has been made to extract a consensus of opinion from the educated or leading Southerners. . . . The composition and the proceedings of the Conference gave us the uneasy feeling that the South's fate is not to be decided principally on grounds of morality or expediency for the Southerners but as a pawn in the power politics game.[26]

However, the British officials in the Northern Sudan, to whom the governors of the provinces (including those in the South) were subordinated, endorsed the report of the administration. Thus by December 1946, the fate of the Southern Sudan was sealed and a change of policy vis-à-vis the South was to be implemented. The Civil Secretary, Sir James W. Robertson, ruled out the two other options open to the Southern Sudan of (1) becoming an independent self-governing African state and (2) being united with East Africa, on the basis that "neither are in the best interest of the Southern

Sudanese nor desired by the Southern Sudanese themselves."[27] Having made a rapid about-face, Sir Robertson stated the new policy toward the Southern Sudan in the following words:

> The policy of the Sudan Government regarding the Southern Sudan is to act upon the facts that the peoples of the Southern Sudan are distinctly African and Negroid, but that geography and economics combine (so far as can be seen at the present time) to render them inextricably bound for future development to Middle Eastern and Arabicized Northern Sudan; and therefore to ensure that they shall, by educational and economic development, be equipped to stand up for themselves in the future as socially and economically the equals of their partners of the Northern Sudan in the Sudan of the future.[28]

The reversal of the Southern policy was the beginning of a new chapter in African-Arab relations in the Sudan. Under constant pressure from both Egypt and the North, the colonial regime laid plans for a merger of the two regions seen as allegedly "in the best interests of the Southern Sudanese."[29] Yet it is difficult to comprehend how Southern interests were to be served when intense hostility existed, having deep roots in North-South relations since precolonial times, coupled with a profound distrust and a greatly inferior level of social and economic development on the part of the South with respect to the North. Moreover, the South was not consulted at any time during the decision-making process which undoubtedly explains the conclusion reached, contradicting the alleged basis for the union.

British administrators in the Southern Sudan were horrified by the plan for merger and based their criticisms on pragmatism and sound principles. One of the British Southern governors, Richard Owen, accused the Civil Secretary of "sacrificing his conscience" warning that as a result of his decision, the Northerners "will dominate the Southerners and treat them as their fathers did and that the sins of the fathers shall be visited upon their children unto the third and fourth generation."[30] Opposition to the new Southern policy and arguments for retaining the separate administration of the Southern Sudan also came from the Fabian Colonial Bureau in London. In a pamphlet the bureau argued cogently that:

> the problem of the South is the biggest human difficulty in the Country. Educated (Northern) Sudanese regard the South as Egypt regards them. The loss of it would become a matter of prestige and to some extent of anxiety, but there is also the fear that in the South might subsequently be discovered the wealth which could guarantee the Sudan's independence. The South, like the Northern Sudan to Egypt, is also a source of cheap labour and servants. On all other grounds the South ought not to be united to the Arab North. In human terms it belongs to the African South of it. There is a great deal to be said for maintaining the present policy of administering the South almost as a separate mandate, without making any decision to separate it in sovereignty from the North, a step which would be bitterly opposed politically just now in Egypt and in the Northern Sudan. Time, education, and gradual economic development may show in the end and whether it can be more suitably attached to the Middle East or to Africa.[31]

However, such arguments fell on deaf ears in Khartoum where British officials stubbornly clung to their decision. Having formulated the new policy, a number of measures were necessary to put it into effect. These included:[32]

1. Northern Arab Sudanese in senior government posts were brought to the South and Southern Sudanese were recruited to junior administrative positions.
2. The rules restricting Northern traders in the South were lifted and Southerners were now allowed to go and work in the North if they so wished.
3. Prohibition of propagation of Islam was lifted for, as the government now argued, "freedom of the facilities for worship for all sects is indispensable, and religious discrimination such as has existed, though it may not have been admitted, must cease. A creed must prevail by administration of its own truth and not by suppression of other creeds."
4. The government now decided that Arabic should be taught in Southern secondary schools and that, instead of sending Southerners to Makerere College (in Uganda) for the post-secondary studies, they should go to Gordon Memorial College in Khartoum.
5. The cost of manual labor in the South was increased and, similarly, prices of produce in the region were raised to "world market prices."
6. It was now realized that the gap between pay, status, and conditions of Northern and Southern staff was unjustified: a principle of equal reward for equal work was initiated.
7. The courtesy title of "Mr." was to be used with Southern staff just as the courtesy title of "Effendi" was used with Northern officials.
8. Holidays were to be standardized throughout the country.
9. Facilities were to be provided to Northern Sudanese to enable them to tour the South for educational purposes, with the hope that many preconceived ideas would be dispelled.

All the above measures were intended to promote a sense of shared outlook and citizenship among the peoples of the North and South of the Sudan. The colonial regime saw the need to embark on a program that would eliminate the prevailing sentiments of distrust and animosity and that would cultivate confidence among the peoples of the two regions. But this change of policy came on the eve of decolonization and did not succeed in altering the attitudes of the North toward the South nor vice versa, nor in accelerating the process of modernization in the South as it had in the North.

Decolonization and Preparation for Self-Government

The recommendations of the Sudan Administrative Conference led to the new Southern policy of merging the North and the South into one political and administrative territorial unit: the Sudan. As we have already pointed out, the British administrators in the Southern Sudan had objections to the new policy. Some had silent reservations but consented; another group expressed open criticisms of the policy and the measures designed to implement it. The governor of Bahr el Ghazal, Richard Owens, having failed to persuade the Civil Secretary to change his new policy, addressed himself to the subject of "safeguards for the integrity of the South which most needs discussion for the formulation of a concerted attitude."[33] The governor saw the need for "a measure of regional autonomy, or eventual federation of two rather different entities on an equal basis, and a plain statement that the British will hold the fort till the South doesn't need a garrison."[34] Fourteen British administrators working in the Southern Sudan stated that they felt "seriously perturbed by the minutes of the Administration Conference." They signed a collective letter to the Civil Secretary protesting the exclusion of Southerners from the conference, adding that "the peoples of Southern Provinces were only represented by two Governors." They called for an Administration Conference for the Southern Sudan to meet in the South.[35] In his reply, the Civil Secretary reassured the signatories of the letter that the colonial government was fully aware of its responsibilities, that it had not reached a decision about the Southern provinces, and that the recommendations of the Sudan Administration Conference had not yet been considered. As chairman of the conference, he added, "the Civil Secretary simply allowed the Northern Sudanese to speak their minds and they did so."[36] But the Civil Secretary indicated that he was "willing to call a conference such as suggested to meet in Juba."

Hence, to allay the fears of the British administrators in the South, the Civil Secretary convened the Juba Conference. At the meeting the terms of reference of the conference were fivefold:

> (1) To consider the recommendations of Sudan Administration Conference about the Southern Sudan; (2) To discuss the advisability of the Southern Sudanese being represented in the proposed Assembly, and if it is decided to be advisable, to decide how such representation can best be obtained in the present circumstances; and whether the representation proposed by the Sudan Administration Conference is suitable; (3) To discuss whether safeguards can be introduced into the forthcoming legislation setting up the new Assembly, to ensure that the Southern Sudan with its differences in race, tradition, language, customs and outlook is not hindered in its social and political advancement; (4) To discuss whether or not an Advisory Council for the Southern Sudan should be set up to deal with Southern affairs from which representatives might be appointed to sit on the Assembly as representatives of the Southern Sudan; (5) To consider the recommendations of the Sudan Administration Conference in paragraph 13 of their report which deals with matters not strictly relevant to the political development of the Sudan, which the Conference recommended as essential if the unification of the Sudanese people is to be achieved.[37]

The Juba Conference was attended by the governors of the Southern provinces, the director of establishments, seventeen Southern Sudanese chiefs and junior government officials, and six well-educated Northerners.

More often than not, it has been argued by Northern Sudanese scholars and practitioners of politics that the Juba Conference concluded that "it was the wish of the Southern Sudanese to be united with the Northern Sudanese in a united Sudan"; and that the majority of the Southerners in the Conference had "decided for unity with the North."[38]

The above arguments tend to overlook the fact that the unity of the North and South was already unilaterally decided by Sir James Robertson, the Civil Secretary, as a result of pressure from Northern Sudanese politicians and on account of British Middle Eastern interests. Moreover, the main items for consideration were whether the Southern Sudanese would be represented in the proposed Legislative Assembly, whether an Advisory Council for the Sudan would be set up, or whether some political or constitutional safeguards would be established so that the Southern Sudan was not hindered in its social and political advancement. The conference was intended to be a rubber stamp to endorse decisions that were already made by the colonial officials in Khartoum.[39] The Southern Sudanese participants in the conference were not free agents; they were handpicked by the administration and most of them were chiefs who were, with a few exceptions, illiterates, and the rest were either clergymen or government officials. So whatever decision they might have made, they had no mandate from the people. Furthermore, "even if they had any mandate, Southern Sudan would still pull out of any agreement that turns out to be for its political enslavement and economic exploitation."[40]

The Southern participants, however, did not disappoint their people. They were fearful of the North and reminded the conferees of the bad precolonial relations between the Arabs and the Africans. They stressed the danger of close association with the Northerners and warned that the North would dominate the South in a united Sudan:

> Chief Tete said he wanted to study in the South until he was clever enough to go to the North. One could not begin to do work which one did not understand. . . . Chief Lappanya thought that if representatives were to be sent to a legislative assembly, they should have had previous experience in councils of their own. It was impossible to send untrained recruits into battle. When the Governor thought they were sufficiently trained, he would send them into the firing lines. . . . Chief Luath Ajak emphasized the fear of the Southerners that a crowd of hungry Gellaba would invade the South and swamp them and cheat the people. . . .[41]

The most senior Southern chief in the conference, Chief Lolik Lado, pleaded for caution in establishing a unified administration between South and North. He painfully recalled the violent relations between the two regions in the past and expressed the fear that it might be difficult to realize any change for the better. Chief Lolik Lado said, however, that he was prepared to observe the new generation of Northerners before the South made up its mind about its future relations with the North.[42] He perceptively observed that ". . . a girl who had been asked to marry a young man usually wanted time to hear reports of that young man from other people before consenting; likewise Southerners before coming to any fixed decisions about their relations with the Northerners need time. The ancestors of the Northern Sudanese were not peace-loving and domesticated like cows. The younger generation said that they meant no harm, but time would show what they would in fact do."[43] Evidently, the Southerners in the conference sufficiently indicated their fear and suspicion of the North. The British officials acted as "brokers" at the conference, while Northern Sudanese made North and South administrative and political unity appear attractive. No resolutions were passed but the Civil Secretary concluded that the following points had been agreed upon: that it was the wish of the Southern Sudanese to be united with the Northern Sudanese in one Sudan; that the South should, therefore, be represented in the proposed assembly; that the number of Southern representatives should be more than thirteen as had been recommended by the Sudan Administration Conference; that these representatives should be elected by province councils in the South and not by an advisory council for the Southern Sudan; that trade and communications should be improved between the two regions; and that steps should be taken toward the unification of the educational policy in the North and South.[44]

The British colonial administration felt calm after the Juba Conference, trusting that a Northern-Arab-Sudanese-dominated central government would be moderate and conciliatory. One important message they did receive from the South was the demand for safeguards for the protection of the South's political and cultural rights in the united Sudan which the colonial regime was now prepared to institute through a unified administration. The Northern Sudanese nevertheless saw proposals for setting up a separate advisory council and safeguards for the South as another design by the British to "separate" the North and the South. While political safeguards were given immediate and serious consideration by the colonial regime, the draft of the Legislative Assembly Ordinance of 1948 did not include any specific safeguards for the South.

The British colonial officials in the South protested against the decision to exclude specific safeguards for the South in the Legislative Ordinance. They pointed out that "without protection the Southerners will not be able to develop along indigenous lines, will be overwhelmed and swamped by the North and will deteriorate into a service community hewing wood and drawing water. To pretend that there are no fundamental differences between them is like covering a crack in the tree trunk with moss. Such a process, like any obscuring of the truth, is unsound."[45] They complained in vain against the Civil Secretary's opinion that specific references to the South could harm the British position in negotiations with Egypt over the Condominium Agreement. The Civil Secretary was persuaded to believe that the union of North and South was the only solution for the problem in the Sudan. Hence, he did not see any necessity for sympathizing with the Southern Sudanese demands for safeguards.

Again for the second time, to allay the fears of the British colonial officials in the South, the Civil Secretary eventually decided to include specific safeguards for the South but they were embodied in the reserve powers of the Governor General. These safeguards were contained in Articles 14 and 100 of a draft of the Self-Government Statute. The Governor General in Article 100 was given special responsibility for "the public service and the Southern provinces," and also the power to protect special interests of the Southern provinces. He was authorized to refuse his assent to any bill passed by the Legislature which in his own opinion adversely affected the performance of the duties conferred on him. Also he was empowered to issue orders which appeared to him necessary for the performance of his special duties, and these orders were to have the force of law and to prevail over any existing or future legislation, and administrative or executive act of the government. In Article 14.2 (where the second constitutional safeguard was stated), the Governor General was authorized "to appoint not less than ten or more than fifteen ministers . . . on the advice of the Prime Minister; provided that not less than two ministers in each council shall be elected Southerners."[46] These two "safeguards" for the South were bitterly attacked by both the press and the legislature in the North.[47] They were, however, eventually passed by the Legislative Assembly.

The other aspects of the 1948 ordinance, aside from the reserve powers of the Governor General, concerned the composition and duties of the Legislative Assembly. The ordinance (1948) created an Executive Council of twelve members, at least half of whom had to be Sudanese. The Legislative Assembly was composed of sixty-five elected members, ten nominated members, and eighteen Executive Council members and under secretaries—making a total of ninety-three members in all. There were thirteen representatives from the South. This meant that only 14 percent of the representatives came from the South and the remainder from the North. The South was therefore heavily underrepresented.

The Executive Council prepared all government legislation for submission to the assembly and finally to the Governor General for his approval. He also had supreme power of veto but the exercise of such power was subject to notification by Condominium powers. The Governor General, however, never exercised his power of veto.

The Sudan was now moving rapidly toward independence. In March 1951, the Governor General appointed a Constitutional Amendment Commission composed of thirteen Sudanese (only one from the South), with a British judge of the High Court as chairman, to recommend the next steps to be taken to complete self-government. The only Southern member on the commission put forth a case for federation between the North and the South. Professor Vincent Harlow[48] (of Oxford University) who was consulted on the projected Measures of Constitutional Reforms in the Sudan, suggested two proposals to deal with the special political status of the South. These were: (1) to vest in the Governor General powers to protect the special interests of the Southern Sudan; and (2) to establish a Ministry of Southern Affairs. As regards the first proposal, the Governor General was to be given the right to withhold his assent from any executive act and to reserve for the consideration of the Condominium government any legislative measure which in his judgment would adversely affect the interests or the well-being of the Southern Sudanese. For the second proposal, the Ministry of Southern Affairs was to be headed by a minister who himself must be from the South, and who, besides assisting the Governor General in the exercise of his special powers in respect of the South, would be responsible for promoting in the Council of Ministers and introducing in the assembly measures for economic and other benefits in the South. The Minister of Southern Affairs was, in turn, to be assisted in the discharge of his functions by an advisory board on Southern affairs, the personnel of which would be selected by the minister in consultation with governors of the three Southern provinces.[49]

The Legislative Assembly accepted the constitutional amendment commission's recommendation on the special powers for the Governor General, but rejected the recommendation for the establishment of a Ministry of Southern Affairs.[50] The assembly stated that instead of creating this ministry, at least one of the members of the Council of Ministers should be from the South. The Southern members of the assembly opposed this motion, unsuccessfully.

In May 1952, the Northern political parties submitted proposals for self-government to the Condominium government. A conference was convened by the colonial regime to discuss these proposals. All the Northern political parties were represented in these negotiations, but the South was not invited to participate. By the time the negotiations were finalized, a new regime had come to power in Egypt under the leadership of Mohammed Nequib, who had been born of a Sudanese mother and Egyptian father, had been educated at Gordon Memorial College in Khartoum, and who knew many Northern Sudanese politicians. Nequib made the Egyptian position more flexible than before: while insisting for the unity of the Nile Valley, he was prepared to "ensure for the Sudanese the freedom of self-determination without foreign influence." Egypt now dropped its demand for "outright annexation of the Sudan."

The major issue of contention between Britain on one side, and Egypt and the Northern political parties on the other, was the special responsibility of the Governor General for the Southern provinces incorporated in Article 100 of the draft Self-Government Statute. Egypt and the North saw in Article 100 a hidden scheme to separate the South from the North and so insisted on its removal. Hence, it was dropped and replaced by an enlarged special responsibility of the Governor General "to ensure fair and equitable treatment to all the inhabitants of the various provinces of the Sudan."[51]

Thus, the Anglo-Egyptian Agreement of 1953 and the Self-Government Statute did not contain any special safeguards for the Southern Sudan.

Under the agreement (of 1953), the following points were of significance:[52] Egypt for the first time expressly recognized the right of the Sudanese to self-determination to be exercised at the appropriate time and with the necessary safeguards. It was agreed that there should be a transitional period not exceeding three years during which the dual administration would be dissolved. The agreement provided for three international commissions: one to supervise elections; the second to control the exercise by the Governor General of his discretionary powers; and the third, consisting of representatives of Egypt, Britain, and three Northern Sudanese, to complete Sudanization of the administration, the police, the defense force, and any government post that might affect the freedom of the Sudanese at the time of self-determination. Finally, it was agreed that self-determination was to be exercised by Sudanese through a Constituent Assembly, which was to have the political right to choose between union with Egypt or independence for the Sudan. The agreement also stipulated that the North and South were one united territory and that elections to the first Sudanese Parliament would embrace both regions.[53]

While the Northern Sudan participated fully in the discussions leading to the crucial decisions embodied in the Agreement of 1953 and in the Self-Government Statute, the South was neither represented in nor even consulted during the negotiations. It is often argued that "the South had no political organizations to send representatives to Cairo where the Conference took place,"[54] that unity had already been established between the North and South in 1947, and consequently, that it was quite legitimate for Northern Sudanese politicians to govern the Sudan in its entirety as a single political unit. This argument may be valid on technical grounds; that is, if representation at the conference was based solely on political parties, the South could not be represented since it had no political parties. But such an argument overlooks the profound schism between the North and the South. There is no persuasive argument to justify the exclusion of the South at the pre-self-government negotiations. The destiny of the Southern Sudanese was decided behind their backs just as the union of the North and South was unilaterally decided upon by the Civil Secretary with the support and pressure from the North, but without the prior consultation or the blessing of the South.

Preparations for self-government involved elections for Parliament: the Senate and the House of Representatives. Colonial policy dictated that political power be handed to those indigenous leaders who commanded the majority support of members in Parliament.

Elections and Transfer of Power

The Sudanese Nationalist Movement for independence crystallized in the late 1940s in the Northern Sudan where much of the political activity was centered.[55] Five political parties eventually emerged and all were characterized by ethnic, religious, and sectarian cleavages. The National Unionist Party (NUP) was the oldest of all the political parties and it developed out of four groups: the Ashigga Party (founded in 1944), Unity of the Nile Valley Party, the Unionists, and the Sudan Federation of Trade Unions. Initially the NUP had the backing of the Khatmiyyah, an orthodox Islamic sect of the Sufi order. But after independence, the Khatmiyyah sect transferred its support to the Peoples' Democratic Party, whose leaders had defected from the NUP. The NUP gradually became wholly an urban organization and also tended to be secular in its orientation. It campaigned against the political power of religious groups which, it was argued, had no proper place in the political life of a modern country. Its support came largely from the towns and cities where professionals, civil servants, traders and laborers, and, particularly, young people backed it. Its greatest strength was in Khartoum province and in Northern Blue Nile province, especially in the Gezira area. The Kababish tribe almost wholly supported the NUP for it was historically anti-Mahdist.

The other major party, the Umma, was the most highly unified and best organized during the decolonization period and shortly thereafter. It acted as the political voice primarily for the Ansar sect (Mahdists), but it also attracted traditionalist elements on the basis of its generally conservative policies. Its political strength was derived almost entirely from the Ansar organization among farming people and on the adherence of nomad tribes bound by tradition to the Mahdist cause. Its main support was in the central belt stretching from Kosti in Blue Nile province west to Darfur. The Baggara Arabs who were largely Ansars supported Umma, and many of the party's regional leaders were members of the families of the heads of tribal or local administrations. Outside its main territory, the Umma Party gained support from the ruling families of the Hadendowa and the Bakr in Kassala province and from the Dongolla area in Northern province from which the first Ansar spiritual leader, the Mahdi, came.

The third party was the Socialist Republican Party, which was created in December 1951 to counteract the alleged ambitions of Sayeid al-Mahdi to become King of the Sudan. This party was composed mainly of some educated persons under the leadership of Ibrahim Yusif Badri. It called for independence of the Sudan from both Egypt and Britain and the pursuit of socialism as an ideology of development.

The fourth party, the Sudan Communist Party (SCP), was founded in 1946 but gained no legal status under both the colonial and postindependence governments. The leaders were drawn largely from the educated middle class while the party's rank and file generally were drawn from the urban workers, particularly unskilled and detribalized. It also drew some support from the organized agricultural workers of the Gezira scheme and from the Railway Workers' Union.

The fifth party was the National Front Party (NFP). It was backed by the religious leader of the Khatmiyyah tariqa, Sayeid Ali al-Mirghani (the rival of Sayeid el-Mahdi). The NFP stood for some form of unity with Egypt.

In the Southern Sudan, by 1953, political groups such as the Southern Party and the Southern Political Association, with offices in the three southern provincial headquarters of Juba, Wau, and Malakal, were established. The colonial authorities did not, however, recognize these organizations as political parties and saw fit to continue to exclude the Southern region from crucial negotiations leading to self-government. The Southern politicians felt neglected and reorganized in December 1954 into a Liberal Party which stood publicly for federation of North and South, but essentially worked to ensure a greater political voice for Southern Sudan.

In an effort to prepare the Sudanese people for a parliamentary system of government in an independent Sudan, the colonial autarchy organized the first general elections in late 1953. This was the first time in the history of the country that the people were to be involved in choosing their leaders on such a scale. According to Karal J. Krotki,[56] out of the ninety-two territorial constituencies, the eleven fully urban constituencies represented on the average populations of 43,000 each, while the remaining eighty-one constituencies (different combinations of urban and rural) represented on the average 120,000 each. He argues that "if we further accept that the five non-territorial constituencies represented predominantly, possibly exclusively, urban areas, we shall see that the 16 members of the House of Representatives from urban and graduate constituencies represented 30,000 citizens each, that is to say, urban inhabitants were four times more important than country people." The inequality between the North and South was substantial:

> A Northern member represented on the average 104,000 people, while a Southern member represented on the average 127,000 people, i.e. the influence of every citizen from the North was 22% greater than that of his brethren from the South. In fact, because all the fully urban constituencies lie in the North, more than half of this difference of 23,000 (127,000-104,000) is due to the advantage enjoyed by the urban areas. If we compare the non-fully urban constituencies, we will have 117,000 in the North, and 127,000 in the South. Another 2 or 3 additional Southern members would do away with this difference of 10,000 (127,000–117,000), but it is doubtful whether in the circumstances of the then prevailing knowledge and administrative boundaries this would have been practicable.[57]

In all, 1,687,000 people were registered as voters in an estimated population of over nine million people.[58] The total number of voters was slightly more than 20 percent of the estimated population of the whole country. There were ninety-seven seats in the House of Representatives (sixty-eight direct election constituencies, twenty-four indirect election constituencies, and one graduate constituency returning five members); and fifty seats in the Senate (thirty elected members by province constituencies and twenty nominated by the Governor General).

The candidates in the countryside encountered immense difficulties in campaigning: long distances with few *murram* roads, scattered and unreliable transport, and lack of funds. Correspondence among the candidates and their party leaders was impossible. These problems made it exceptionally prohibitive for them to mobilize support among voters who had not had the benefit of political socialization. In some parts of the Northern Sudan, candidates found it also difficult to organize meetings among the nomads, who kept on moving from one place to another in search of water and grass for grazing their animals.

The NUP waged the most efficient and effective political campaign and made the most of mass rallies, ward organizations in the cities, and efforts to get out the vote. It won the elections on a platform of unity with Egypt partly due to considerable support from many who opposed union with Egypt but feared that an Umma victory might mean creation of a Northern Sudanese monarchy headed by the late leader of the Ansar sect, Sayeid Abdal-Rahman al-Mahdi. The popular appeal of the NUP leader, Ismael el-Azhari, with full Egyptian backing also accounted for much of the NUP electoral victory.[59]

The main campaign issue in this first act of mass involvement in political participation in the Northern Sudan was the rapid drive for independence. The two sectarian groups: the Ansars (Mahdists) and the Khatmiyya mobilized their supporters behind the two rival parties—the Umma and the NUP respectively. Political discussion centered mainly on the personalities of the candidates rather than on policies of development. Most of the traders, regardless of sect, voted heavily for the NUP. The Umma Party, on the other hand, drew most of its support from the rural areas, with a solid appeal in Darfur and Kordofan provinces.

But whereas the Northern political parties demanded self-determination from the colonial power, the Southern Sudanese wanted self-determination from both the British and the Arab Sudanese. That is, the people of the two regions looked at independence from the British in different ways:

> Two ethnic communities can suffer joint domination from an external colonial power, particularly when there is no immediate hope for either of them to attain independence. When prospects for independence do materialize, each may define its limits of self-determination. In the Sudan, the Northerners, because in the majority and with better prospects of taking over as successors of the British, defined self-determination for the entire Sudan as one entity. The Southerners, because in the minority and apprehensive of domination by the Arabs of the North, defined self-determination to mean separate independence for the North and the South. The clash between the two was, therefore, inevitable.[60]

The concern in the Southern Sudan was the fear of betrayal by the British to Northerners whose ancestors had carried on slave trade in the South. But the South was handicapped from the beginning in arguing its case: it lacked educated and sophisticated leadership which could match that of the North and, above all, the colonial regime was not ready to reverse its policy of a united Sudan.

Hence, following the 1953 elections, Parliament was formally inaugurated by the Governor General on January 18, 1954, and five days later, Ismael el-Azhari, leader of the NUP, became the first Sudanese Prime Minister. An elected Sudanese government was now in full control of internal affairs while foreign and constitutional affairs were still controlled by the Governor General. The days of colonial rule were numbered. It is therefore in order to make an overall assessment of the Colonial era in the Sudan, with particular regard to its impact on African-Arab relations.

The Pax Britannica and the Sudan: An Appraisal

The British occupied and colonized the Sudan in 1898 ostensibly on behalf of Egypt. The control of the Nile Valley was seen as necessary for both the economic livelihood of Egypt and for the strategic interests of Britain. A joint Anglo-Egyptian military expedition was thus sent to annex the Sudan lest other European powers such as France and Belgium should occupy it. Although Egypt and Britain were to have a dual control over the Sudan, policy decisions up to the post-Second World War period were made exclusively by the British colonial administrators.

The colonial regime decided to treat the Northern and the Southern regions as separate territorial entities. This plan of separate administration and development of the two areas was formally formulated and announced in 1930 and came to be known as the Southern policy. It was not a departure from the preexisting situation. The North and South were two different areas geographically, religiously, culturally, and to some extent racially. Moreover, there existed already a deeply rooted mutual hatred and distrust between the people as a result of memories of Arab slave raids into the South before and during the Anglo-Egyptian military occupation of the Sudan. Hence, the policy of separate administration of the two regions was logically based on the facts of the situation: it was, by default, a correct colonial policy.

The greatest error of the British colonial administration was in its reversal of the Southern policy after the Second World War and its consequent failure to provide the kind of social development and constitutional transition that might have had the chance of safeguarding the political position of the South in independent Sudan. In 1946, the British officials in Khartoum decided, without either consulting the Southern Sudanese or sounding out the views of the British administrators working in the South, in favor of the merger of North and South. The reversal of the Southern policy came as a result of a combination of factors: pressure for one Sudan from the Northern Sudanese politicians who were entertaining cultural imperial interests in the South; pressure from Egypt which was hoping that after the British withdrawal the Sudan would become one of its provinces; and of no less importance were the British interests in the Middle East—the Suez Canal was becoming a bone of contention between Britain, France, and Egypt, and Britain did not want to antagonize Egypt in the Sudanese affair. The

Southern Sudan was to be sacrificed to appease Egypt. Indeed, after the war, Egypt acquired an effective role in the shaping of policy on the future of the Sudan.

The Southern Sudan was not well prepared for the rapid political transition to self-government in 1953. Southern Sudanese had no concept of one Sudan together with the Arab Sudanese. The colonial policy of separate administration had kept the two peoples of North and South apart and there also developed wide disparity in social and economic development between the two regions. For, whereas education and social services were left in the hands of the missionaries in the South, the colonial regime was actively engaged in expanding education and economic development and modernization in the North. Many Northern Sudanese also went to Egypt for education.[61] In short, the colonial regime knew that the merger of North and South in essence meant handing of the latter and weaker region to the former and stronger one. Protests from British colonial officials working in the South against the new policy of one Sudan were not taken seriously by their superiors in Khartoum. Southern Sudanese fears were also deliberately ignored.

When self-government was ushered into the Sudan, there was an absence of a sense of national belonging on the part of the Southern Sudanese. The new "united" Sudan lacked the centralizing process that can help promote in a population "mutual identification as nationals of the same country"; there was an absence of "a collective cumulation of shared moments of national experiences." The Negroid Africans of the South and the Arab Sudanese of the North did not have experiences which would lead to "shared prejudices and shared emotional dispositions."[62] Instead, whereas the various ethnic groups in the South possessed and shared prejudices and emotional dispositions against the Arabs in the North and vice versa, there was no sense of nationality between Southerners and Northerners.

Therefore, as the British gradually transferred institutional political power to the Arab Sudanese in the North, African-Arab relations in the country deteriorated. While the situation required understanding, tolerant, and imaginative leadership, it was not forthcoming in independent Sudan.

PART II
Praetorian Politics and Civil War

CHAPTER IV

Parliamentary Politics and African-Arab Confrontation

With the Sudan well on its way to independence and the colonial regime having decided to relinquish political power to the North, the Southern politicians had no choice but to participate in the new politics in Khartoum with the hope that they might help influence policies affecting the South. They also hoped to secure a federal arrangement with the North before complete independence was achieved. Thus, they reorganized under one united front.

The Southern Party, formed prior to the 1953 elections, was now renamed the *Liberal Party* in order to avoid the word "Southern," which "might imply that the region is separated and to the use of which the Northerners objected." While membership in the Liberal Party was open to the Northerners, none joined so it remained an exclusively Southern party. It had the support of the Southern intellectuals as well as that of the great majority of the Southern people. The top three posts in the party were filled by politicians from the three Southern provinces, which gave the party a representative and balanced leadership. The President, Benjamin Lwoke, was from Equatoria; the Vice President, Stanislaus Paysama, was from Bahr el Ghazal, and the Secretary General, Buth Diu, was from Upper Nile.

Although the Liberal Party formed branch committees throughout the South, it was more actively a parliamentary group than a mass party. It also suffered continually from personal clashes and disagreements over strategy and policy. However, it did achieve to a considerable degree its initial objective of representing the South as a united front in crucial issues affecting the region.

Southern Reactions to the Sudanization Report

In the general elections preceding the formation of self-government under Ismael el-Azhari, the Northern political parties made wild promises to the

South in an attempt to win the support of the Southern members of Parliament. The NUP, for instance, promised regional autonomous institutions for the South:

> Our approach to the question of Sudanization shall always be just and democratic, not only shall priority be always given to Southerners in the South, but also shall the employment of the Southerners be greatly fostered in the North, especially in the highest ranks of the central government service. Not only government jobs but also membership of the different local government institutions, development committees, etc., shall be as far as possible in the hands of competent Southerners in the Southern province.[4]

The process of Sudanization, that is to say, the taking over of jobs by Sudanese from the departing colonial administrators, was however, disappointing to the South. When the report of the Sudanization Committee was announced in October 1954, only six Southerners were given administrative posts out of 800 posts Sudanized.[5] The highest post given to a Southerner was that of an Assistant District Commissioner. The Sudanization Committee used three criteria for filling the posts: seniority, experience, and academic qualifications. All these conditions favored the North—the committee acted on a built-in inequality to the detriment of the South which viewed the three criteria as a "deliberate and malicious plot"[6] to exclude it from participation in the administration of the new unified Sudan.

The Southerners perceived relative social and economic deprivation as the fear of domination by the North became real and widespread among them. They were embittered irretrievably. The results of Sudanization confirmed the feeling in the South that the region was being cheated and that its lot in the future was to be dominated and exploited by the North. One Southerner expressed the feeling of his fellow compatriots in these words: "The results of Sudanization . . . mean our fellow Northerners want to colonize us for another hundred years."[7]

The Liberal Party MPs, accompanied by some opposition MPs from the Umma Party, toured the South and held public meetings in which:[8] (a) the NUP government was criticized for failing to honor its election promises to the South; (b) the Northern traders (most of whom were illiterate or only semiliterate, arrogant, and supporters of the NUP) were accused of exploiting Southerners; and (c) a demand was made for Southern MPs who joined the NUP to resign from it. Henceforth, the Liberal Party increased its campaign activities in the South and called for a federation with the North. Everywhere highly inflammable speeches were made against the Northerners labeling them as oppressors and "slave traders."[9]

Meanwhile the Southern MPs who joined the NUP and were made ministers presented to Prime Minister Ismael el-Azhari their own version of what they considered to be the genuine "demands of the South."[10] They called upon the government to pass special legislation to accelerate the appointment and promotion of Southerners to higher administrative posts.

They also asked the Prime Minister to appoint Southerners as governors and deputy governors for the Southern provinces to replace the Northerners who took the positions from the British. Unfortunately, the Prime Minister ignored these demands from the Southern members of his own party. Instead, he decided to tour the South, in company with a large number of NUP politicians, in an attempt to win the confidence of the Southerners.

The Prime Minister was, however, ill-received, being booed wherever he went. In an attempt to counter the effects of the campaign mounted by the Liberal Party against his policies, the Prime Minister announced an increase in salaries of prison wardens, policemen, and clerks in accordance with Northern scales, but the Southern leadership regarded such a move as politically motivated calling it a bribe, which was considered an insult to the dignity of the people of the region.

The relationship between the North and the South progressively deteriorated. In May 1955, one Southern MP who was made a minister in the NUP government resigned his post, left the NUP, and joined his fellow Southerners in the Liberal Party.[11] He resigned in sympathy with the general grievances of the South and because he thought the NUP government was not interested in allaying the mounting fears of the South by embarking on a program of development aimed at redressing the imbalances between the two regions. A second Southerner in the cabinet was dismissed for openly criticizing the government for doing nothing for the South.[12] The Liberal Party welcomed both of them and one Southern parliamentary bloc was formed to pursue the rights and demands of the South.

Northern Administrators and Politics in the South

The NUP government decided to use the Northern administrators in the South to frustrate the activities of the Liberal Party. Two events will be discussed here to illustrate the extent to which civil servants became involved in politics, particularly in Equatoria province.

The first event was the Liberal Party Conference held in June 1953. All Southern MPs, including those in the NUP, were invited to attend the conference: it was meant to be a family gathering for all Southerners regardless of differences in political persuasions. The NUP government was, however, infuriated by the invitations sent to Southern Parliamentary members in the NUP, and it therefore decided to frustrate the conference: "it appears a hint was sent from a Government source to some politically minded administrators in Equatoria to arrange for telegrams to be sent to Khartoum deprecating the aims of the Juba Conference, and supporting the Government."[13] When the Prime Minister was informed by one Southern MP,[14] who was a minister in his government, of the forthcoming Juba Conference and its main subject of "federation," the Prime Minister threatened that his government would not hesitate to use force if the unity of the Sudan was at stake. The Prime Minister's attitude and his reaction to the news of the Juba Conference was unbecoming of a head of a political party.

At the time the Liberal Party Conference convened, the following telegram was allegedly sent by the Prime Minister to Northern administrators in the South:

> To all my administrators in the three Southern Provinces: I have just signed a document for Self-Determination. Do not listen to the childish complaints of the Southerners. Persecute them, oppress them, ill-treat them according to my orders. Any administrator who fails to comply with my orders will be liable to prosecution. In three months' time all of you will come round and enjoy the work you have done.[15]

This telegram was circulated widely among Southern politicians in all three provinces. It is difficult to establish its authenticity but it was not unlikely that the Prime Minister could have sent such a message to his administrators in the South. What is important here is not whether such a telegram was actually sent by the Prime Minister but the fact that it was widely believed in the South that the telegram existed. Moreover, the substance in the alleged telegram reflected the attitude of some of the Northern administrators.

At the Liberal Party Conference a resolution calling for a federal relationship between the North and the South was unanimously endorsed. Although the nature of such a "federation" was not defined, the term "federation" became a household word in the Southern Region. Henceforth, the situation in the South became tense, and increasingly potentially explosive.

The second incident in which Northern administrators interfered in politics in the South occurred in Yambio District, and Azandeland, where the District Commissioner (DC) and the Assistant District Commissioner (ADC) forced chiefs to affix their signatures to a statement supporting the government. Other forms of pressure were employed as well to obtain the consent of the chiefs.

One chief, Basia Renzi, felt bitter because of the way in which the DC and his assistant coerced and tricked his fellow chiefs to support a statement of confidence in the government and in the Northern administration in the South. He sent a letter of protest to the Governor General of the Sudan, in which he explained his conflict with the two administrators:

> I, Chief Basia Renzi of Tembura, was compelled by the D.C. Yambio, A.D.C. Yambio, A.D.C. Tembura and Executive Officer Tembura Rural Council to sign an Agreement. I refused to do so giving him the following answer: I have to call my Sub-Chiefs first and bring to the public notice what I am going to sign for: if they approve of it then I am at liberty to sign. . . . The D.C. and his colleagues refused and frightened me that they have the power to take me away from being a Chief and take my car and my guns including whatsoever I have got and made me a poor man in the sense of the word poor.

> The D.C. then asked me whether I could write. I admitted to him that I was able to write. Then he gave me a piece of paper to write my name to prove that I can. As a proof to him I wrote my name. He immediately took the piece of paper and put it in his pocket, taking for granted that I have signed for the political idea he has in his mind which I cannot undermine for the moment. A very cowardly attack which means slavery for Southerners during self-determination which will mean our doom.
>
> The third request of the D.C. who was of course the chief speaker was that I should with immediate effect lend my car for relief of the government lorry which got broken on its way to Tembura carrying money to the District. This I did at once without any argument. After all this was only a trick no lorry was broken on its way to Tembura. The D.C. and his colleagues took my car driving all over the district compelling other chiefs to sign on the ground that I have signed and pointed at my car as an example that I too have signed and given the car as proof for them to believe and sign likewise. So all the Tembura chiefs have signed in cold blood like me under childish circumstances.[16]

Thus, although civil servants were not supposed to indulge and interfere in politics, this was not the case in the South where the NUP government used them to further its policies. The findings of the Commission of Inquiry into the Southern Disturbances of 1955 indicted the government for allowing the civil servants to meddle in politics.

> The fact that the Assistant District Commissioner himself interfered in politics in such a way, whilst preaching to his subject people not to do so is deplorable both in a moral sense and in an administrative sense. It is manifestly wrong for an administrator to allow his party loyalty to carry him beyond his duty to his people and the public service. It certainly led into his public losing confidence in his impartiality. There is also reason to believe that the Governor and Deputy Governor in Equatoria were well aware of the activities of their subordinates. . . . We are led to the irresistable inference that some form of intimidation had been sent out to some administration—in Equatoria by a Government agency (the exact source of which we are unable to establish) to try and suppress it (the Liberal Conference). Such methods would ultimately lead to corruption of the whole civil service and for the sake of a temporary and a doubtful party gain in Khartoum. A population which was passively anti-Northern was transformed, by such administrative meddling, into becoming actively so. The telegram of support for that matter, would not create such excitement if it had been the spontaneous feeling of the people.[17]

The telegram, allegedly sent in the name of thirteen chiefs in the Yambio District, had unanticipated repercussions. At the same time that it was sent, a Liberal Party Member of Parliament, Elia Kuze, was holding political meetings in his constituency. In these meetings, he criticized the NUP government for failing to honor its election promises to the South and he also attacked Northern Sudanese in general. When he heard about the telegram allegedly sent by chiefs in his area in support of the government, he immediately seized the opportunity to organize more public meetings in which he denounced the chiefs who signed the telegram. Kuze enlisted the support of Chief Bangasu, who had already sent a letter to the Governor General in protest against the method used to obtain the signatures of chiefs. They organized a meeting in Yambio and the following resolutions were passed:[18]

1. That Mr. Elia Kuze, M.P., being the Parliamentary Member duly elected by the people to represent them in Parliament, is the only person to talk on their behalf, and he should have been consulted prior to sending the telegram by the Assistant District Commissioner.
2. That all the chiefs who had signed the statement of support for the Government should be removed from their offices.
3. That they do not wish to be ruled by Northerners.
4. That it is not fair that Northern Sudanese should be superior in both Houses of Parliament, and the administration. They were completely lost and dominated by their "false so-called Northern brothers."
5. That if the organizers of this meeting were put in jail, all other Azande would go to jail too, and that a lawyer brought from outside the Sudan, should come to try them.
6. That the Assistant District Commissioner, by calling and asking the chiefs to sign the declaration had himself interfered in politics, contrary to Government Regulations.

These resolutions undoubtedly showed the strength of public feeling against the Northern Sudanese in general and against the newly installed NUP government in particular. The Avungara chiefs who signed the telegram took great offense at resolution (2), which was directed against them.[19] The Azande chiefs refused to sign the telegram and fully supported the six resolutions. Chief Nyaka, an Avungara and the President of the Chiefs' Court (the presidency of the court rotated monthly among the chiefs), together with another chief, lodged a complaint to the DC against the organizers of the Yambio meeting. The DC supported them and signed the court summonses. Elia Kuze, who had by then left to attend the Liberal Party Convention in Juba, was arrested and sent back to Yambio at the request of the DC. The DC argued that Elia Kuze and his supporters who organized the meeting which passed the six resolutions had to be tried to "restore the authority and prestige of chiefs which suffered considerably in consequence of the resolutions passed in the meeting."[20]

The trial of Elia Kuze, the Liberal Party Member of Parliament and five of his supporters opened in Yambio in July 25, 1955. They were charged with "criminal intimidation under Section 441 of the Sudan Penal Code." The prosecution argued that the accused had on July 7, 1955, at their political meeting resolved that the chiefs who signed the declaration of support for the government be removed from their offices (resolution 2).[21] The Chiefs' Court found the accused guilty and sentenced each to twenty years' imprisonment. The DC who was in the courtroom at the time of the trial intervened and explained to the chiefs that the maximum sentence laid down by the law for such an offense was only two years and that the court had no jurisdiction to pass a sentence of twenty years. The court promptly reduced the sentences of the accused to two years, the maximum it could impose.

When the sentence was announced, there was a spontaneous demonstration by the crowd of about 700 people in sympathy with the accused.[22] In order to disperse the crowd, the DC called in troops, who used tear gas against the people. In the midst of the confusion, two Northern Sudanese merchants shot at the mob, killing eight and injuring eleven people. A shop of a Northerner was raided and some of the merchants were beaten up by the crowd. This incident was handled badly by the authorities as evidenced by the widespread repercussions. The Southerners regarded it as the beginning of a war and thereafter lost confidence completely in the Northern administration.

In the eyes of the Southerner, the government and the Northern Arab merchants and traders were one institution: wrongdoing by one meant collaboration by both. Indeed, in many instances, the Northern traders became agents of the government, and their close social interactions with the Northern administrators in the South confirmed the equation: administrators plus traders equaled Northern Arab dominators and oppressors.

The Report of the Commission of Inquiry into the 1955 disturbance in the South found that the trial of Elia Kuze and five others was "a farce and a usurpation of the machinery of Justice."[23] The report gave six reasons for this conclusion. First, the District Commissioner's motive for the trial was simply the restoration of his prestige and that of his chiefs. Second, some of the members of the court were themselves involved in the action, thus in fact sitting as judges in their own case. Third, the trial was contrary to the spirit and intention of the Chiefs' Court's Ordinance, legislation primarily passed for the trial of ordinary offenders according to native law and custom, was never intended to be used for the trial of political or quasipolitical offenders. When the Governor General's council debated this piece of legislation, it was firmly understood that it would not apply to sedition and other political offences.[24] Fourth, the report contended that it was unlawful to try a Member of Parliament by a Chiefs' Court since government officials were exempted from its jurisdiction except by consent of the District Commissioner. Although his conduct might have implied such consent, it was the opinion of the members of the Commission of Inquiry that he at least should have consulted the Province Judge Southern Circuit, particularly since he had been anxious to consult him in previous cases where Northerners were involved. The report noted that it was "a pity that the Self-Government Statute does not bestow on the Sudan Members of Parliament immunities normally accorded to such Members by other democratic Parliaments."[25] Fifth, no consideration was taken by the court of Section 7 (3) of the Chiefs' Court's Ordinance, which provided that attention be paid to the age and character of the first offenders; and that by reason of the first sentence of twenty years' imprisonment, the court was obviously prejudiced. Sixth, the report concluded that the often repeated golden rule that "justice must not only be done, but *must be seen to be done*" was flouted.

The conviction of Elia Kuze was quashed by the Chief Justice on revision and a retrial was ordered.[26] But the damage was already done and relations between Northerners and Southerners in Equatoria province reached a low ebb. Moreover, it was known by the Southern elites that in the case of Elia Kuze, the Governor and Deputy Governor of Equatoria province, who were first-class magistrates, did not intervene to see that justice was carried out. The case demonstrated misuse of power by the Northern administration in the South, and the Liberal Party Members of Parliament thereafter united to campaign against the NUP government and called for a "federal constitution."

The Nzara Riots

After the colonial administration decided unilaterally to unite the North and the South of the Sudan, it found that all economic projects were concentrated in the North, which became, relatively, more economically advanced. Thereafter, the administration designed an agricultural scheme in Zandeland (the Zande Scheme) in Yambio district, for the growing, spinning, and weaving of cotton. The cotton mill was established between 1946 and 1949 and was located in Nzara, a few miles from Yambio.[27] This was the only scheme of its kind in the South.

By 1955, the Zande Scheme was a flourishing industry employing many thousands of Southerners, mainly Azande. The textile workers had a well-organized trade union movement to further their interests. Another important political organization also emerged in the area: the Anti-Imperialist Front. There was a similar group (Communist Front) in the North, and, although the Southern Anti-Imperialist Front gained its inspiration from its Northern counterpart, the strategy was not only anti-imperialism but also anti-Northern Sudanese.

The Anti-Imperialist Front published leaflets in English and these were translated into the Azande language and distributed to chiefs, government employees, and to the literate natives. The tone of the leaflets varied depending to whom each was directed:[28] some emphasized the strength of collective industrial strikes for demanding wage increases; others explained the cause of Southern Sudanese poverty and ways to combat it; still others denounced the newly instituted Northern government for not raising the wages of workers in the South. One of the leaflets complained that cloth made from the cotton grown by the workers in Yambio was sold more cheaply in Khartoum than in Nzara; the workers saw that their inexpensive raw materials and cheap labor were turned into cloth so expensive that they were unable to buy what they had produced. They complained bitterly:

> Our economic standard must be raised by the Government. And this by seeing that things are sold in the shops at reasonable prices, and also that our local cash crops and other articles are bought from us at fair prices. It is too much to buy our local cotton at 1½ piastres per rottle and after weaving its damuria (cloth) at Nzara, it is sold to us for thirteen piastres per yard. That is simply cheating us simply because we are yet largely ignorant and backward.[29]

The Southern Anti-Imperialist Front advocated local autonomy for the South. In pursuit of this objective it issued the following statement at the end of December 1954:

> Malakal, Wau, and Juba should be states each having its own Parliament: but the Central (Southern) Parliament should be at Juba, and from this Juba Central Southern Parliament Members should be selected to represent us in the Khartoum Central Sudan Parliament. In this way, we shall have our own Governors, District Commissioners, etc., but as far as we are going to be ruled by Northerners as it has begun now, there is no difference for us with the time when the English were our rulers, and worse still it means very surely that we are to be only slaves.[30]

Political consciousness among the Nzara workers increased considerably during the period of self-government and parliamentary politics. Some of the cotton growers in the Iba subdistrict of Yambio, influenced by the leaflets, became reluctant to sell their cotton for the low prices offered by the Equatoria Projects Board (EPB), the organization set up to run the Zande Scheme. On the whole, however, the campaign by the Southern Anti-Imperialist Front did not gain wide support in the South. The Southern political elites agreed in general with their grievances, but they did not care for the use of radical and Communist slogans. Some of the chiefs were thoroughly perplexed by the leaflets and took them to the District Commissioner's office at Yambio. Three points at least did interest most Southerners even if they abhorred the rhetoric of the leaflets: (1) equal pay for equal work for all Sudanese people; (2) three parliaments, in Juba, Wau, and Malakal; and (3) the criticism of the excesses of Northern administrators and of the anti-Northern passages.

The management of the EPB was Northernized as part of the Sudanization program. The Northern Sudanese managers arrived in June 1955, and a month later they dismissed *en masse* some three hundred Southern workers allegedly for financial reasons. Although the Northern Sudanese technical staff increased comparatively as a result of Sudanization, the dismissal of Southerners was a major blunder in that the decision, though necessitated by reason of economy, did not take into consideration the repercussions it might involve in the political situation prevailing at the time. To the Southerners it appeared to be a deliberate attempt to deprive the South of its livelihood.[31] The mass dismissals coupled with the evidence of corruption at the trial of Elia Kuze, engendered an increasingly tense political atmosphere.

Indeed, it was no surprise that on July 26, 1955, one day after the Elia Kuze episode, about sixty workers in the weaving and spinning textile mill at Nzara sent a petition to the Northern Sudanese Acting Manager demanding "higher wages." The petition explicitly stated that if the demand was not granted, a strike would ensue.[32] A day after the petition was presented, it was alleged that the workers abused their Northern Sudanese bosses and that they had shouted at them to go "back to their country" (meaning Northern Sudan). The Northern Sudanese officials complained to the Acting General Manager who tried in vain to exert his authority and to restore discipline. Police and soldiers were called in from Yambio, and the ensuing confrontation resulted in the death of eight people, six from gunshots fired by the police forces and two from injuries sustained in the resultant stampede of the crowd.

The news of the Nzara incident spread like wildfire throughout the South. As the Northern administrators in the South received the message "to get tough," hostility in Zandeland and throughout Equatoria province increased. Southerners concluded that there was no reason to expect any form of equal treatment with the Northerners in one united Sudan. They asked themselves once again why the grandchildren of the slave dealers who had plundered the South would become their masters. The Nzara incident was the last straw: "If there was some confidence left in the administration, it had then disappeared completely,"[33] which rendered inevitable the Nationalist uprising in the South.

The Issue of the Southern Corps and Eruption of the Civil War

The Anglo-Egyptian colonial administration created two separate army establishments: one for the Northern region (composed of the Northern, Western, and Eastern Corps) and the other for the Southern provinces (the Southern Corps). The two armed forces were recruited from the two respective regions and before the attainment of self-government, no Northern troops were stationed in the South. However, following the replacement of British officials by Northern Sudanese officials there was a persistent demand by the latter for stationing of Northern troops in the South, as one of them put it, "just in case of eventualities."[34] What eventualities did the Northern official have in mind? He must have foreseen North-South confrontation in the offing as a result of the Northerners' own colonial behavior toward the South.[35]

While the commander of the armed forces (Kaid) vehemently disapproved of sending troops to the South on the basis of mutual distrust and hostility existing between the local inhabitants and the Northerners, as well as for strategic and financial reasons, he was eventually pressured into carrying out these transfers. He gave orders that Company No. 2 of the Southern Corps was to leave Torit for Juba and thence by steamer to Khartoum. Also Company No. 5 of the Southern Corps stationed in Malakal was to leave for Khartoum.[36] Some Northern troops in return were to be flown to the South. These orders took place at a time when the atmosphere in the South was charged with suspicion and rumor. The most explosive of these rumors were that Northern troops which were coming to the Southern Sudan would be used to exterminate the Southerners, and that the Southern Corps was to be disbanded or to be transferred to the North where all the Southern soldiers would be massacred, and that a Northern army unit in Juba had murdered all Southern civilian natives including patients in hospitals.[37] These rumors were widely spread in the South by branch committee members of the Liberal Party. Moreover, the NUP government made no attempt to allay the fears and misapprehensions in the region, and actually fomented the belief that the rumors were possibly true.

When the government, therefore, decided as a concession to Northern administrators in the South to transfer Company No. 2 of the Equatorial (Southern) Corps to the North, the soldiers, fearful of their fate if shipped North, disobeyed the command to enter the waiting lorries to take them from Torit to Juba. This amounted to a "mutiny"[38] on the 18th of August 1955 when the troops ran amok and killed any Northerners they could find, including some of their Northern Sudanese Army officers. This incident in Torit sparked a nationalist uprising throughout the Southern region and it was the beginning of the African-Arab war in the Sudan.

The Northern government in Khartoum, with the help of the British, responded decisively: 8000 Arab troops were airlifted in British Royal Air Force planes to the South where they opened a violent and brutal campaign of repression which was to last for seventeen years. Soon after the Northern military occupation of the South,

> Firing squads worked overtime, suspects were shot in the bush, villages burned, crops destroyed, livestock killed, and Southern politicians intimidated as the wave of terror continued month after month. All Southern schools were closed and normal life ended in large areas. The fearful rushed into the wilds or across the convenient borders into exile. Except for a few towns, administrative order depended on a military presence coupled with random shooting. By October, Khartoum could feel that all was quiet. Although there was no coherent resistance, there still was no effective restoration of order—the South was slipping toward anarchy.[39]

Most of the Southern uprising was concentrated in the politically conscious Equatoria province which remained the focus of Southern resistance throughout the war years. The reported casualties resulting from the "Army Mutiny" totaled 261 Northerners and 75 Southerners, but the degree of Northern revenge was so brutal that there must have been a greater number of Southern casualties. In fact, the only Southerners included in the count were soldiers shot in action and prominent elites while natives killed in the countryside by Arab soldiers in pursuit of Southern members of the Equatorial Corps were excluded. Besides the Arabs, no foreigners were ever molested even when they gave refuge to Northerners.[40]

The wish of the Southern troops, who controlled Torit as well as most of the districts in Equatoria province in the month of August 1955, was the return of their British officers. They requested the British colonial government in Kenya to intervene as a mediator between themselves and the Northern administration after having refused the Prime Minister's order to surrender. The British authorities in Kenya rejected such results calling upon the Southern troops to do as commanded.

Meanwhile, the Governor General of the Sudan, Sir Knox Helm, who was on leave in Britain when the civil war broke out, returned to Khartoum. He immediately wired the following message to the Southern troops in Torit:

> I am most deeply shocked by your mutiny. When I visited Torit last May, I was very pleased with the spirit and efficiency of the Southern Corps. I never thought that three months later you would bring shame and disgrace on the name of the Southern Corps by breaking the oath which each of you has taken to serve me truly and faithfully and to obey lawful orders of your superior Officers. As Supreme Commander of the Sudan Defence Force I now order you to obey this direct order from me and by facing like men the consequences of your acts you will help to stop further bloodshed and to reduce the disgrace of your mutiny. The Prime Minister of the Sudan has told you what surrender means. He has also given you his personal word about a full and fair investigation and about your treatment as military prisoners if you surrender. I myself now give you some assurance. If you are ready to obey my order fully and without question I will send Mr. Luce, who is my Advisor and who was Deputy Governor of Equatoria in 1950 and 1951, as my personal representative to Torit to tell you the detailed arrangements for your surrender. You must acknowledge this message immediately and send me your reply within twenty-four hours. Unquote. Acknowledge.[41]

Thus, the Governor General's message to the Southern troops was the same in substance as the one previously sent by the Prime Minister—an order for the troops to surrender and face the consequences. The British officials in Khartoum even at this time could not understand the tension between the North and the South and acted on the assumption that the Southern troops had "mutinied" against the "legitimate authority" of the Northern government. The Governor General was either incapable of comprehending the deep political implications of the incidents in the South in the months of July and August in 1955, or he deliberately decided to ignore them and pretended that nothing was serious in North-South relations and that all would be well once the Southern troops surrendered to the Northerners. Presumably, he suffered from the former condition and trusted the Northerners to behave in a civilized manner in an attempt to cultivate the confidence of the Southerners. The British were prepared, at any rate, to leave the Sudan having handed political power to the North.

The Southern troops acknowledged the Governor General's message with a prompt response in which they contended that they did not mutiny but that a Northern Camel Corps in Juba was the cause of the disturbances when their plot to kill drivers of the Southern Corps Company No. 3 became known. They now requested an evacuation of Northern troops from Juba or at least, supervision by British troops to safeguard their surrender. Finally, they promised that there would be no more bloodshed if these requests were fulfilled.

Sir Knox Helm refused, however, all the requests of the Southern troops and insisted that they must surrender. He firmly rejected intervention by British troops and assured them that, although the Northern troops would not be evacuated from Juba, they would do no harm to the Southerners.

Eventually, the Southern troops surrendered in deference to the pressure and assurances from the Governor General. But when the Northern troops entered the town of Torit, where the Southern Corps was headquartered, they found no more than four soldiers, including the one who had acted throughout the period as their spokesman. Most of the Southern troops did not trust the Northern troops and fled the town into the bush and stayed in hiding. Many others, seeing the Northern reinforcements and having no hope of British help, went into exile in the then British East Africa, where they surrendered their weapons.

The revenge of the Northern troops was unprecedented: the Southern soldiers and policemen who surrendered were summarily executed and many innocent people were killed.[42] Sir Knox Helm having arranged the surrender did not intervene to see that a fair trial was conducted or that justice was carried out.

This incident serves to demonstrate, as had long been the case, the inability of the British to fully understand the predicament of the South in its struggle against the North and the consequent lack of cooperation between the two. What occurred, in the eyes of the South, was not a mutiny but a responsible nationalist reassertion of Africanism over Arab hegemony in the South. The Southern troops miscalculated in believing that the British would intervene to arbitrate and possibly to alter the political arrangement before complete independence was achieved. Actually, there was no proper coordination of plans and strategy between the Southern troops and politicians. Most of the prominent members of the Liberal Party in Juba were immediately arrested after the outbreak of the war.

The North viewed the situation differently. The Prime Minister argued that the Southern troops, as mutineers, must surrender and face the consequences of their actions or else confront the military might of the Government forces who were being flown to the South daily in the month of August 1955. The British authorities concurred with the Northern view and mobilized all power remaining with them to help the Northern government to defeat the Southern uprising.

It is necessary here to remember that the British colonial administrators in the South had warned against their bosses' decision in Khartoum to unite the North and the South on the eve of self-government and had asked for guarantees for the South. The guarantees were not specified in a separate article in the self-government statute but were embodied in the powers of the Governor General. When Southerners found themselves in an inferior position and took up arms in an attempt to encourage Her Majesty's government to review the North-South relationship, the response of the Governor General was profoundly sympathetic to the North and he refused to consider the possibility of a "federal structure" of government as demanded by the Liberal Party. In view of the British government, the time had come for the Northerners and Southerners to sort out their differences. Even so the Royal Air Force planes were used to transport Northern troops to the South, and the Governor General, still the Supreme Commander of the Sudan Defence Force, ordered the surrender of Southern troops.

Declaration of Independence

While Northern Sudanese leaders were able to unite against the South in response to the "Army Mutiny" of August 1955, members of the Parliament became increasingly critical of many NUP policies as evidenced by the indecisiveness in policy implementation. This prompted the Umma Opposition Party to call for the formation of a nonpartisan cabinet to hold a national plebiscite as a means of self-determination. The NUP government rejected this suggestion and, thereafter, it was censured in the House of Representatives on a budget issue by forty-nine votes against it compared to forty-five votes in its favor. The Prime Minister and his cabinet resigned, but five days later, the vote in Parliament was reversed by forty-eight votes to forty-six. This incident set the precedent for the pattern of parliamentary politics in independent Sudan.[43]

The Southern Members of Parliament were preoccupied with the future constitutional relationship between the South and the North, and did not participate in the censure motion. The Southern MPs concluded that since all the Northern political parties supported the NUP government's decision to deal violently and brutally with the Southern troops after their surrender, it made little difference which party in the North was in power. Of crucial concern to the Southern MPs now in the face of Northern occupation and consolidation of control in the South, was to delay total British withdrawal and subsequent Sudanese independence, as it inevitably signified Northern domination and repression. They proposed that a plebiscite be held in the South under the auspices of the United Nations to determine the desires of its peoples with regard to the nature of the political relationship they wanted with the North. Alternatively, the MPs called for a team from the International Red Cross to assess the deteriorating situation in the Southern region.[44]

The government as well as the departing colonial regime rejected both proposals. The Marquis of Reading echoes the British position in these words:

> The dispatch of United Nations' observers would almost certainly revive and strengthen the movement for some sort of self-rule in the South, thus widening the gap between South and North and running counter to the declared intention of the Anglo-Egyptian Agreement that the future of the Country should be decided as one integral whole.
>
> H. M. Government is strongly of the opinion that the future interests of the Sudan can be served only if the authority of the Sudanese Government is maintained and strengthened.[45]

For the British government, the events of July and August 1955 were not substantial evidence to confirm the fears and warnings of the British colonial officers in the South with regard to the inevitable outcome of a unitary government: Northern domination.

In the Northern Sudan, pressure for immediate independence continued to build. On December 3, 1955, Britain and Egypt signed a formal agreement in Cairo giving the Sudan the right to self-determination by means of a national plebiscite, to be supervised by a seven-nation committee. Elections to create a constituent assembly were to take place at the same time. Having accomplished this, Governor General Sir Knox Helm returned to Britain to resume his holiday, which had been interrupted by the nationalist uprising in the South.[46] The departure of Sir Helm provided the Northern Sudanese political leaders with a golden opportunity for a shortcut to immediate independence. The Prime Minister Ismael el-Azhari, and the leader of the opposition in the House of Representatives, Mohammed Ahmed Mahgoub, collaborated in a daring maneuver whereby the Sudanese Parliament bypassed the projected popular plebiscite and confronted the Condominium powers with a proclamation of independence to take effect January 1, 1956.[47] The resolution which was introduced in Parliament and intended for presentation to the Governor General stated explicitly:

> We, the members of the House of Representatives in Parliament assembled, declare in the names of the Sudanese people that the Sudan is to become a fully independent state, and request your Excellency to ask the two Condominium Powers to recognize the declaration forthwith.[48]

Although this proclamation was unanimously endorsed by the House of Representatives, the Northern politicians ran into difficulty in their attempt to persuade the twenty-two Southern MPs to accept it. The Southern MPs were concerned about guarantees for the South and the military situation in their area. The manner in which the North had responded to the uprising in the South made the Southern MPs insistent on a federal relationship. In order to win their support, the Northern leaders inserted the following clause in the Independence Resolution:

> That the House is of the Opinion that the claims of the Southern Members of Parliament for federal government in the three Southern provinces be given full consideration by the Constituent Assembly.[49]

This clause was inserted as a political maneuver rather than as a genuine promise on the part of the North. It was later explained by the then leader of the opposition, Mohammed Ahmed Mahgoub, in the following words:

> We canvassed all the parties to secure unanimity. We encountered some difficulty in convincing the Southerners so *we inserted a special resolution to please them* (emphasis mine) pledging that the Constituent Assembly would give full consideration to the claims of Southern Sudanese Members of Parliament for a federal Government for the three Southern Provinces.[50]

The Southern MPs naively believed that the Northerners were honest about their commitment and therefore decided to support both the Independence Motion and later the Transitional Constitution, which was passed unanimously on December 31, 1955. The following day, the Sudan formally became an independent state, and both Britain and Egypt promptly recognized the Sudan's new status.

Subsequently, the Sudanese Parliament appointed a five-man Supreme Council to take over from the Governor General. The Supreme Council acted as the head of state on the advice of the Council of Ministers through the Prime Minister, and the Council of Ministers in turn was collectively responsible to Parliament, of which all were elected members. The Prime Minister was elected by the House of Representatives and appointed by the Supreme Council. The members of the Supreme Council were elected by Parliament, and its chairmanship rotated among its members on a monthly basis. The two Houses of Parliament, the Senate and the House of Representatives, were both retained in the new arrangement. But while the former was composed of both elected and nominated members, the latter was composed solely of elected members. The Transitional Constitution provided for an independent judiciary directly responsible to the Supreme Council for the discharge of its functions. It also guaranteed fundamental human rights and freedoms which were justifiable before the courts.

The parliamentary system as worked out above by colonial as well as Northern Sudanese officials was intended as a temporary arrangement to facilitate the orderly transition to independence. But as it happened, Sudanese politics acquired a praetorian nature wherein leaders did not stand for periodic elections as specified, and no consensus was reached for a permanent constitution until 1973.

The Federal Issue and the Search for a Constitution

In September 1956, Parliament appointed a National Constitutional Committee of forty-six members, three of whom were from the South. Sayed Babiker Awadalla[51] was appointed chairman of this committee to which Parliament entrusted the preparation of a draft Constitution to be presented to Parliament sitting as a Constituent Assembly. The three Southern members of the committee called for a federal constitution, while the forty-three Northern members advocated a strong, centralized, and unitary system of government. The Southern members argued that the Independence Resolution had specifically promised full consideration of the Southern demand for a federal arrangement and therefore that the Constitutional Committee should present concrete proposals which would accommodate and adequately reflect the character, the needs, and the aspirations of all Sudanese people. The federal issue was rejected on grounds that it was not feasible. Thereafter, the three Southern members boycotted the meetings of the Constitutional Committee.

The Northern members of the Committee continued their deliberations. They recommended to Parliament that: (1) the Sudan should become a unitary Parliamentary Democratic Republic (Article 1); (2) Islam should become the official state religion of the Sudan (Article 5); and (3) that Arabic should become the official and national language (Article 4). The draft report of the Constitutional Committee was presented to Parliament in May 1958, after the general elections of 1957. The Southern members protested against the report, particularly Articles 1, 4, 5 (above), and when they realized that they were making little impact in the debate, they walked out of the assembly. The Northern MPs then decided to submit the draft report to a forty-member committee of the House of Representatives to study it and report back to the Constituent Assembly.[52] The composition of the forty-member committee was as follows: Umma Party, seventeen; NUP, nine; Peoples Democratic Party (PDP), seven; "Southern" Liberal Party, six; the speaker of the House of Representatives became the chairman and the fortieth member.

The forty-member committee did not succeed in producing a report because its work was constantly paralyzed by disagreements between the Southern and the Northern members over the question of federation. The Southern members refused to discuss any aspects of the draft constitution before the issue of federation was resolved. The Northerners on the other hand thought that federation was not necessary and that federal arrangement would be used by the South to further their separationist tendencies. This feeling prompted a Southern spokesman to make the following statement in Parliament:

> The South has no ill-intentions whatsoever towards the North; the South simply claims to run its own local affairs in a united Sudan. The South has no intention of separating from the North for had that been the case nothing on earth would have prevented the demand for separation. The South claims to federate with the North, a right that the South undoubtedly possesses as a consequence of the principle of self-determination which reason and democracy grant to free people. The South will at any moment separate from the North if and when the North desires, directly or indirectly, through political, social, and economic subjection of the South.[53]

The North was adamant and rejected a federal structure of government. This rejection of a Federal Constitution for the Sudan became another source of disillusionment for the Southern Sudanese. The state of emergency in the South declared in August 1955 remained in force, and harassment of Southerners by the occupying Northern army continued.

The North was not itself united on the draft constitutional proposals. Its political parties disagreed over the position and powers of the President. Thus the forty-member committee did not produce a report to the Constituent Assembly, which went into recess in August 1958. It was rescheduled to reassemble on November 17, but it never did.

The Failure of Parliamentary Politics 1956–1958

The period of self-government was intended to ensure a smooth transfer of political power and administrative responsibilities to Sudanese leaders (in this case Northerners) by the departing colonial regime. It was thought that the decolonization phase would enable the Sudanese politicians to learn the art of parliamentary politics and would ensure regular political participation at both local and national levels. This, however, did not happen after independence. The party machinery in the countryside dried up as the power contests and maneuvers were concentrated in Khartoum. The sectarian cleavages of the two Ansars and the Khatmiyya characterized parliamentary politics. Personalities of the traditionalists and to some extent of the secular-minded Azhari dominated the political scene. Consensus politics never took root. Political bickering among the leaders coupled with corruption in high circles soon led to disillusionment among party supporters. The parliamentary system soon became unstable and, only eighteen days after independence, the government of Prime Minister Azhari was defeated on a budget issue in Parliament. Azhari refused to resign but instead called for a vote of confidence in his government and won it. Those who voted against his budget proposals were afraid to go to the people for election before their parliamentary term was over.

While the politicians were engaged in parliamentary feuds in Khartoum, the workers and the farmers, in the South, who had been promised increases in their wages and prices of their products, became restive as the election promises were not kept. One incident that showed this restiveness took place in Kosti[54] when farmers were joined by the town workers in a large demonstration in support of their demands for higher crop prices. A violent clash occurred between the demonstrators and the police, in which 281 of the demonstrators, including women, were jailed overnight in a small windowless room—192 persons died of suffocation during the night. This workers' participation via demand for higher prices was seen by the opposition parties as an issue intended to exploit and embarrass the government. A delegation of lawyers led by the president of the Bar Association, Mohammed Ahmed Mahgoub (who was also one of the prominent leaders of the Umma Opposition Party in the House of Representatives), delivered a note to Prime Minister Azhari demanding his resignation and accusing him of negligence in the deaths of the 192 farm and town workers. A second demonstration was organized including government workers (civil servants) in Khartoum in protests against the Kosti affair. The government moved in swiftly and arrested its political opponents who had taken part in the demonstration, including Hassan al-Tahir Zarrug, Deputy President of the Anti-Imperialist Front Party, Abdal Rahman Abdal al-Rahim, Secretary of the Party, and Mohammed al-Sayyid Salam, President of the Workers' Syndicates Union. All these persons were subsequently tried and sentenced to six months' imprisonment for taking a leading part in the Kosti protest. However, the true question of responsibility for the 192 persons killed was answered when the government, having accepted the burden of guilt, earmarked 19,000 Sudanese pounds as compensation to their families.

The aftereffects of the Kosti incident became apparent when labor leaders hardened their attitude against the government and demanded wage increases for their union members. The worsening of the relations between the government and the labor organizations subsequently eroded the support which the NUP government had enjoyed among the workers.

The government failed to meet most of its election pledges, and its program of action was not comprehensive enough to sustain enthusiasm among its old supporters. Moreover, it was unable to formulate decisions on the most urgent problems of the economy. The opposition Umma Party did further damage by announcing its plan to form an Islamic Democratic Republic advocating a legislative policy based on religious laws. This policy statement was expected to appeal to the predominantly Moslem Northern Sudanese.

As the opposition criticism of the government became increasingly intense, the ruling party faced an internal leadership crisis. Prime Minister Ismael el-Azhari was accused by his rivals in the NUP of becoming too secular minded in his approach to politics. Indeed, Azhari was making a strong bid to take Sudanese politics from under the sway of the religious sects. Of no less importance were the personal clashes within the NUP, and these internal dissensions eventually led to the withdrawal of the Khatmiyya elements from the NUP to form the Peoples Democratic Party. The NUP became a purely secular party (like the Sudan Communist Party), the majority of its support being civil servants, professional groups, traders, and workers. In other words, it was essentially an urban party in contrast with the Umma Party. Soon after the rift in the NUP, Azhari lost his position as premier, following a vote of no confidence in the House of Representatives. Succeeding him was the Secretary General of the Ansar-dominated Umma Party, Sayed Abdullah Bey Khalil who won by sixty votes to thirty-two votes in the House. The PDP joined Umma to stabilize the government while the NUP, now devoid of sectarian support became the opposition. As regards the Southern Liberal Party, its members were preoccupied with the status of the South in the new Sudan and alternatively supported one party or another, depending on the issue. They sought backing for a federal arrangement.

The term of the First Parliament came to an end; and so by January 1958, nominations for the House of Representatives and the Senate were completed: 637 candidates were nominated for 173 seats in the House, and 135 for the 30 contested seats in the Senate. The Southern region was divided into 46 constituencies and the North into 127 for the House of Representatives.[55] Extensive campaigns were conducted in both North and South. In the former, the main political parties were dominated by old-guard politicians and by the two sectarian groups: the Ansar and the Khatmiyya, supporting Umma and the PDP respectively. Among the informed public, the main campaign issues were the management of the economy and conduct of foreign policy, especially Sudan's relationship with her Northern neighbor —Egypt.

In the South, a new leadership emerged, better educated and more politically militant than the representatives of the 1954 Parliament. Most of the former MPs lost their seats. The new MPs were generally single-minded in their approach to issues, although they were concerned with the creation of a unified parliamentary bloc which would press for federation. The most sophisticated and dynamic leader of the new militant group of Southern MPs was Fr. Saturnino Lohure, who was elected President of the Southern parliamentary group.

There was a large turnout for voting throughout the entire country. The ruling coalition of Umma and the PDP under Abdullah Bey Khalil was victorious. In the House of Representatives, the Umma Party won sixty-two seats, followed by the NUP with forty-five, the PDP with twenty-six, and the SLP with forty. The other six Southern seats were won by supporters of Northern parties.[56]

The Southern MPs generally voted with the coalition government, but being loosely organized, were never a dependable arm of the Umma-PDP alliance. There was, however, agreement among all Southern MPs, including those who joined the Northern parties, on the demand for a federal constitution and also for an increased Southern share of the country's development program. Although the new Southern MPs had deplored the frequent floor crossings and constant divisions among their predecessors, they, too, soon failed in maintaining a cohesive Southern bloc. They disagreed on parliamentary tactics, as when for example, during the crucial vote on whether the Sudan should accept U.S. aid as advocated by the government or should reject it as some Northern opposition and even PDP MPs preferred. When Fr. Saturnino Lohure and Luigi Adwok voted in support of the government motion calling for acceptance of the U.S. aid, they were both promptly dismissed from the Liberal Party positions by their colleagues and replaced by Elijah Mayom and Franco Garang, as President and Secretary General respectively. Hence, although the 1958 Southern MPs were more assertive in pressing Southern interests than their predecessors, they also suffered from personality clashes and divisions.

Other minority groups in the Northern Sudan, such as the Beja and the

Nuba, also made demands for inclusion in decision making. For instance, on August 13, 1958, the Beja MPs and chiefs called for the right of their people to run their own affairs: this was the same demand that the Southern Sudanese were making. It was, however, easy for the dominant Arab group to use pay-off mechanisms for containing the Beja and Nuba leaders. Islamic solidarity in the North helped forge a sense of primary consensus;[57] the sharp polarization only remained between the South and the North.

The Umma-PDP coalition was a very uneasy one. The two parties differed in foreign affairs policies. Umma was anti-Egypt and was more inclined toward the West, while the PDP was more oriented toward the Middle East and the Arab League, and was anti-West. The coalition was at best the result of political opportunism and sectarian loyalty, all held together by parliamentary manipulation. And when the tactics of party management were exhausted, parliamentary institutions were left debased, benefiting only those politicians who continued to reap the rewards of power and patronage. The government, which had become very ineffective, could hardly govern in the South and there was a lack of responsiveness to the pressing problems of economic development. Politics in Khartoum became characterized by sectarianism, corruption, and misallocation of national resources. The government could not control the rising rate of inflation. The Umma Prime Minister, Abdullah Bey Khalil, was indecisive, inactive, and lacked political foresight and astuteness. His political boss, El Mahdi (the Ansar religious leader) was not happy with Umma's sharing of power with the PDP and, consequently, entered into negotiations with Ismael el-Azhari concerning the possibility of a coalition between Umma and NUP. It was believed that the wide respect for El Mahdi and the appeal of Azhari to the educated elite and the commercial class in the nonsectarian society of the towns would ensure political stability and would terminate the parliamentary crisis. The future of Abdullah Bey Khalil in such a coalition was, however, uncertain. Bey Khalil, who was himself an ex-brigadier, was now convinced that the firm government which the Sudan needed would not be forthcoming by democratic means. He confided his desire for the Army to take over the government to his son-in-law, Major General Ahmad Abdal al-Wahhab, Brigadier Hassan Beshir Nasr, and the Commander-in-Chief, Lieutenant General Ibrahim Abboud. The Army responded with enthusiasm and took control of the government in a bloodless, predawn coup d'etat on November 17,1958. It was invited to take over Prime Minister Bey Khalil, to put an end to the efforts being made to form an Umma-NUP coalition, and to dismiss a Parliament which was hostile to his domestic and foreign policies. Bey Khalil later boasted that he knew of the coup in advance and approved of it, because it saved the country from a "foreign sponsored" move to end Sudanese Independence.[58]

An analysis of the social and political relations of the Army general who carried out the coup reinforces the thesis of a behind-the-scenes compromise. The Commander-in-Chief who led the coup, Lieutenant General

Abboud, is a member of the Khatmiyya sect and was vaguely inclined politically toward the PDP. The possible displacement of PDP by NUP from the government in a new coalition was distasteful to him but the prospect of becoming a leader of a government was attractive enough to cause him to discard his party loyalty. Major General Ahmed Abdal al-Wahhab, who became the first Minister of Defense in the new Army government, was a member of the Ansar sect and was associated with the Umma Party but was ready to support his father-in-law against the move to oust him from power. Brigadier Hassan Beshir Nasr was sympathetic to the NUP but was an advocate of closer relations with Egypt and thought that a military government in which he would play an influential role would achieve the goal of union with Egypt.

Parliamentary democracy was thus promptly brought to an end in the Sudan after only three years of independence. The politicians failed to reach a compromise on a coalition government before the Army intervened. Prime Minister Abdullah Bey Khalil lost faith in parliamentary politics. Party disputes became more acute and the economic situation deteriorated. Parliament was reluctant to pass a bill that would have enabled him to receive aid from the United States. He also feared that the weakness of the government might prompt Egypt to annex the Sudan. Relations with Egypt at this time were at a low ebb following disagreements on whether the twenty-second parallel should be the boundary between the two countries or whether the Sudan should continue to administer two regions north of this latitude. Egypt eventually withdrew its army from the area after the Sudanese coup. An additional motive for Prime Minister Bey Khalil to solicit the Army to take over the government stemmed from the crisis between the North and the South. He thought that the continuing deterioration of the situation could not be solved by parliamentary maneuvers short of a Southern autonomy and that the brutal suppression of the South could only be continued by a military dictatorship. More irritating to Bey Khalil was the possibility of exclusion from a coalition that was being negotiated by the patron of his Umma Party, El Mahdi, and the leader of the opposition, Ismael el-Azhari, the NUP President. All these factors persuaded him that what the Sudan needed was a military government. Hence on November 10, 1958, he met the Army Chief of Staff Lieutenant General Ibrahim Abboud and evidently discussed the handing over of power to the Army. Bey Khalil thus knew of the 1958 Army coup and encouraged it, but he was ignorant of the details and timing. He naively thought that he would remain the power behind the scenes, but General Abboud on seizing political control, retired him along with Ismael el-Azhari on pension and both were banned from participating in public affairs. Parliamentary politics was thus abruptly terminated by "the barrel of the gun."

The parliamentary experiment after independence did little to consolidate the parliamentary system which was established by the departing colonial power. Development of informal factional politics which seemed to replace the regular party machinery in Khartoum (for example, factional alliances were formed to replace el-Azhari only a few months after independence, and the same thing was going to be repeated in the case of Bey Khalil) somehow rendered government leaders insecure and ineffective. That was the beginning of the development of praetorianism in the Sudan.

As far as the North-South conflict was concerned, the existence of the parliamentary system served at least two functions. First, parliamentary politics helped restrain Northern Sudanese who advocated the use of force to suppress Southerners who called for separation or federation. Second, it also provided a free atmosphere for continuing a dialogue between the leaders of both regions from which it was hoped an honest and realistic compromise could be reached. Hence, although the parliamentary regime was generally ineffective in responding to the urgent needs of the people, it was less brutal in dealing with the South when compared to the military junta that followed.

Conclusion

In many conflict situations, aggression is unleashed only when frustration becomes intolerable and conditions are not expected to improve in the future without a confrontation with the sources of it. In the Sudan, a series of both deliberate and malicious policies carried out by the Northern Sudanese administrators led to the buildup of frustration and to the breakdown of tolerance of the Southern Sudanese. The Southern Sudanese saw the policies of the Northern government as consciously conceived to thwart their need for self-preservation. These policies constituted the immediate precipitants of the "army mutiny" of 1955 and of the secessionist war. Some of these governmental measures, most of which were mentioned earlier, will be summarized below:[59]

1. The government did everything in its power including the use of administrators to intimidate Southern chiefs, to block a projected meeting of Southern leaders of all parties and shades of political opinions in Juba in June 1955. The aim of this meeting was to create a united Southern organization whose objective would be the pursuit of the demands of Southerners, particularly their demand for a federal constitution to allay their fears of Northern domination.

2. In the Zande Scheme about three hundred Southern employees were dismissed (but replaced with Northerners) for alleged redundancy. Besides, following a demonstration at Nzara, an industrial town, eight Azande were killed and many injured by the police, but the government, instead of investigating the causes of the disturbances, issued threats and ultimatums from Khartoum through the mass media.

3. A Southern MP, Elia Kuze, was imprisoned on July 25, 1955, after a trial which the Commission of Inquiry described as a "travesty."

4. The manner in which the Sudanization policy was being implemented was disappointing in the extreme to the Southerners who hoped for a fair share of the

> posts being vacated by British Government officials. For out of the posts to be Sudanized only about .75 percent went to Southerners and all these posts held by the Southerners were relatively unimportant. More than anything else this Sudanization policy was an eye-opener to the Southerners; it was indeed the realization of one of their worst fears. The meritocracy argument to defend its policy is very unconvincing where no visible attempt has been made to improve the educational and training facilities available in the South where there was still only one secondary school.

Such measures and many others reinforced by long-standing and deep hostilities led to mounting tensions and feelings of frustration in the South. Fears and uncertainties were pervasive everywhere; and as it is usually the case in such ambiguous and tense circumstances, rumors were created to clarify the situations. These rumors which were believed by Southerners made the Southern troops fight for the survival of their people.

The Report of the Commission of Inquiry pointed to the underlying differences existing between the North and the South, in terms of race, culture, and history. It also found that "there was too much mutual suspicion and mistrust between the administration and the missions in the Southern Sudan which is widening and not narrowing the cleavage between Northern and Southern Sudanese."[60] But the report concluded that the real trouble in the South:

> . . . was political and not religious; and neither slave trade nor the difference in religion played a part in the disturbances. . . . In the extensive disturbances that took place in Equatoria, Christians, pagans as well as Moslems took part; in fact some of the leaders of the anti-Northern propagandists are Southern Moslems.[61]

Perception by Southern elites of their relative social and economic deprivation in comparison to their counterparts in the North was, according to the report, one of the precipitant causes of the war:

> Since the Southern Sudanese benefited very little from Sudanization they found little or no difference between conditions now and conditions previously; and independence for them was regarded merely as a change of masters. We feel that the Southern Sudanese by finding themselves holding secondary positions in the Government of their country have a genuine grievance.[62]

The members of the Commission of Inquiry were shocked when they received confirming reports about the behavior and attitude of Northern Sudanese administrators who replaced the British officials in the South. The attitude of the administrators toward the Southerners led a great majority of opinion leaders in the South to regard the Northern administration as colonial. As the report pointed out:

> Some Northern Sudanese, including high officials in the administration, refer to the Southern intelligentsia as half-educated. Education is a relative term and largely a matter of opinion, but experience has taught, time and again, even

> nations with a very long history in colonial rule, that it always pays to gain the confidence of the intelligentsia whether they are fully educated, half-educated or quarter-educated. The Northern Administration in Southern Sudan is not colonial, but the great majority of Southerners unhappily regard it as such, and as long as that is so it is just as important to gain the confidence of this group as the people living in the bush.[63]

Most of the Northern Sudanese administrators in the South were young and inexperienced. Their encounter with the Southerners, who regarded tham as "the new colonial officials," did not provide a friendly atmosphere in which to become acquainted with their new environment; nor did they make an effort to impress on the people in the South an attitude of understanding and friendship. Instead, they liked to appear as bosses, and more often than not, intimidated the Southerners.

The Report of the Commission of Inquiry also pointed to the presence of basic dysfunctional cleavages between the North and the South. On the whole, the report produced a critical account of the genesis of the African-Arab conflict in the Sudan. Unfortunately, the Northern political leadership either did not study the report or ignored it completely, in favor of the pursuit of policies of assimilation of the South through the processes of co-optation, Arabicization, and Islamization. These policies were laid down by the short-lived parliamentary regime and were vigorously pursued by the succeeding military government.

CHAPTER V

The Military Regime of the Generals: Benevolent Dictatorship in the North and Arab Hegemony in the South

The November 1958 coup d'etat of Lieutenant General Ibrahim Abboud was generally well received in the North. It was widely believed that the politicians had been venal and ineffective. Hence, the army accession to power was hailed and considered appropriate under the circumstances. In the North, it was believed that the army would bring political stability, that it would silence the South with an iron hand, and that it would bring economic prosperity. Accordingly, the Khatmiyyah sectarian leaders publicly welcomed the coup and called on their followers to support the Army. The Ansar leaders also welcomed the army's seizure of power, but they qualified their support: the Ansars would back the army only so long as it was necessary. The professional politicians did not deem it wise to issue a statement although a few power opportunists were reported to have made favorable remarks in anticipation of ministerial appointments.

While the Army coup met no opposition in the North, it came as a blow to the Southerners who viewed it as a step backward in the process of achieving a federal political arrangement between the two regions. Moreover, there were no Southern officers in the ruling junta and those few who were in the army were of junior ranks. It meant, therefore, that the South was to be under Northern Arab hegemony so long as the army ruled. This belief was reinforced by the excesses of the Northern administration in the South, as well as by the military regime's decision to embark on the use of military force as a means of containing the South.

Governmental Structure and Divisions Within the Army

On coming to power, the military junta abolished the five-man Supreme Council, suspended the 1956 interim Constitution, dissolved Parliament, and pensioned off the two ex-premiers. The regime made no pretense about its dictatorial nature.

The supreme authority for legislative, executive, and judicial affairs was vested in the Supreme Council of the Armed Forces consisting of thirteen officers under the chairmanship of Lieutenant General Abboud acting as both Prime Minister and President. Abboud also retained his position in the Army as Commander-in-Chief of the Armed Forces. Second in prominence to General Abboud was Major General Ahmed Abdal al-Wahhab, Bey Khalil's son-in-law. Abdal al-Wahhab had a satisfactory background, general education, and solid military experience. Below the Supreme Council of the Armed Forces, there was established a Council of Ministers comprised of seven senior Army officers from the Supreme Council and five civilians, only one of whom was a Southerner.[2] The Army officers held the most important cabinet positions in the Council of Ministers.

General Abboud tried to neutralize the sectarian groups during his regime. Most of the civilian ministers were close to the Umma-Mahdiyya circles, while a majority of the members of the Supreme Military Council were associated with the Khatmiyya sect and the NUP/PDP parties. Abboud's policy was aimed at ensuring the supremacy of the Officer Corps and he eventually succeeded in neutralizing the traditional party-sectarian influences in the decision-making process.

The Supreme Military Council granted the ministers powers of arbitrary arrest and detention, of closed trial by military court, with the right to remove cases from civil jurisdiction, and of censorship of the press. Freedom of speech, assembly, and association was denied, and for a period of time the Northern Sudan was placed under a state of emergency. The Southern region was already declared an emergency area in 1955, and remained as such throughout Abboud's rule (1958–1964), and up until March 1972.[3]

The first two years of Abboud's regime were characterized by crises and unrest within the Army. Struggles for control of the Supreme Council produced factions within the Council. General Abboud remained quiescent, above the frequent squabbling. Then in March 1959, he made the surprising announcement to the country that all the members of the Supreme Military Council had resigned. This happened as a result of pressure exerted by Brigadiers Abdal Rahim Shenan and Mohieddin Ahmed Abdullah, both of whom amassed troops in Khartoum to back their demands for inclusion in the Supreme Council. A new Council was appointed including these two Brigadiers and a third one, Magboul el-Amin el-Haj. General Abboud was pressured to drop five members of his previous Council. The Minister of Defence, Major General Abdal Wahhab, who was rivaled by Brigadier Hassan Beshir Nasr, refused to accept the composition of the new Council and would not swear allegiance to it. Subsequently, he was relieved of his duties, retired with a pension, and given three thousand *dunams* of state land as compensation for his loss of office.

In an attempt to gain more prominence in the Supreme Council, Brigadiers Shenan and Abdullah conspired with other officers to launch an armed attack on Khartoum with the aim either of gaining more concessions from General Abboud or, as a last resort, of overthrowing the regime. Both of them were arrested and sentenced to death. However, the sentences were commuted by Abboud to life imprisonment. The internecine struggles among the Army officers erupted into open attempts in late 1959 to seize control of the government. The ringleaders were tried and executed. Thus, after a turbulent period, Abboud's regime came to enjoy a relatively calm and stable period.

By mid-1961, however, the public had become restless with the lack of a timetable for return to civilian rule. There were sporadic demonstrations in various parts of the country, leading to the arrest and detention of fifteen politicians, including Sayed Ismael el-Azhari, the NUP leader and first Prime Minister, Sayed Abdullah Bey Khalil, former Prime Minister and Umma Secretary General, two former foreign ministers, Sayed Mohammed Ahmed Mahgoub and Sayed Mubarak Zaroug, and Sayed Abdel Khaliq Mahgoub, the Secretary General of the Sudan Communist Party. President Abboud declared that these arrests were necessary to bring an end to the unscrupulous invention and spread of false rumors and criticisms with regard to the regime. Most of those arrested were detained in Juba in the Southern Sudan. These repressive measures did not, however, put an end to demands for a return to civilian rule.

The Search for Legitimacy

General Abboud stated in his first official announcement to the country that the purpose of the military takeover was stability rather than revolution: "in changing the prevailing state of affairs, we are not after personal gain nor are we motivated by any hatred or malice towards anyone. Our aim is stability, prosperity, and the welfare of this country and its people."[4] He added that "bitter political strife, instability, failure to safeguard independence, and misuse of the National resources" were faults of the past. He then committed his regime to ensure the participation of the people as a prelude to the ultimate goal of attaining a constitutional framework which would suit the nature of Sudanese environment in the hope of avoidance of the defects of systems imported with neither forethought nor understanding. The military regime outlined three goals in its policy statement: to bring about stability in the political system through gradual rather than revolutionary reforms; to produce a viable economy; and to ensure participation of the people in the political process. Abboud's six years of power fell short of reaching these objectives.

What follows is an analysis of the attempts of the military autarchy to import the Egyptian local government system into the Sudan.[5] No significant results were obtained from the experimentation with the Egyptian model because the regime had no intention of institutionalizing a participatory framework.

In an attempt to legitimize its authority through a controlled participatory system, the military junta appointed a commission under the chairmanship of the Chief Justice to recommend a blueprint for the "best ways for the citizens to take part in the government of the country and to play an effective role in the development of their own affairs." In a memorandum to the commission, the government stated explicitly that it was:

> To carry out an extensive survey of the present administrative machinery (local and central) and to submit its recommendations as to the best system from all points of view for an efficient, unified administration in the Sudan—whether through local government as practised now, centralized government or both—taking into consideration the objectives and principles of the present regime which aim at the prosperity and well-being of the citizens through taking quick decisions and handling problems and difficulties in an impartial way, and in an atmosphere of confidence and trust which will considerably strengthen the public security, stability and prosperity of the country.[6]

The government statement emphasized the dire necessity of an efficient and unified administration in the Sudan. The form of government to be achieved was not explicitly mentioned. The commission recommended that the spread of democracy should be the objective of a government. To achieve these aims, the commission recommended the formation of councils on three levels: local, provincial, and central to be filled by partial elections. The underlying aim of such a system was to achieve effective administrative unity. The local councils were to be free in exercising their powers under the directives from the central government. On the third anniversary of his regime (November 17, 1961), General Abboud accepted the recommendations and pledged his government to the attainment of a parliamentary system based on general elections.

In April-May 1963, the military junta conducted the first elections to local councils under the constitutional changes introduced following the recommendations of the commission. The country was divided into eighty-four local councils, both urban and rural, nine provincial councils, and one central council. Voting was restricted to male adults, and while the franchise qualifications were much the same as those of the parliamentary elections of 1958, the age limit was raised from twenty-one to twenty-five. Campaign organizers ran up against some difficulties. It was necessary to secure government permission to hold meetings, which, when appearing critical of the status quo, were forcibly dispersed, the organizers arrested, only to be released soon afterward without trial. Thus, most preelection meetings in the rural districts were of an informal nature being characterized by personal relations and tribal associations.

The banned political parties reacted differently to the elections. The Umma Party, which continued to maintain rigid party discipline among its followers through religious meetings, opposed the elections, and there was a very low turnout in its strongholds in Kordofan province. The NUP was opposed in principle to participation in the elections but could not ensure adherence to this position among its followers. In some cases the party leadership was defied. The PDP, representing the political face of the Khatmiyya sect, was enthusiastic about the elections, and its support explained the high percentage of voting in the Northern province where the party enjoyed a favorable influence and following. The Communist Party decided to contest the council elections but did not gain much support as the regime, being suspicious of its participation, had put its members under surveillance.

No campaign meetings were held in the Southern Sudan, where the government intensified its policies of coercion and repression. The Southerners showed no interest in such elections and viewed them as being irrelevant to their basic demands. They argued that participating in the government-controlled elections would have given the regime the impression that the South was supporting it. A few Southerners were, however, brought into the councils.

In general, people in the North were apathetic toward the elections because of the inadequate power and responsibility of the new councils. Moreover, the banning of the political parties deprived the electorate of the vehicles of political socialization. The "guided democracy"[7] the government claimed to introduce could not be achieved without difficulties in a society where district, political cynicism, and indifference prevailed. Active political participation could not be attained in restricted elections whose results were a foregone conclusion (there was a large number of unopposed candidates: 502 out of 1581 [about 32 percent] compared to only 2 out of 173 [or 1.16 percent] in the parliamentary elections of 1958). Voter enthusiasm was noticeably absent and candidates were interested in office solely for the financial allowance to be received if elected.

The reins of power continued to be in the hands of the Supreme Council of the Armed Forces. The councils were mere rubber stamps for the regime council rather than forums for genuine participation in the political process. At any rate, they were not meant to be used as effective instruments of democracy, for their powers were so greatly circumscribed that they could function neither freely nor effectively as agencies for discussing and implementing government policies nor could they provide feedback to higher authorities. Subsequently, in the Northern Sudan a United National Front was created in opposition to the military regime—a clear indication that the regime's search for political legitimacy through faked elections and controlled local, provincial, and central councils had failed.

In the economic sphere, however, the military junta was considerably successful in bringing about some progress in the North. It abolished a fixed cotton price, an action which resulted in surplus revenue. The military junta also concluded the "Nile Waters Agreement" with Egypt, an agreement which enabled the government to use a greater supply of water than previously for irrigation.

The Abboud Regime and the Southern Sudan

With the advent of the military junta in November 1958, all open political activities came to an end. The conservative Army generals embarked on a policy of cultural integration of the South into the Northern fold through the processes of Arabization and Islamization. This practice was a reversal of the colonial Southern policy of the 1930s whereby the South was treated as an entity separate from the North. The military regime reasoned that the South and its educated elites were the products of a system of Western acculturation which the British colonialists in conjunction with their agents, the Christian missionaries, had devised to divide the Sudan according to their colonial interests. Nationalism and national integration were henceforth equated with Arabization and Islamization. Northern values were imposed on the Southerners by use of force, giving the system an internal colonialist character. This characterization is evident in the definition of internal colonialism:

> A structure of social relations based on domination and exploitation among culturally heterogeneous, distinct groups. If it has a specific difference with respect to other relations based on superordination, it inheres in the culture heterogeneity which the conquest of some peoples by others historically produces. It is such conquests which permit us to talk not only about cultural differences (which exist between urban and rural populations and between social populations and between social classes) but also about differences between civilizations. . . . It is the result of an encounter between two races, cultures, or civilizations, whose genesis and evolution occurred without any mutual contact up to one specific moment. The conquest or the concession is a fact which makes possible intensive racial and cultural discriminations, thus attenuating the *ascriptive* character of colonial society.[8]

In pursuing a colonialist-line policy in the South, the Abboud regime initiated specific measures for the achievement of such a goal. It used intimidation and arbitrary arrests of suspected Southerners as a means of consolidating its control over the South. It set a ring of spies around some members of the Southern intelligentsia:

> . . . the secondary school and university students on leave, the Government officials and the ex-members of Parliament. The spy was not to detect crimes or intention to commit crimes only but he was to cooperate in the fabrication of charges against persons the Government had made up its mind to mistreat. To increase the number of offences and make their committal more likely, parting hair by a Southerner was interpreted as a separation between North and South; wearing a watch on the right-hand wrist by a Southerner was interpreted as a desire to be different from the Northerner who wears his on the left-hand wrist; leaving hair and beard uncut by a Southerner was interpreted as a sign that he resented the situation in the South which further meant that he was a Southern Nationalist.[9]

The pace of Arabization and Islamization was stepped up. A Department of Religious Affairs was set up for the supervision and organization of Islamic schools and institutes. Some newspapers in the North called on Northerners to join efforts with the military regime in converting Southerners to Islam. For instance, the daily *Rai el Amm* wrote:

> There is no doubt that many in this country know how much need Islam has in the South of efforts on the part of the government. The administrative authorities and men of the Ministry of Education and of the Department of Religious Affairs continue to make gigantic efforts; but this by itself is not enough.[10]

The weekly *Anba el Sudan* also called for expansion of Islamic teaching in the South: "this religion [Christianity] continues to expand in the South notwithstanding the measures adopted by the government in its regard. . . . It is the duty of the government to call into the South Islamic missionaries from India and Pakistan and from other Moslem countries."[11] Attempts to propagate Islam in the South were widely shared by most Northern Sudanese. As Collins succinctly put it:

> These attempts to proselytize in the mid-twentieth century originate from the deepest religious traditions of the Muslim past. The emotional appeals of the Sufi orders, which have played such a vital role in Sudanese history, fused with the apocalyptic mission of Mahdism to continue the spirit of the *jihad* without its more violent overtones. Whether in the name of Allah or a unified Sudan, to spread Islam throughout the country was a duty upon which most Northern Sudanese could agree irrespective of political persuasion.[12]

Thus the Abboud regime through the Department of Religious Affairs constructed mosques, established Islamic schools (*ma'had*), and subsidized Moslem propaganda in the South. The policy of nationalizing the missionary schools laid down as early in 1954 by the el-Azhari Ministry was pursued vigorously. All the missionary schools after being nationalized, were "integrated into the system of government schools which flourished in the North, while the missions or any Southerner were prohibited from opening a private school in the South although such privately owned schools continued to provide a valuable supplement to the government schools in the North. In addition six intermediate Islamic Institutes were opened, and the military administrators worked assiduously to spread Arabic and Islam."[13]

In pursuit of this new Arabized educational system for the South, the military regime decided in February 1960 to change the day of rest in the South from Sunday to Friday. This change of the official day of rest provoked a vigorous reaction of protest from students in the Rumbek and Juba Commercial Secondary Schools, who later were joined by pupils from intermediate schools. The Southern students in the only two existing secondary schools in the South considered the abolition of Sunday as the official day of rest to be a last straw which had to be resisted for three principal reasons. First, the government was clearly indicating that its policy in the Southern Sudan was one of dechristianization and, unless it was resisted early enough, it would gather momentum, becoming increasingly ruthless. Second, the policy aimed at removing one of the main differences that distinguished the South from the North, thereby asserting the idea of unity and making more remote the possibility of separate political status for the South. Third, the government action was yet another instance in which the Arabs deliberately humiliated Southerners. In Rumbek, the Student Executive Committee produced and distributed leaflets throughout the South encouraging resistance to the government policy through its advocation of strikes in schools and public services. This proved successful when, by mid-April 1960, all the schools in the South were on strike and closed down.

The genuine and widespread opposition to the Northern policy of Islamization is expressed clearly in this passage of the leaflet:

> . . . . But the recent decree of our Government saying Sunday, the religious holiday, becomes an ordinary working day, and that Friday, the Moslem religious day, is the only resting day for all citizens of every creed, clearly states that we [Christians] should disregard the tenets of our Christian faith and Islam must be imposed on us by the present regime. . . . Since the day of our independence . . . never such an order was given. . . . Is it because we are now ruled by guns, and our mouths closed, that we should be made to turn our backs to Jesus Christ, being forced to give up our dear religion? . . . Let us resist, therefore, unanimously with our soul, our heart, our body, using the peaceful means. We appeal to all Christians in every walk of life and occupation, from Assistant Governors to the last street sweeper to boycott work on Sundays.[14]

Having become aware of the leaflets, the government sought and arrested the main authors, including a Roman Catholic parish priest of Rumbek, Fr. Paulino Dogale. They were prosecuted under the Defense of the Sudan Act of 1958 for having written, printed, and distributed the leaflets. Fr. Dogale was sentenced to twelve years imprisonment, and the three Rumbek students to ten years each. These sentences were reduced on appeal by the Chief Justice to five and three years, respectively.

The war against Christianity and promotion of Islam in the South went on unabated. The Northern administrators regarded the missionaries as subversives and accused them of being the source of the growing discontent among Southerners. Hence, efforts to restrict their work were intensified: all religious gatherings for prayer, except in a church, and all catechistic teaching were forbidden, and missionaries who were on leave were not permitted to return. These measures were followed, in May 1962, by the enactment of The Missionary Societies Act.[15] The Act was promulgated to regulate missionary activities, from social and health services to religious functions. The prohibitions of the Act were so sweeping that the missions were left at the whim of the government. The following sections of the Act emphasize this point. Section 3 provides that:

> . . . no missionary society or any member thereof shall do any missionary act in the Sudan except in accordance with the terms of a license granted by the

> Council of Ministers. Such license shall be in the prescribed form and shall specify the religion, sect or belief of the missionary society, and the regions or places in which it may operate and in addition may impose whatever conditions the Council of Minsters may think fit either generally or in any specific case.

According to Section 6, the Council of Ministers "might refuse to grant or renew or even revoke a license at its discretion." Section 7 prohibited a missionary society from doing "any missionary act towards any person or persons professing a religion or sect or belief thereof other than that specified in its license." Missions were not allowed to "practice any social activities except within the limits and in the manner laid down from time to time by regulations." Section 8 states that "no missionary society shall bring up in any religion or admit to any religious order, any person under the age of eighteen years without the consent of his lawful guardian. Such consent shall be reduced to writing before a person appointed for that purpose by the Province Authority." In Section 9, the Act states explicitly that "no missionary society shall adopt, protect, or maintain an abandoned child without the consent of the Province Authority." Section 10 subjects to ministerial regulations "formation of clubs, the establishment of societies, organization of social activities, collection of money, famine and flood relief, the holding of land, and the publication and distribution of papers, pamphlets, or books."

The reasoning behind such encompassing restrictions was explained as follows:

> It is clear that the missionary organizations have directed most of their internal and external efforts against the national government. Their main objective has been to have the confidence in the Government shaken and the unity of the nation undermined. It became necessary, therefore, to pass an Act aiming at the regularization of the work of the missions.[16]

It was, however, obvious that the government saw the missionaries more as rivals of and obstacles to its policy of Arabization and Islamization of the South rather than as instigators of disunity. The *Missionary Societies Act of 1962* and the subsequent propaganda critical of the missionaries may be viewed as Northern Sudanese reactions to the British Southern policy of 1930 whereby the propagation of Islam was excluded in favor of Christianity. Now the military regime initiated an exact reversal: Islam was supported by the government machinery to the detriment of Christianity, which was embraced by the overwhelming majority of the Southern elites.

In March 1964, the government went further in its crusade against the missionaries and accused them of sowing seeds of discord among the peoples of North and South:

> It has now been proven beyond doubt that the foreign missionary organizations have gone beyond the limits of their sacred mission. . . . They . . . exploited the name of religion to impart hatred and implant fear and animosity

> in the minds of the Southerners against their fellow-countrymen in the North with the clear object of encouraging the setting up of a separate political status for the Southern provinces thus endangering the integrity and unity of the country.[17]

Soon, the government expelled all foreign missionaries from the Southern Sudan. Although satisfied with its action in that it had at last removed foreign witnesses to its repressive policies and brutalities in the South, the government later discovered that such tactics widened rather than narrowed the cleavages between the two regimes.

The relations between the North and the South were even further aggravated by the government's differential treatment of the regions in its allocation of funds for economic development projects. All economic enterprises were concentrated in the North, and the numerous schemes that the British colonialists initiated in the South, on the eve of its departure, were abandoned. Collins describes this preferential treatment carried out by the military junta thus:

> Although the military government had steadily imposed its policies throughout the Southern Sudan, it had noticeably failed to gild the bitter pill of Arabization and Islamization with the economic development. When the British left the Sudan in 1956 there were numerous schemes for developing the Southern Sudan. Like education, however, most of these projects had been postponed or abandoned in favor of economic undertakings in the North. The plans for growing sugar cane at Mongalla and Malakal in conjunction with a sugar refinery constructed in joint partnership between the Sudan Government and the Boxall Company were given up in favour of inferior sugar schemes in the North at Junayd and Khashm al-Girba. A paper factory planned for Malakal was quietly forgotten as well as a fish canning plant, which was moved north to Jabal al-Awliya. Plans for a meat packing factory in the Bahr al-Ghazal remained stillborn. To be sure, the important strategic railway was extended from Babanusa in Kordofan to Wau, but the line represented as much an iron tie to bind the South to the North as an important link in the Sudan's economic infrastructure.[18]

The government policy made the knowledge of and fluency in the Arabic language essential for advancement, which handicapped many Southerners. For instance, between 1956 and 1964, out of 211 candidates accepted in the police college, only 21 were Southerners; and in the Army, there were 20 Southerners out of 589 commissioned officers during the same period.[19] Such was the pattern in every field.

The Southern Reaction to Arab Hegemony

The Southern reaction to the accumulation of grievances was "sullen resentment, flight, and finally rebellion."[20] Southerners saw subjection in the political, educational, economic, social, and religious systems being forged for the country by a Northern-Arab-dominated government. The rejection of a federal form of government by the Northerners meant for the Southerners a denial of well-deserved autonomy. Educational repression in the South was represented by the introduction of compulsory Islamic education with Arabic as the medium of instruction throughout the country. Economic suppression and deprivation took the form of siting all industrial projects in the North in addition to the more painful policy of assisting Arabs to settle in the South and appropriating land from Southerners. The practice of open segregation of Southerners from Northerners in ordinary social life was as oppressive as it was insulting. Finally, the abolition of Sunday as a day of rest for students and public employees was considered the most indiscreet example of the repressive policies aimed at the South, occurring in such an important sphere as religion.

Most Southerners envisaged themselves repressed by the Northern Arabs in every way and by every means. Whether or not they were objectively correct, it was what they believed to be the case that determined their reaction to the Northerners. Perhaps the situation would have improved if the government had tried to examine the causes of the Southerners' fears and frustrations. For between 1955 and 1963 there was mere tension without serious open violence. However, the military regime, which did not encourage political discussion and even stepped up Arabization and Islamization, did not improve matters. The blockage of a legitimate outlet for built-up frustrations only helped to drive the disgruntled elements in the South underground in search of other means of achieving their objectives.

The Southern Sudan was full of rumors of trouble ahead. In December 1960, a number of former MPs in the South were forewarned of an alleged plot by the government to arrest them on Christmas Eve. Prominent among them were Fr. Saturnino Lohure, Joseph Oduho, and Marko Rume, who were shortly joined by William Deng, an Assistant District Commissioner at Kapoeta in Equatoria Province, who was regarded as a trusted civil servant.[21] Subsequently, refugee traffic to neighboring countries, particularly Uganda and Zaire, resumed. While in exile, the Southern politicians founded, in February 1960, a political organization called the Sudan African Closed Districts National Union (SACDNU) which, in 1964, was simplified to Sudan African National Union (SANU). Joseph Oduho, Marko Rume, and William Deng were elected President, Vice President, and Secretary General, respectively, while Fr. Saturnino Lohure became the "patron" of the movement. The main objectives of SACDNU were twofold: (1) to publicize the problem of the Southern Sudan by petitions to the United States (and later also to the Organization of African Unity), by interviews in the press, and through publication of pamphlets; and (2) to organize guerrilla attacks within the Southern Sudan against the Arab army.

The SACDNU leaders were based in East Africa, but Oduho, Lohure, and Deng roamed throughout Europe and the rest of the tropical Africa explaining the Southern cause. Vice President Rume, who was stationed in Kampala, Uganda, began in the middle of 1962 to send letters to the Sudan.

The letters said that preparations were being made for military invasion of the Southern Sudan and that Ugandan independence on October 9, 1962, would be the signal for such an operation. For fear of reprisals, the students were urged in the letters to leave schools and go to neighboring countries to join the Southern Sudanese forces. Rume also advised people to withdraw their money from banks. What Rume wrote was completely without foundation, but the letters had an enormous effect. A school strike in October 1962 spread throughout the South as the students, fearful that they would be the target of any Northern Sudanese retaliation in case of a Southern uprising, refused to attend classes ostensibly because of bad food and government harassment.[22] The numbers of exiles in the bush and moving across the borders into Uganda, Zaire, and Ethiopia continued to increase along with the rumors of the military invasion. Although no military activities of significance occurred in 1962, the letters helped the progress of the liberation movement in the South.

In September 1963, soldiers of the old Southern Corps, who had taken up jobs in East Africa following their abortive uprising in August 1955, returned to the bush in the Southern Sudan. They founded the Anya-Nya guerrilla army movement and planned a series of coordinated attacks against the Northern Army in the South. The words in which the Anya-Nya declared their open hostilities were good indicators of the magnitude of the Southern Sudanese frustration and desperation:

> Our patience has now come to an end, and we are convinced that only use of force will bring a decision. . . . From today onwards we shall take action . . . for better, for worse. . . . We do not want mercy and we are not prepared to give it.[23]

The decision by the South to resume the war was not an easy one; the reasoning behind it was highly subjective. For although the Anya-Nya raised poignant war cries they had hardly any arms. The odds against them were overwhelming and obvious to outsiders, but both the present and the expected conditions were too threatening to the existence of Southern Sudanese to deter them. They saw their war as a struggle for their survival not only as individuals but as a people.

The Anya-Nya movement did not, however, have an effective political front. Almost from the outset SACDNU's effectiveness was compromised by personal and organizational conflicts. The personalities of Oduho, Deng, and Lohure were such that it was difficult for them to work together. None of them found it necessary to be accountable to the SACDNU Executive Committee. Each saw himself as a leader restricted by authority. Such lack of cooperation among the politicians rendered SACDNU ineffectual however much they were individually committed to the Southern cause. Moreover, their differences were carried to the ranks of the Anya-Nya, which became divided along ethnic lines.

In late 1964, an attempt was made to reorganize SACDNU and elect a new executive. The name SACDNU gave way to SANU. Aggrey Jaden, a former Assistant Secretary General of SACDNU, became the new President of SANU, with Philip Pedak as Vice President. William Deng was retained in the executive as Secretary for Foreign Affairs, and Joseph Oduho was also retained as Secretary for Justice. Fr. Saturnino Lohure remained as "patron" of the movement while Rume went into seclusion for a while. But William Deng and Joseph Oduho did not recognize the new leadership and refused to cooperate with it. Indeed, William Deng did not even attend the convention.

Despite the divisions within the political ranks, the Anya-Nya made sporadic attacks against the Northern Sudanese forces in the South. A few examples will illustrate their activity. In October 1962, a small police post near the Uganda border (nine miles from Kajokaji township) was attacked and a Northern Arab policeman was killed while his colleague, a Nuba, was taken alive. On September 9, 1963, an Anya-Nya column attacked a police post at Pochala on the border between the Upper Nile Province and Ethiopia. The Anya-Nya operations began to spread across the South with the backing of the population in the countryside. The response of the government was to intensify the traditional policy of pacification through violent repression. Such a policy naturally engendered further evacuations into the bush and enlistments into the ranks of the Anya-Nya.

Southern employees in the South became suspect and were eventually transferred to work in the North. But "their stay in the North, supporting families and paying comparatively high house rents, and being put in offices where they practically did no work because of their lack of knowledge of the Arabic language created frustration and sometimes bitterness."[24] The Army generals were so blind to the aspirations of the Southerners and were so devoid of imagination in their dealings with them that they systematically alienated the majority of the informed sections of the Southern community. For instance, an abortive attempt to capture Wau, the provincial capital of Bahr el Ghazal, was followed by the burning of the villages and destruction of crops around the scene of military confrontation.[25] Livestock was mutilated and killed while suspects were shot on sight. Most parts of the South became a battleground as the Anya-Nya increased their attacks from their border sanctuaries. More than a third of the Sudanese Army was engaged in the war but to no avail. The Anya-Nya soldiers were fighting in their own environment, and the Northern Army faced a hopeless task in trying to contain their bands in the vast, unfriendly, unmapped wilds. Gradually, the situation was slipping out of the Abboud regime's control into endless rounds of massacres with further repression producing further resistance. The deteriorating situation was finally acknowledged even by the complacent in the North.

But the generals still refused to admit to the existence of a problem in the South. The missionaries and the "imperialists" were seen as the instigators of the war, and the solution from the Army perspective was more force. The regime "drifted on a tide of growing discontent hopeful that there would soon be light at the end of the tunnel."[26] No light appeared and eventually the regime began to openly show recognition of the seriousness of the situation in the South.

The Civilian Coup

By the middle of 1964, the military regime had become worried about the daily deterioration of the Southern situation. As the Anya-Nya gained momentum and confidence, the Northern Army's morale was diminished, doing injury to its effectiveness. So, in September 1964, General Abboud appointed a Commission of Inquiry[27] under the chairmanship of Sayyid Ahmad Mohammad Yassin to investigate the causes of unrest in the South and to study the factors which hindered harmony between the North and the South. The commission was asked to make recommendations with a view to achieving internal stability without infringing upon the principle of unitary government enshrined in the relatively new constitutional structure. The commission was empowered to consult with whomever it deemed necessary, including nationals in particular from the Southern Provinces. And it was to submit its report to the Minister for Headquarters Affairs. The formation of such a commission in the words of Collins

> was itself a confession of the government's failure to acquire control or to restore confidence, and with every passing month, the magnitude of this failure became increasingly apparent to the Northern Sudanese and even to the world beyond. Although many Northern Sudanese had little sympathy for their Southern countrymen, they were able to use the government's failure there to assail military rule in the North. The Northern Sudanese had at first welcomed General Abboud's government and then tacitly accepted it. By 1962, however, numerous urban elements, including the intelligentsia, the trade unions, and the civil servants, as well as the powerful religious brotherhoods, the tariq, had become bored and disenchanted with the military regime. In 1958, these groups had applauded the efforts of the patriotic and progressive army officers to clean the Augean stables of Sudanese parliamentarianism and to solve pressing economic and international problems. But within a few years, after the military government had consolidated its power, the intelligentsia resented its exclusion from the Councils of government, the trade unions chafed at the restrictions placed upon their activities, and the civil servants sulked at orders from their military superiors. Even the conservative religious brotherhoods grew restless when they were unable to carry on their former political activities. Moreover, the tribal masses and growing proletariat had become increasingly apathetic toward the government, for even if the parliamentarians were corrupt, they were at least exciting and colorful. Military reviews, parades, and heroic pronouncements were no substitute for the enthusiasm generated by party politics and the passions stirred by political action. The military government never provided an outlet for the political frustrations of the Sudanese, and, in the end, the regime was overwhelmed by

> boredom and overthrown by the reaction to its lassitude. The means, not the cause, was the Southern Sudan.[28]

The appointment of the commission was the beginning of an open discussion of the Southern problem and criticism of the military government in its management of state affairs. Discontent was also brewing in the Army as the prospect of military victory in the South receded and the corruption of the military leadership in Khartoum became evident. The civil service was weak and inefficient as it increasingly became alienated by the constant interference of the Army officers in administrative matters. In October 1964, a public debate at Khartoum University on the Southern problem triggered a series of events. After the debate the students and some of their teachers staged a demonstration outside the university premises and when security forces tried to disperse them, they were joined by crowds.

The demonstrations led to disturbances and clashes that lasted three days, during which time a student and two other persons were killed and more than a hundred were injured. A curfew was imposed at night. Businessmen, government officials, and blue-collar workers all went on strike. The old traditional parties with their veteran leaders reemerged and combined with other new organizations to form a National Front, which demanded the withdrawal of the Army from power, the dissolution of the Supreme Council of the Armed Forces, the immediate resignation of the government, the restoration of the 1956 Constitution, elections, and a solution to the agonizing problem of the South. Criticism of the military regime found expression primarily among the left wing intellectuals.

The Communist Party gained some supporters among the workers and the intelligentsia. After the death of a Communist student on the first day of the demonstration, the Communist Party was able to act as an organized body and take the initiative, thereby gaining a decisive voice in the formation of the National Front. The religious and political leaders and the mass of their supporters in the three towns of Khartoum, Khartoum North, and Omdurman joined in mounting the mass demonstrations against the government. No group rose to defend the junta—not even the junior officers. The ruling generals were hated because of the corruption so widespread through their ranks. The army was itself divided: the strong man of the Army, Major General Hassan Beshir Nasr, who acted as Deputy to Lieutenant General Abboud in the Army Command, wanted to use the full power of the Army to suppress the opposition. He did not, however, win the support of the senior officers and, in fact, heard strong criticism from the junior officers who threatened to attack the Presidential palace should Abboud refuse to hand over the government to the civilians. Another group of neutral senior officers, composed of three major generals, a brigadier, and three colonels, served as mediators between the Army and the civilian leaders and were more inclined to persuade the junta to surrender to a civilian group. The leader of this group was Brigadier Mohammed Idris Abdallah, a relative of Ismael al-Azhari. He was a provincial military governor (Kassala) but had brought a division of troops to Khartoum to counter any move on the part of Abboud and others to use force against the demonstrators. Most of the young officers were frustrated, having become disenchanted with their conservative senior officers and wanted a change of leadership in the running of the affairs of the country. Most of these young officers were revolutionaries with Pan-Arabist philosophy. Finally, in the third week of October 1964, the concerted effort of the Sudanese people eventually overthrew the repressive regime of Abboud and ushered civilian rule into the country once again. The manner in which Abboud's regime was overthrown was unprecedented in the annals of modern military dictatorships in that the junta was removed from power not by a military coup but by a popular uprising, and he was compelled to yield to civilian authority.

What should be emphasized is that the desire on the part of many diverse ideological groups in Khartoum to actively participate in politics prompted them to unite against a military government which excluded them from political participation and decision making. The military government refused to allow outlets through which the people could voice legitimate complaints, and it successfully alienated many sectors of the people, whose disenchantment with the junta was shown in their massive uprising to dislodge it from power. The October Revolution, as the event came to be known, was carried out by politically conscious urban elements, including the unemployed who were easily mobilized against the government by the United National Front. General Abboud decided against massive repression to maintain his position and subsequently resigned in accordance with the people's desire.

Conclusion

When the Army seized power, it was generally assumed in the North that it would provide an effective leadership and that it would give a sense of direction to the government. This, however, did not prove to be the case: the first two years witnessed many divisions within the Army ranks. General Abboud became conciliatory leader of the Supreme Military Council. The economy gradually improved in the North as a result of an increase in cotton prices and as a result of good harvests of both cotton and gum arabic.

The Abboud regime in its search for legitimacy, introduced a system of participatory local government. But there was so much control from above that the degree of free participation was minimal. The generals were intolerant of criticisms and arrested some of their vocal critics among the politicians. On the whole, it was, however, a benevolent dictatorship in the North.

As regards the South, the regime systematically attempted to establish Arab hegemony in the region through the pursuit of policies of Arabization and Islamization. These policies provoked a further sharpening of the cleavages already in existence between the North and the South. Every educated Southerner became a suspect in the eyes of the Northern administrators. The expulsion of foreign Christian missionaries from the South further confirmed to the Southerners the Northern desire to wage war against other religious practices in order to give Islam a foothold. Brutal use of force against the Southern voices of dissent led to the flight of Southerners to neighboring countries for refuge. The Southern soldiers, who dispersed rather than surrender in 1955, reorganized and formed the Anya-Nya movement, whose sole objective was to liberate the South from the Arab Sudanese.

Although the success of the coup was made possible by a concerted effort of all political groups and by divisions within the army command in the North, it was the failure of the military to defeat the Anya-Nya in the South that precipitated the mass uprising. The North did not really oppose the use of force in the South but it was the army regime which was blamed because it was not successful in defeating the Anya-Nya. Indeed, the regime was praised by many Northern intellectuals, poets, and musicians and, if it had succeeded in suppressing the Southern movement for self-determination, nothing but praise in the North would have gone to it. As will be shown in the following chapter, successive civilian governments also did not succeed in defeating the South through the use of force. Indeed, the politicians did not learn from the mistakes of the army regime and, in fact, they followed the same policies of repression which had exacerbated the war.

CHAPTER VI

The Southern Sudan Question and the Failure of the Politicians

Following the successful civilian coup (in late October 1964) against Lieutenant General Abboud's military regime, Sir el-Khatim el-Khalifa, then Deputy Permanent Secretary in the Ministry of Education, was selected by the United National Front to head the new government. It was thought that his long service as Assistant Director of Education in the South, his knowledge of the South, and the fact that many Southerners held him in high esteem—all these positive factors—would make him an asset to the new government which was attempting to find a compromise solution to the Civil War.

The Transitional Government

A provisional government of sixteen cabinet members was created to represent all shades of political opinion. It was comprised of persons of diverse ideological persuasion and differing personalities. The United National Front demanded that the transitional government should include in its program a restoration of personal freedoms, a reorganized and independent judiciary, freedom for all political prisoners, and a foreign policy free from close ties to either the Western or the Eastern countries. The new government subsequently did rescind censorship of the press, and prohibition of political parties, and released all political prisoners. The system of government was based on the 1956 Interim Constitution, and the transitional cabinet was mandated by all political groups which participated in overthrowing the Army from power to arrange for general elections for a Constituent Assembly not later than the end of March 1965.

At the beginning of the new era of return to civilian rule, the United National Front obscured the political factionalism which brought the Sudanese Republic to a standstill in 1958. There was a continuing popular hostility to the reappearance of political parties because of their divisive effects and this was clearly reflected in the composition of the caretaker cabinet: only five of the sixteen cabinet posts went to party politicians, two posts were given to nonparty Southerners, and the rest were given to both the Professional Front, which was formed during the turbulent days of Abboud's overthrow, and to the Communist Party. Differences in religious orientations and in foreign policy issues, coupled with the opposition by the rural notables to control of the government by urban dwellers and progressives, contributed gradually to the reemergence of support for the old political parties. Soon after, internal dissensions and strain in the new government prompted the old traditional political parties (Umma and NUP) to demand more representation in the Cabinet. Eventually disagreements between the right-wing groups, on the one hand, and the Communists, pro-Nasserites, and their supporters, on the other, came into the open. The right-wing parties accused the representatives of the professional organizations in the government of being Communists enabling the left to dominate the cabinet. One immediate cause of the crisis was a dispute over the date of general elections, the prelude to restoration of a parliamentary government. As a show of strength in mid-February 1965, the Ansar supporters of the Umma Party gathered in Khartoum and with the concurrence of the NUP and the Moslem Brotherhood demanded the resignation of the caretaker government calling for general elections and a quick return to party politics. Prime Minister Sir el-Khatim el-Khalifa resigned but was persuaded after a week of negotiations to form an all-party national government of representatives of the popular allegiances rather than of the professional elements. The second Khalifa Ministry was given a mandate by the dominant parties to remain in office until June 7, 1965, when an elected party government would be ready to take over.

The Khartoum Round Table Conference on the Southern Question

After the fall of Abboud's government, William Deng,[1] who was then in Europe, wrote to Prime Minister Sir el-Khatim el-Khalifa suggesting that a conference be convened composed of Southerners, Northerners, and observers from neighboring African and Arab countries. Deng had not consulted his colleagues in the SANU Executive when he wrote to the Prime Minister, but it was thought in Khartoum that because of Deng's seniority in the Southern Sudanese movement outside the Sudan, his colleagues were in accord with his suggestion. Hence, Prime Minister Sir el Khatim el Khalifa, who felt considerable concern about the situation in the South, as evidenced in his declarations on assuming office that it is "the most urgent national issue of our time and therefore (one which) must be tackled very quickly and energetically,"[2] readily accepted the idea of a national conference. He appointed the vice-chancellor of Khartoum University, El Nazir Dafallah, as chairman. A secretariat was also created to assemble data on the conflict and to coordinate preparations for the conference.

The new SANU Executive, headed by Aggrey Jaden, was at first reluctant to travel to Khartoum after efforts to hold the talks in Juba in the South or outside the Sudan failed.[3] However, after various visits from the Sudan to East Africa by representatives of Northern political parties, by Vice Chancellor Dafallah, and by members from the newly formed Southern Front Party,[4] SANU agreed to participate in the conference. Meanwhile, William Deng had already flown to Khartoum at the end of February 1965 as the leader of a group of eight SANU members.[5] Deng's sudden departure for the Sudan proved popular and it undoubtedly forced the rest of his SANU colleagues as well as the Southern Front to take part in the discussions. Official observers came from Algeria, Ghana, Kenya, Nigeria, Tanzania, United Arab Republic (Egypt), and Uganda.

The South was represented officially by three groups: the Southern Front, and the two SANU factions—the Jaden wing still operating outside the Sudan, and William Deng's faction, which had flown to Khartoum a month before the conference began. The North insisted on the attendance of other so-called "informed opinion bodies representing the South," such as Santino Deng's Unity Party, which were subsquently seated, but as observers, with no right to vote.[6] Six Northern political parties—Umma, the Peoples Democratic Party, the Sudan Communist Party, the Islamic Charter Front, the Professional Front, and the National Unionist Party were represented in the conference.

The objectives of the Khartoum Round Table Conference, as agreed upon by the various Sudanese political parties and associations in their preliminary meetings and consultations, were: "to discuss the Southern Question with a view to reaching an agreement which shall satisfy the regional interests as well as the national interests of the Sudan."[7] Both Dafallah, the chairman of the conference, and Khalifa, the Prime Minister, emphasized in their opening addresses the necessity for reaching a solution by the conferees.[8]

Three options were proposed by the Southern representatives: separation, federation, or self-determination. Aggrey Jaden who spoke on behalf of SANU (in exile) reviewed North-South relations and concluded that in the past the South and the North had not been one country politically and that whatever political union might presently exist developed without the consent of the South, and that the colonial regime decided upon union of North and South unilaterally (with Northern pressure) in 1946; the Anglo-Egyptian Agreement of 1953 leading to self-government was an agreement made between Britain, Egypt, and the Northern Sudan; and the Independence Resolution of December 1955 had been based on a quid pro quo arrangement—the South agreed to it with a clear understanding and assurance that the South and the North would be two federal states. The North, Jaden argued, dishonored its part of the agreement when it rejected federation in the 1957 Draft Constitution, and consequently the South was not bound to respect its part. Moreover, Jaden contended, the South was different from the North and it was in the best interests of the South to be left on its own. This was the argument for separation of the two regions by Jaden, who concluded by warning that "there could be no settlement of differences until separation and independence had been granted (to the South). . . . Apart from posing a threat to African peace, the Southern problem has the seeds of damaging Afro-Arab relations. To avoid this, the Southern Sudan must be given its own independence if further damage is to be avoided."[9]

William Deng, who spoke on behalf of his SANU faction, did not differ from the other Southern representatives; he too rejected a unitary system of government as impracticable on the grounds that it did not allow each region to maintain its own culture (the North had encroached upon the cultures of the South through its Islamization and Arabization policies). Deng, however, proposed that the undertaking of the North in the Independence Resolution to create federal states, of which the South would be one, should be reaffirmed by the North. He defined in detail the kind of federation that should be created.

The Southern Front argued that "the relationship which exists between the North and the South has been imposed by an external body. The wishes and aspirations of the inhabitants of the South have not been considered. What is more, this relationship has been strained by actions of Northern governments and Northern individuals and groups with influence . . . that it requires a reexamination by the Southern Sudanese alone."[10] Hence, in response to the facts of history and to the Northern Sudanese politicians argument that all Southerners wanted unity and that only a handful of adventurers wished to disturb the status quo, the Southern Front argued that the South should be entitled to decide its destiny in the way it thought best. This could be done through the free exercise of self-determination.

The Northern political parties agreed on a unified platform regarding the Southern Question as decided upon during their preliminary consultation preceding the conference. The broad aspects of their platform were sevenfold:[11] (1) The Sudan, in its present boundaries, is one country having an international character and no part thereof is entitled to claim separation; (2) There are economic, political, cultural, and racial differences between the South and the North; (3) The South has a special status; (4) The political aspirations of the Southerners are to be recognized; (5) The South should have a Southern House of Parliament and a local Council of Ministers; (6) The South must have a special representation in the civil service as well as its own civil service commission, and finally; (7) The Central Sudan Parliament is to deal with major issues such as defense, finance, foreign affairs, and so forth, while the Southern Parliament is to authorized to deal with matters of education, health, agriculture, etc. Other issues will be dealt with by the two Parliaments jointly. All the Northern political parties rejected the three proposals of separation, federation, and self-determination put forward by the Southern representatives. They blamed colonialism and foreign actors in the North and the South for instigating the Civil War.[12]

The observers from the seven African and Arab countries played an influential role in keeping the conference going as wide differences in perception of the issues by the Northern and the Southern representatives existed. All of them agreed that there was no place in the Sudan for a centralized unitary form of government. Although the Southerners were willing to consider a federal system as a possible alternative to separation and self-determination, the Northerners contended that there was no place for such an arrangement in the Sudan. As we have already pointed out, these differences sprang from a lack of consensus on the fundamental philosophy and principles upon which a Sudanese system of government should be based and from disagreement on the conclusions drawn from the analyses of the historical relationship between the North and the South up to the time of the conference. Table IV shows the positions taken by the two regions in the conference.[13]

Although the conferees, from the North and South, disagreed on the principles upon which a system of government for the Sudan should be based, they eventually made specific proposals for one another to take into consideration. The Northern parties proposed a regional system of government for the South which would have its own Parliament, executive, public service commission, development committee, and a university. They also suggested that "a citizen from the Southern region shall be appointed Governor by the Central Government to preside over the Regional Executive Council."[14] The Southern parties on the other hand proposed a system of government in which each region would have control of its own financial and economic planning, foreign affairs, armed forces, and internal security. Hence, even though the representatives from both regions agreed on devolution of powers between the center and the regions, they disagreed on the kinds of powers to be assigned to each level of authority.

Confronted by a deadlock, the conferees decided to adjourn, having proposed a twelve-man committee to be composed equally of Southerners and of Northerners to resolve the constitutional issues and report back in three months. It was also agreed to send a Peace Commission to tour the South in an attempt to restore "law and order" within two months.[15] It was agreed that the campaign for peace would begin with a series of short-term reforms that the conferees recommended to the government. The most important of these reforms were:[16] (1) resettlement in the Sudan of Southern Sudanese refugees then in Uganda and in other neighboring countries; (2) more rapid Southernization of police, military, and administrative positions in the three Southern provinces; (3) equalization of wages between South and North; (4) assurance of freedom of religion and missionary activity for Sudanese nationals; (5) early establishment of a university in the South as well as girls' secondary schools and a crash program for agricultural training; (6) creation of a Southern development planning agency as well as increased expenditures.

The Khartoum Round Table Conference did not find a solution to the Southern question. It did, however, provide an opportunity for Northerners and Southerners for the first time to meet face to face and listen to each

TABLE IV

Fundamental Principles for the Government of the Sudan

The Northern Sudanese Position	*The Southern Sudanese Position*
A. The system of government shall be based on principles that guarantee the continued existence of the Sudan as one sovereign entity. 1. No sovereign state would accept the settlement of any internal problem in a way that would prejudice its national unity. This is a generally accepted principle even in federal states such as the United States, Australia, Canada, etc. 2. The trend toward unity is an international, and especially, African phenomenon. There is no place in Africa (which aspires for unity) for the multiplication of regional divisions and the Balkanization of the continent in a manner that would complicate its political set-up and undermine its pace and progress. 3. The economic development of any country (and especially of underdeveloped countries) calls for a wide geographical basis which would provide sufficient human and natural resources, and facilitate the efficient	A. The trend toward unity is voluntary in nature. As to the question of self-determination we shall not question whether it is a right absolute or conditional. We have in our opening speeches shown that peace and international security have been threatened in the Southern Sudan during the last hundred years and particularly during the last decade (since independence). So we wish to avoid its continuing. We shall further remind the Conference that the unity of Africa and the world is based on: (i) Justice (ii) Equality (iii) Dignity of individual alone or in a community. This is the basis of the Charters of the Organization of African Unity, the United Nations and the Universal Declaration of Human Rights 1948. These pillars of African unity and in fact of all nations in the international community are abused in the Southern Sudan because of the present unity we are maintaining. To refuse the legitimate claims of the South because of African unity or the international communities, is to turn the idea of unity into an instrument of oppression. 1. The implications of self-determination as we see them are as follows: (i) The Southern Sudanese in choosing what they consider to be best for them will certainly not be worse than they have been during the last decade; perhaps they will contribute more effectively to the unity of Africa. (ii) The probability is that the Southern Sudanese will have the opportunity to develop economically, socially, and politically.

exploitation of a wide market. Separation between North and South would seriously compromise development of both regions.

4. Considering the human, economic, and geographical ties that bind North and South, separation would precipitate numerous human and political problems which would enfeeble both regions and invite imperialist intervention which would aggravate the dissension.

5. The right to self-determination is not an absolute right which may be used, or abused, by any faction without due regard to the interest of the international community nor in a manner detrimental to peace and security. Nor is it a course which may be lightly followed without the proper understanding of its implications and consequences, and/or due regard to the requisites of national independence.

6. Relations between North and South are not based on any exploitation or colonization which would justify the claim for separation. Nor does the Sudanese way of life tolerate racial

(iii) Peace and friendship are likely to be established between the North and the South on the basis of equality (assuming that the South opted for independence).

2. The argument for economic integration as claimed to call for a wide geographical basis which would provide sufficient human and natural resources does not in the least preclude the demand for self-determination. In fact, economic integration can and has been achieved without political integration. The East African community and the European Common Market are two of the many examples that can be cited.

3. We reemphasize the following points:

(i) Sudanization was in fact Northernization as far as the South is concerned. The Northern administrators continued to act the same as the British colonizers.

(ii) In the field of economic development, the South has been deliberately subjected to stagnation. Of the nine industrial and productive schemes opened since independence, only one has been allocated in the South. Furthermore, pre-independence industrial schemes such as the establishment of a sugarcane plantation and refinery in Mongalla, and the establishment of paper and fish canning factories in Malakal have been diverted to the North.

(iii) Equally, the South has been subjected to retrogression in social advancement. There is only one academic senior secondary school in the South opened since 1948 as compared to 20 government senior secondary schools in the North. While there are 9 secondary schools for girls in the North, there are none in the South. Out of more than 70 hospitals opened, there are only 17 in the South.

(iv) Finally, the means of communications in the South have remained more than inadequate.

TABLE IV (continued)

The Northern Sudanese Position	*The Southern Sudanese Position*
discrimination. There is no evidence in the history of the Sudan since independence that shows the North has exploited the resources of the South or discriminated against it in social services and development schemes.	B. The Northern political parties do not make a convincing case for unity in their arguments. But their offer of a ''Regional Government'' shall be included in the list of possible choices to be presented in a PLEBISCITE to the people of the South. The list will therefore read: (1) Unity with the North (2) Local Government (3) Federation (4) Separation
B. The administrative system of the Sudan shall be established on a geographical basis that will guarantee for the South a regional government suited to its special circumstances and likewise guarantee to other regions of the Sudan degrees of regional government that suit each.	

other's points of view. The press coverage of the conference helped to educate the Northern Sudanese public concerning the magnitude of the North-South conflict. Also, the conference pointed the way for a future compromise toward a solution in the future. Undoubtedly, of no less importance, the observing delegations lifted the conference to an African-Arab plane in that they came from both black and Arab Africa.

Nevertheless, subsequent events underscore the reality that the conference was essentially a failure. It was "never reconvened, none of its resolutions were ever implemented, and even the agreement concerning the composition of the Twelve-Man Committee designated to conclude a settlement was immediately violated."[17] Indeed, the twelve-man committee did make some important recommendations, which included: (1) the rejection of a centralized unitary system of government, and (2) a detailed system of regional autonomy for the Sudan. But these recommendations were marred by disagreements on two significant points:[18] (1) the number of regions that would constitute the South, and (2) the method for electing the regional commissioner or governor. In essence, the potential achievements were eradicated by the lack of implementation of the conference recommendations.

The Transitional Government and the Southern Sudan

Earlier in this chapter, we mentioned that Sir el-Khatim el-Khalifa was chosen by the United National Front to become Prime Minister with the hope that his knowledge and understanding of the Southern Sudan, and the respect he commanded among its educated elites, would make him an asset in efforts to resolve the African-Arab conflict. Now, we shall assess his performance in handling the Southern question.

Prime Minister Khalifa was sensitive to the feelings of Southerners and therefore, unlike his predecessors, he allowed the Southern elites and other politicians in Khartoum to advise him as to who should represent their region in his cabinet. For instance, he was ready to abandon Ambrose Wol in favor of Ezibon Mondiri[19] after public expression of resentment by Southerners against the former. In addition to Ezibon Mondiri, who was appointed Minister of Communications, another Southerner, Clement Mboro, a Deputy Governor for a number of years, was named Minister of Interior. The appointment of a Southerner to the sensitive and powerful ministry for internal security was the first of its kind and it was well received by Southerners, who thought that the act indicated both a sign of change on the part of Northerners and a determination on the part of the Prime Minister to genuinely confront the conflict between North and South. This action partly explained why the Southern Front Party of which Clement Mboro later became President, was keen to participate in—and also eager to persuade Southern politicians in exile to attend—the Khartoum Round Table Conference.

The appointment of a Southerner to head the Ministry of Interior, however, later proved to be a token gesture for powers commonly associated with the Ministry of Interior were transferred either to the Ministry of Local Government or to the Ministry of Defence (both of which were headed by Northerners). As a consequence, Clement Mboro was not fully involved in security affairs in the South. Even if he had been informed and had wanted to act, his powers were circumscribed. For instance, when Clement Mboro wanted to present a report to the cabinet on Southernization of the administration (police and prison warders) in the South and the transfer of Southerners back to their region, the cabinet refused even to listen to his report.[20] To placate the Southerners and to save his own face at the same time, the Prime Minister decided to visit the South, ostensibly to explain the new policy of peace to the Northern administrators in the South, but in actual fact to reassure the Northern administrators and traders that the Army was to continue military rule in the South.[21] The evidence of this was that, although the transitional government was ruling under the 1956 Interim Constitution, the Prime Minister conferred the security powers in the South on the Army.

Nevertheless, Prime Minister Sir el-Khatim el-Khalifa did make a personal effort to see that arbitrary arrests and killings in the South were minimized during his government. He also acted decisively to save Southerners from Arab mobs following communal riots at the Khartoum Airport.[22] These riots, which resulted in deaths of many Southerners, further confirmed the deeply rooted North-South tension. The Khalifa Ministry at any rate had been given the mandate to solve the Southern Question. While acting as a caretaker administration, it did, however, provide an opportunity for politicians from both North and South to meet and exchange views on the salient issues surrounding the Civil War.

After the Round Table Conference was adjourned, pressure for general elections was reactivated. The Supreme Council was deadlocked with Northern members on whether or not to hold elections immediately in the North. The deadlock was eventually broken by the Southerner in the Council, Luigi Adwok, who was a member of the executive of the Southern Front. Although the Southern Front opposed elections in the South before the lifting of the state of emergency, the party did not realize that elections in the North would undoubtedly vitiate the transitional government, which did show rather considerable interest in a solution to the North-South conflict. Instead, it explained Luigi Adwok's "yes" vote in the Supreme Council in the following way.[23] The Southern Front was not a party to the National Charter, which was drawn following the fall of General Abboud's regime and in which holding of elections within a specified period was indicated. The Southern Front argued that the National Charter was an exclusively Northern document and that the real issue before the Supreme Council was that of holding elections in the North. The Southern Front also desired a change from the transitional government, whose internal divisions had rendered it so inept that it was unable to stop the killings and burning of villages in the South. After all, the transitional government, despite some of its good intentions, had declared that it had no mandate to end the Civil War. Therefore, unless elections were held in the North and a party government took the reins of power, no Northern political group could be held wholly responsible for the Army atrocities which continued unabated in the South. The Southern Front also was incorrect in thinking, as events later showed, that a Northern Party government might come out to boldly address itself to the war.

When it became obvious that elections were going to be held in the North, the Southern Front submitted a memorandum to the transitional government and to the Northern political parties demanding a number of guarantees for the South. These demands, among others, included:[24] (1) That the Northern political parties along with the transitional government should take overt steps toward the solution of the Southern problem. This implied the implementation of the resolutions of the Round Table Conference and the reconvening of the conference not later than the second week of June 1965. (2) That the South should be represented in the cabinet on the basis of Sudan population ratio. (3) That the Southern members of the cabinet should be nominated by the South and appointed by the Prime Minister. (4) That the Parliament elected on April 21, 1965, should serve only to indicate the strength of the participating parties which should form the government; the elected Parliament should not sit until the Southern problem was solved or at least until such a time when the South decided to elect its own representatives to Parliament. (5) That it should be the policy of the government that elections would not take place directly or indirectly in the Southern region on April 21, 1965, as might be the case in the North.

The transitional government and the Northern political parties refused to give definite answers to the Southern Front demands,[25] and arrangements for the elections went ahead according to procedures agreed upon by the United National Front. The PDP was the only political party in the North which officially boycotted the elections on grounds that the time was not opportune to hold them.

The legal voting age was lowered to eighteen years, and for the first time, women were given the right to vote. Another interesting feature of the election was a special fifteen-seat national graduates constituency created to give an added voice to the educated elite. About 17,000 secondary school graduates registered to vote in this special constituency without losing their right to vote in the regular 158 territorial constituencies in the North. However, less than a quarter of the eligible voters actually went to the polls. The low turn-out was due to the lack of a well-coordinated organizational structure by the parties—the parties had not had enough time to organize themselves following their suppression during the six years of the military regime. The Communist Party was, however, able to retain much of its organizational base through its underground organization. The Umma Party also retained its structure through its strength in the Mahdiyyah religious brotherhood. The Communist Party, over the objections of some of its internal factions, for the first time entered the campaign openly. But in some constituencies, its candidates ran as independents or as members of the Tenants and Workers Party Front.

The May 1965 parliamentary election results were inconclusive. Interestingly enough, they were amazingly similar to those of 1958 before the accession of the generals to power. The two traditional parties (Umma and the NUP) once again shared most of the seats. The six years of military dictatorship left no mark on the party strengths in that the regime had no effect on the political and the social relationships of the people. The results were:[26] Umma, seventy-five; the NUP, fifty-three; Communists, eleven (the Communists and their supporters won their eleven seats from the fifteen graduate constituency seats); the Beja Congress, ten; the Nuba Independents, nine; Islamic Charter Front, five; PDP, three (officially the Party did not contest the elections and the three members were independent PDP); Darfur Front, six; and Independents, fifteen.

Although elections were canceled throughout the South because of the state of emergency, at the request of the Southern political parties, twenty-one Northern Sudanese, mainly traders living in the South, claimed that they had been elected as unopposed candidates. Elections were, indeed, effectively boycotted in the South because the people refused to have anything to do with them even under threats of coercion from the Army.[27] But the twenty-one Northerners insisted that they had been duly elected without opposition. Of course, they had nominated themselves in order to go "unopposed" to the Constituent Assembly, having taken the chance of there being a Southern boycott. They appealed to the Supreme Council to declare them as the duly elected representatives from the South. The Supreme Council decided that the twenty-one persons were not members of the Constituent Assembly because their claim to have been elected unopposed took place in circumstances, in places, and at the time when "freedom" of elections as such did not exist.[28] Surprisingly enough, a Khartoum High Court upheld the claim of the twenty-one persons and declared them as duly elected representatives of the South and members of the Constituent Assembly. Protests by Southern parties to such acts of provocation by the Northern establishment were of no avail.[29]

After the elections which did not produce an absolute majority party, Umma and the NUP agreed to form a coalition government in which Mohammed Ahmed Mahgoub of Umma became Prime Minister, and Ismael el-Azhari of the NUP became President of the Committee of Five which collectively acted as Head of State. The Sudan was once again back to party policies and parliamentary government.

The Coalition Government and North-South Relations

Prime Minister Mohammed Ahmed Mahgoub had an antipathy for the Southern Sudan and argued persistently that the only language Africans in the South can understand is force. Therefore, it was not surprising that on assuming the office of Prime Minister he resorted to use of force in the South. This policy of application of military force as a means to solve the conflict was detailed in various statements in which the Prime Minister said, among other things that: (1) the government would disarm the Anya-Nya to restore law and order; (2) the Army would be given full power and would be reinforced to deal with the rebellion in the South; and (3) the resolutions of the Round Table Conference would not be implemented until law and order were restored in the South. Mahgoub also resumed the policies of Arabicization and Islamization of the South. He never learned a lesson from the errors of General Abboud's regime and embarked immediately on implementing his policies of repression. The situation increasingly deteriorated:

> Throughout June and July 1965 the army appears to have attempted to crush the Southern political movements by systematically eliminating educated Southerners. In virtually every major town throughout the South, but particularly in Equatoria, the leading educated Southerners were killed or if forewarned fled into exile. Some have attributed the murders to isolated incidents by ill-disciplined troops but the timing, geographical extent, and the discrimination employed by the troops in singling out the educated Southerners remains powerful circumstantial evidence that the Army was acting on orders from the Prime Minister determined to annihilate the terrorist gangs which abuse security.[30]

Indeed, the Mahgoub Administration introduced sinister laws in the South, and the Army was left at large to do what it considered "appropriate and good." The civilian population became a target of attack: entire villages were burned to the ground and those inhabitants who escaped vanished into the bush while many fled to the neighboring countries.[31] The entire village life of the Southern Sudan was disrupted. The most ruthless massacres[32] were in Juba where over 1400 helpless Southerners were machine-gunned on July 8 and 9, 1965, and in Wau, where Southern elites (mostly government officials) numbering not less than seventy-six were butchered by Northern forces while attending a wedding on July 11, 1965.

In Khartoum, Mahgoub was opposed to the work of the twelve-man committee appointed by the Round Table Conference to explore areas of constitutional compromise between the North and the South.[33] In June 1966, he announced his own proposals for ending the war: the establishment of a regional government in each province in the South to deal with local affairs, while the central government in Khartoum would be responsible for foreign affairs, defense, economy, planning, and higher education. These regional governments would consist of provincial legislatures formed through direct elections. Such pronouncements were a departure from the resolutions of the Round Table Conference and rendered the twelve-man committee obsolete. Some members of the committee also became increasingly disinterested, as was shown in their absence from meetings, but the committee did protest the Prime Minister's attitude as reflected in his statements.[34]

In the South, the situation had progressively deteriorated since General Abboud's military regime. The prospect of a quick military solution grew fainter as the Anya-Nya determination stiffened. Also in the North, the high hopes of the civilian coup that overthrew the military government dribbled away as the old parliamentary games resumed—cabinet reshuffles, mergers, coalitions, deals, and maneuvers, and no specific programs of policy implementation. Before we examine the pattern of praetorian politics in the North, we shall analyze the trend of divisions in the Southern Sudanese resistance movement.

Divisions in the Southern Sudan Liberation Movement

The resumption of increased military operations in the South by the Umma-NUP coalition government of Mohammed Ahmed Mahgoub proved a complete failure. The flight of more educated Southerners to the bush and to neighboring countries brought more support and some new leadership to the liberation movement. When the Congolese (Zairean) Civil War ended in the defeat of the Simba rebels, the Anya-Nya were able to acquire a large quantity of weapons abandoned by the Simba rebels. As Sarkesian has pointed out:

> . . . ironically, the Sudan government assisted the Congolese rebels, but in so doing, it also provided an opportunity for the Anya-Nya to gain access to a reasonable assortment of modern weapons. Some of the convoys moving to the Congo were ambushed by the Anya-Nya and the weapons used to arm impoverished military bands. Additionally, a number of "Simbas" fleeing into the Sudan were relieved of their weapons. Thus, the Anya-Nya were able to initiate more active military operations against the Sudanese army. Until this period, weapons and supplies had been too few to engage in any substantial military effort. Parenthetically, only much later did the Southern resistance movement receive some aid from external sources—aid that was negligible and primarily non-military.[35]

By mid-August 1965, the Anya-Nya began to increase their attacks on Northern government forces. They established many camps and started for the first time to coordinate their activities throughout the South. Although they inflicted heavy losses on the Northern Sudanese Army, they suffered from lack of coherent planning and an effective military organization mainly because of ethnic differences. Ethnicity was a drawback in the Anya-Nya organization, particularly in Equatoria province where numerous camps were created. The Anya-Nya also failed to introduce political education to the masses and they had no propaganda machinery. The masses in the rural areas, however, gave them full support even though they often suffered from some excessively ruthless actions of a few Anya-Nya commanders.

The weaknesses of the Anya-Nya were generally not of their own making. They did not have a strong and effective political wing, because, following the Khartoum Round Table Conference, three political parties emerged: SANU outside the Sudan under the leadership of Aggrey Jaden, SANU inside the Sudan under the control of William Deng, and the Southern Front now headed by Clement Mboro operating within the Sudan. The SANU group in exile tried to work closely and identified with the Anya-Nya, but SANU actually had little control over the Anya-Nya. Internal divisions and confusions within it were further aggravated by Joseph Oduho and George Kwanai, who formed another Southern political group calling it the Azanian Liberation Front (ALF). Joseph Oduho became President of the ALF which was dedicated to complete independence of the Southern Sudan. Soon after the formation of ALF, Aggrey Jaden announced the dissolution of SANU in exile and the formation of yet another Southern political movement, calling it the Sudan African Liberation Front (SALF). Both these groups were divided not over policies, but by personality conflicts of their leaders. In December 1965, the two parties, ALF and SALF, were merged under the name of the Azania Liberation Front (ALF), with Joseph Oduho as President, and Aggrey Jaden as Vice President.[36] The preamble to the combined group's (ALF) Constitution read:

> We, the African people, owners and masters of the country presently known as the "Southern Sudan," victimized by the perpetuation of political, cultural and economic domination and oppression, and all forms of colonial policies and practices which have been rejected by the African Continent . . . have therefore formulated and bound ourselves to this constitution for the sole aim of liberating the Southern Sudan and establishing a free and independent African nation so that the black man in his part of the continent may realize security, justice, welfare and his hitherto lost human rights and dignity.[37]

The ALF leadership tried to rally the Anya-Nya behind it. Joseph Oduho toured eastern Equatoria province while the ALF Secretary for Defense Ezibon Mondiri, toured Western Equatoria and Bahr el Ghazal in an attempt to unite all the freedom fighters under the leadership and control of ALF. Despite ALF efforts to win the Southern masses, internal dissension and struggles to control foreign assistance paralyzed its organization. Oduho dismissed Jaden from the Vice Presidency of ALF allegedly for having met William Deng in Nairobi and for having discussed the war in the Northern Sudan without his permission.[38] He later also dismissed Ezibon Mondiri and Elia Lupe from the ALF's Executive and appointed George Kwanai to replace Jaden as Vice President. The reason for all these dismissals was basically personal animosity between Oduho and Jaden—the two men hated each other. Mondiri and Lupe were dismissed because they criticized Oduho for the way he tried to run the party. Oduho was continually accused by his critics of tribalism, nepotism, and of using financial aid for the Anya-Nya for his own petty interests.

Fr. Saturnino Lohure joined to help Oduho rebuild the ALF. He decided to move into the Southern Sudan in eastern Equatoria province and made Tul his headquarters. But it was not long before Oduho and Fr. Lohure quarreled. Fr. Lohure allegedly commanded more support and respect than Oduho in the Southern Sudan movement. Hence, it was not surprising that the latter was arrested following his quarrel with the former. The Anya-Nya in eastern Equatoria confined Oduho for over a year as a prisoner in their camps.[39] The death of Fr. Lohure at the hand of Ugandan soldiers at the Sudan-Uganda border was blamed on Oduho whose supporters were alleged to have betrayed Fr. Lohure to Uganda authorities. The Anya-Nya who arrested and imprisoned Oduho sentenced him to death after they court-martialed him. Fortunately, the death sentence was not carried out and Oduho eventually was released on grounds of ill-health. Subsequently he returned to East Africa.

Following his explusion from the ALF, Jaden worked assiduously to build a rival political group which he called the "Home Front." Eventually, he was successful, and by August 1967 had reunited a number of prominent Southern politicians to form a provisional government inside the Southern Sudan. A convention was held at Angudri near the Sudan-Congo border and it was well attended by politicians and Anya-Nya representatives from many areas of the South. During the convention, the Anya-Nya officers pressured the politicians to put aside their petty and personal quarrels for "the cause of liberating the Southern Sudan." The convention decided to dissolve all political groups and organizations and founded the Southern Sudan Provisional Government (SSPG) with headquarters in Bungu in Yei District. Jaden tried to balance his cabinet evenly among the Southern ethnic groups in an effort to avoid tribal clashes.[49]

The provisional government of Jaden provided the political arm that the Anya-Nya had lacked for a long time. It attempted to educate the masses about the causes of the South, and a gazette was founded to disseminate information about the provisional government and its policies. The Anya-Nya was renamed the Anya-Nya National Armed Forces (ANAF), which were nominally brought under civilian control (the President of SSPG and his Minister of Defense). Large-scale military operations were planned and coordinated by a Defense Council composed of the President, the Minister of Defense, the Commander-in-Chief, Chief of Staff, and Chief of Intelligence. However, the Commanding Officer of each region was empowered by the Defense Council to direct military operations in his region. Civilian administrative officers were appointed to collect food supplies from the rural masses for the Anya-Nya Forces. These civilian officers provided a buffer between the civilian population and the fighting men; thereafter, relations between the two groups greatly improved. The three Southern provinces of Bahr el Ghazal, Equatoria, and Upper Nile were divided into nine administrative regions. Each region was administered by a commissioner who worked closely with his Army counterpart. Regional, provincial, and district councils were formed to coordinate coherent military and civilian organizations. They also generated a sense of national identity and purpose.

The SSPG under Jaden was a militant organization, committed to liberating the South from the Northern Sudanese occupying force. It even decided not to cooperate with the Southern Front which continued to operate within the Sudan. The Southern Front had, of course, acted as the mouthpiece of the Southern politicians in exile.

Although the SSPG provided the first combined political and military organization of Southerners inside the Sudan, it was not long before it underwent serious internal divisions which had characterized previous Southern political groups. Eastern Equatoria had not participated in the founding of the SSPG, nor had much of the Bahr el Ghazal and Upper Nile areas (although these areas eventually submitted to the authority of the SSPG), and some politicians who wielded strong influence in these places remained for a long period outside the command of the SSPG.

However, the greatest setback to the SSPG was in Zandeland and Moruland, where the leaders refused to recognize Emidio Taffeng as Commander in Chief of the Anya-Nya forces. Nonetheless, the SSPG had a firm control of central Equatoria where it launched many successful guerrilla attacks against the government forces.

The reappearance of schism within both the SSPG and the Anya-Nya brought about the final collapse of Jaden's leadership. As I have written on this point elsewhere,[41] in September 1968, Jaden felt that he was not being respected and supported in his leadership. He began to take a cautious and reserved attitude toward issues and decision making. It was alleged by his supporters[42] that there was an underground movement to depose him, championed by his Vice President, Camillo Dhol. The situation became increasingly confused as tribal differences, clashing personalities, and personal ambitions entered the picture. Jaden subsequently abdicated his position as President of the SSPG and fled to Nairobi, Kenya. Undoubtedly, Jaden was a refined and cool-headed man, but he was equally an indecisive politician.

Following Jaden's flight to Kenya, a convention was held in March 1969 at Balgo-Bindi in Yei district under the chairmanship of Camillo Dhol, and Gordon M. Mayen was reported to have been elected President. This happened in March 1969. The convention renamed the Southern Sudan the Nile State. Although the Nile Provisional Government (NPG) seemed to be dominated by the Dinka (four cabinet ministers out of eight), it was so because most of Jaden's supporters—mainly people from Equatoria province—refused to participate in the convention. The policy of the NPA was the same as that of its predecessor, the SSPG: to prosecute the war of liberation for national freedom and complete independence.

However, not long after the formation of the NPG, Jaden's followers, without his consent, solicited some Anya-Nya support, mainly from central Equatoria province, and declared the formation of an Anyidi revolutionary government. A plethora of political parties soon materialized: Sudan Azania, the Sue River Republic, and the Anya-Nya organization, which eventually gave way to the Southern Sudan Liberation Movement (SSLM).[43] The SSLM was headed by an Anya-Nya officer, the then Colonel Joseph Lagu, who established his headquarters in eastern Equatoria province where he had served as the regional commander during the period of the SSPG.

The SSLM eventually gained ground and succeeded in uniting all the Anya-Nya officers and their units under its high command and authority. Colonel Lagu was promoted to the rank of major general and he immediately pensioned off his rival General Taffeng.[44] The Anya-Nya became the sole authority and the only effective Liberation Movement in the Southern Sudan. In the interest of unity, the NPG dissolved itself in mid-1970 and, subsequently, all the other parties followed its example and declared support for Major General Lagu's leadership.

The foregoing description and analysis of the various characteristics of the many Southern Sudanese Liberation Movements show that the South lacked dynamic leadership. All the Southern politicians in exile, in the words of Collins:

> . . . were not the men who make successful revolutionaries. Conservative, mission educated, impressed with rhetoric and titles, they failed to inspire those who were fighting for their dearth of ideology, lack of organizational ability, and their unwillingness to sacrifice their personal interests. They were a pathetic group sustained by clandestine meetings, the resolutions of which were never implemented and kept in business by a trickle of foreign financial assistance which gave them the illusion and the livelihood to afford the luxury of politics. Living in the fantasy world of the political exile, they became convinced that they were the ones who remained behind in Khartoum and in the countryside of the Southern Sudan.[45]

Within the Sudan, the Southern politicians also were not united in an effort to argue their case with their Northern counterparts. After the fall of the Abboud government, Santino Deng, who had been a cabinet minister in the ousted military regime, formed the Sudan Unity Party. This party stood for a united Sudan and shared basically the same philosophy as the right-wing groups in the North except possibly on the issue of religion. Santino Deng, having made Khartoum his permanent home, had lost contact with Southerners in the South. The membership of the Sudan Unity Party was insignificantly small. Two veteran Southern politicians, Buth Diu and Stanislaus Paysma, revived the old Liberal Party, but it did not attract a large following. Also Philemon Majok, another veteran Southern politician and a former member of the defunct five-member Supreme Council, formed his own party which was financed by some sectarian groups in the North. None of these politicians—Santino Deng, Stanislaus Paysma, Buth

Diu, and Philemon Majok—had sources of income so they formed their political parties to attract financial support from Northern groups which saw them as advocates of unity. The Northern political parties exploited the divisions within the Southern political groups.

The principal Southern political parties operating within the Sudan after the Round Table Conference were the Southern Front and the SANU of William Deng. The Southern Front stood for self-determination but its influence was not sufficient to achieve substantial reforms for the South from the Mahgoub government of which it was a partner. Gradually the front became more and more pragmatic in its policies and claimed the role of a "watch dog" for the South. SANU had the largest number of Southern Members of Parliament in the National Assembly during the parliamentary period. It vacillated between secession and federation. All these parties were rivals and each claimed to represent and protect the true interests of the Southern people. But, more often than not, they spent most of their time and effort fighting each other instead of presenting a united front against the North.

However, Southern elites and politicians inside the Sudan were on the whole more politically refined, more responsive to change and had a strategy (this only applied to the Southern Front and SANU) for reaching an honorable solution to the Southern question than those who operated from without. Their political maturity may perhaps be attributed in part to their education: a number of them were graduates and their level of education enabled them to speak to their Northern counterparts on an equal basis. Although they had little influence upon the civilian coalition governments, they were successful in challenging some of the sinister legislations with an intellectual sophistry which their fellow Southern predecessors lacked.[16]

The Failure of the Politicians

The national unity forged among Northern parties in their joint opposition to the military regime soon disappeared and the divisive politics of 1955-58 soon reemerged. Sectarian rivalries were revived between the Ansar and the Khatmiyya and their respective political wings: Umma and the NUP/PDP (the Khatmiyya supported both the NUP and the PDP). Within the Umma Party, there was also a split between the progressive conservatives supporting Sadiq el-Mahdi, the President of Umma, and the traditional conservatives supporting Sadiq's uncle, the Imam el-Hadi, the head of the Ansar sect and patron of Umma. The young Northern elites were generally split into three groups: those supporting Sadiq el-Mahdi, a small group supporting the Islamic Charter Front of Dr. Hassan el-Turabi, who campaigned for an Islamic Constitution, and an articulate and well-organized group supporting the Sudan Communist Party led by Abdel Khaliq Mahgoub. The Communist Party was itself split into two camps:

those who looked to Moscow and those who looked to Peking for both ideological inspiration and financial support.

In general, ideological differences divided these organizations: there were the pan-Arabists who looked to Nasser's Egypt for leadership and ideological reference and advocated union or closer ties with Egypt; and there were also those Northerners who vehemently opposed Cairo influence in Sudanese politics. A small group was opposed to both Eastern and Western alliances and stood for strict nonalignment in foreign policy. Yet another group, the Sudanese nationalists, called for closer cooperation with the black African countries and preferred concentration on national issues to futile ideological competition and wrangling. But the Sudan remained profoundly closer to the Western world than those in power and the elites in Khartoum had often accepted it to be.

The rural masses were beginning to react against the continual dominance of national politics by the educated elite who showed no responsiveness to their problems of social and economic development. They became increasingly disillusioned and apathetic and this was reflected in low turnout for meetings addressed by party leaders. The minority groups—the Fur of Western Darfur, the Beja, and the Nuba—also complained of neglect and lack of proportionate representation in national affairs. They complained they did not get a fair share of the distribution of economic projects and they organized themselves into political interest groups lobbying for rewards from the dominant parties in exchange for support in Parliament.

These political cleavages punctuated the pattern and the trend of politics in the North. After the change from the transitional to the Umma/NUP coalition was effected, the sensitive issue of whether the Sudan should have an Islamic Constitution gained ground. The Islamic Charter Front, which campaigned for a permanent constitution based on Islam, assiduously exploited the issue in the public media. Although the traditional dominant parties (Umma and the NUP) did not initially support the idea of an Islamic Constitution in its totality, they gradually came around to supporting it in fear of being labeled anti-Islam by the Islamic Charter Front. At the same time, an attempt was launched in the Constituent Assembly and in the public media against the Communist Party. Mass demonstrations were organized by the Islamic Charter Front in the three towns of Khartoum, Khartoum North and Omdurman, and it called on the Constituent Assembly to proscribe and ban the Communist Party. Under mob pressure, the Constituent Assembly on November 15, 1965, amended Article 5(2) of the 1956 Interim Constitution, which guaranteed the right of free expression and association, in order to exclude the propagation of atheism and Communism as well as the advocating of the overthrow of government by force.

The Constituent Assembly carried the amendment by 151 votes, with 12 votes against and 9 abstensions. The Communist Party was subsequently banned after the passage of the Communist Party Dissolution Act of 1965, and its eight members of Parliament were expelled.[47] The Communist Party successfully challenged the constitutionality of the amendment and the legislation implementing it before a High Court.[48] The government, however, appealed to the Supreme Council, which passed a decision in support of the action taken by the Constituent Assembly both in banning the Communist Party and in expelling its eight members of Parliament.[49] This was, of course, much against the ruling of the High Court. Consequently, the Communist Party and all the parties of the left formed a new party and called it the Sudan Socialist Party (SSP) and elected as its President the President of the Sudan Bar Association, Amin el Shibly.

The ideological, religious, ethnic, sectarian, and regional cleavages permeated national politics. Soon a crisis developed in the Umma-NUP coalition as a result of personal animosity between Prime Minister Mahgoub and President el-Azhari. This rendered the coalition government ineffectual and without a sense of direction.

At the time that Mahgoub and el-Azhari were quarreling between themselves, Sadiq el-Mahdi wanted to become the effective leader of the Umma Party both in the Constituent Assembly and in the country at large. Therefore, he exploited the differences between Mahgoub and el-Azhari, and instigated a vote of no confidence against Mahgoub within the Umma Party. With the support of el-Azhari, el-Mahdi formed another coalition government and became Prime Minister. Mahgoub became leader of Opposition with the support of the traditional conservative wing of the Umma Party under the patronage of Imman el-Hadi, who disassociated himself from the political ambitions of his nephew, Sadiq el-Mahdi.

Sadiq el-Mahdi reacted to the Southern question with the usual confirmed Northern attitude. He advocated the spread of Islam and Arabic in the South as unifying factors, and he therefore wanted the new constitution to be Islamic. In his maiden speech as Prime Minister to the Constituent Assembly in October 1966, he defined his position thus:

> The dominant feature of our nation is an Islamic one and its overpowering expression is Arab, and this nation will not have its entity identified and its prestige and pride preserved except under an Islamic revival.[50]

Prime Minister Sadiq el-Mahdi believed that the Southern Sudanese culture was not a culture in itself and therefore contended that the Southerners must be converted to Islam and must be Arabicized. In early 1966, as head of the Umma Party, he had written to the Pope proposing a fourteen-point protocol between Christianity and Islam to convert pagans, particularly in Africa: "We should agree that paganism should be eliminated for humanitarian and humanistic purposes. Islam and Christianity have there a common interest. We could agree to coexistence with a view to converting all pagans into believers."[51] What Sadiq el-Mahdi had in mind was actually the Southern Sudan, not the rest of Africa. His policies and attitude toward the South were totally in line with those held by European colonialists toward Africa.[52] He refused to reconvene the Round Table Conference and ignored the report of the twelve-man committee submitted to the government in September 1966. When he toured the South in November 1966, he praised the Northern army and declared a firm policy against the Anya-Nya, whose activities he labeled treason and defined as talk of plebiscites, self-determination, or independence for the South (hereby referring indirectly to the Southern Front which had adopted such a position). He insisted that elections be held in the South ostensibly to enhance the representativeness of the Constituent Assembly.

The Southern Front opposed the holding of elections in the South on grounds that they should be held only after a Constitution was agreed upon by all parties at a reconvened Round Table Conference. Moreover, the front argued, the state of emergency in the South would make it difficult for candidates to campaign. Consequently, the front officially boycotted the elections.[53] SANU, on the other hand, disagreed with the front and contested the elections. In the North, the PDP refused to take part in the elections on grounds that the voting lists were compiled from old tax registers which included deceased persons as well as people living outside the country. As expected, Umma candidates (traders) won most of the seats in the South; in many areas, the only voters were the Northern soldiers.[54]

After only a year in power, Sadiq el-Mahdi lost his political base. On May 15, 1967, his arch rival Mohammed Ahmed Mahgoub, who had been reconciled with President el-Azhari, gathered enough support in the Constituent Assembly to successfully move a vote of no confidence against Sadiq's government. A new coalition government, again with no specific programs of development, assumed office under Mahgoub. Mahgoub continued his predecessor's policies of Islamization and Arabicization in the South and the military situation deteriorated further. The Southern Front became a partner in the coalition government with the hope of forestalling the proposed Islamic Constitution but had little influence in the government.

The Southern politicians of all parties campaigned against the Islamic Constitution on grounds that Africans would lose their identity since they would be subjected to the Shari'a law which would not recognize their cultural traditions. Moreover, such a constitution would perpetually confirm Africans as second-class citizens. Abel Alier explained the Southern position cogently:

> Because of the overriding religio-racial components of the constitution, Christian, Moslem, and pagan Afro-Negro Southerners appeared unanimous in their rejection of such a document. In this situation the Southern representatives, for whom I had the honour to be spokesman, left the constitution commission at the end of December 1968. We did not wish to be party to a document that emphasized the Arab race, Islamic religion and Arab culture to the exclusion of other existing races, religions, and culture. It would have made nonsense of a regional autonomy anyway. The people of the Southern Sudan have learnt something of the religions of Christianity and Islam. But

> these religions have not affected the way of life and the indigenous cultures of the people of the Southern Sudan up to this moment. A person still has the option to follow his religion and preserve his culture and identity. In being told to accept the rule of a constitution based on religion, the Southerners were being told they would become aliens in the Arab world and its cultures, exiles from the negro-African world. They were being told to say goodbye to their cultures and their general way of life. They also saw in the Islamic constitution a legal instrument of state discrimination against non-Moslems.[55]

Southern Sudanese are not opposed to the Northern identification with the Arab world and with its obsession with Islam. What they detest is the Northern disregard for their own African values and their campaign for integrating the South into the Arab fold. For, to argue "the Sudan is an integral part of the Arab world—anybody dissenting from this view must quit the country"[56]—is to assume that the Southerners would have to surrender to Arabism if they were to continue to live in the Sudan. Southerners on the other hand have argued that because they are neither Arabs nor Moslems, they have no desire or right to be part of the Arab World and that the Northern Sudanese should therefore permit them to identify themselves with black Africa to which the Southern region by all criteria belongs. The preoccupation with the question of whether or not the Sudan should adopt an Islamic Constitution further polarized African-Arab relations.

The divisions within the political parties created parliamentary instability when disagreements between Sadiq el-Mahdi and his uncle, Imam el-Hadi, led to a split in the Umma parliamentary group. The equal distribution of parliamentary votes prevented any government action, thereby rendering the machinery of consensus politics ineffective. The Prime Minister, Mohammed Ahmed Mahgoub, who belonged to the traditional wing of the Umma party, became afraid of Sadiq el-Mahdi, who in 1966 had assembled enough votes in the assembly to pass a vote of no confidence in him, and who subsequently replaced him as Prime Minister for a year until he eventually, with the help of the NUP, gathered enough votes to get Sadiq out of power. Sadiq was gradually becoming more and more powerful in Parliament once again and to offset any move from him to gain enough votes to dislodge Mahgoub from power, Mahgoub with the backing of President el Azhari dissolved Parliament.[57] Sadiq and his followers refused to recognize the constitutionality of the dissolution of Parliament, and for a short time, two Parliaments functioned in Khartoum: one inside the Parliament building and the other on its lawn. These divisions prompted the Army commander to request clarification from the Supreme Court as to which faction had the authority to issue orders. The Supreme Court advised him to wait for the outcome of the case before the High Court. The Supreme Council, after much deliberation backed the move toward dissolution which was subsequently upheld by the Supreme Court. New elections were called for in late April 1968.

The NUP and the PDP meanwhile decided to merge and formed a new party, the Democratic Unionist Party (DUP) under Ismael el-Azhari. The DUP and the traditional conservative wing of the Umma Party supporting Imam el-Hadi and his protégé Mohammed Ahmed Mahgoub agreed to form a coalition government to preside over the general elections. The elections were held in April as scheduled despite opposition from Sadiq el-Mahdi, who had preferred postponement until a new constitution was approved.

The turnout at the polls was much greater than in 1965—in some constituencies as many as 85 percent of the electorate voted. In the South, elections were also held under a reasonably calm atmosphere. The Anya-Nya deliberately slowed their activities to allow the Southern candidates to campaign in order to stop Northern Sudanese living in the South from declaring themselves elected unopposed as they did in 1965.

No single party held a majority to form a government.[58] The DUP needed at least eight more votes in order to form a government. The stability of the parliamentary system could not be ensured. Subsequently, a coalition government of DUP and the traditional wing of the Umma Party (Imam group) was formed under Mohammed Ahmed Mahgoub, of the Umma Party, as Prime Minister and Ismael el-Azhari, of the DUP, as Permanent President of the Supreme Council. The Umma Party was given four posts in the cabinet, the DUP and the Southern Front were given five and two posts, respectively.

Soon after the election results were announced, an incident occurred in the South adding more stresses and strains into the already fragile African-Arab relationship in the Sudan. The SANU President, William Deng, was assassinated.[59] Deng was traveling from Rumbek to Tonj in the company of four political aides when his car was ambushed by Northern Sudanese government forces. It seemed that a directive was given by the government in Khartoum to the Northern Army in the South to eliminate Deng, whose political sophistry was resented by the Northern "old guard" politicians. It is also said that he entered into an alliance with Sadiq el-Mahdi, and this was not well taken by the traditional Umma group of Imam el-Hadi and Mohammed Ahmed Mahgoub.

The DUP/Umma (Imam) coalition government proved incapable of breaking the economic and political impasse facing the country. The leaders led the country into bankruptcy and fraudulent activities, emptying the coffers of the state.[60] Since the civilian coup of October 1964, the balance of trade steadily decreased. Because of priority given to the importation of consumer goods and luxury articles, the foreign reserves decreased from about sixty-one million Sudanese pounds in 1965 to only about fourteen million pounds in May 1969. The foreign debt surpassed all previous records: ninety-one million pounds—double the amount of 1964—and foreign loans were used to hide the budgetary deficit, caused by extravagant spending, instead of financing development projects. In 1968, the state enterprise registered a deficit of thirty-one million Sudanese pounds. A flight of capital, mainly of foreign origin, deprived the country of some fifty-two million pounds! All these facts demonstrate the poor condition of the economy.

On the political front, the return of the old guard politicians failed to produce a stable political system. Parliamentary instability rendered coordination of governmental actions difficult. The party leaders who were in power were preoccupied with maintaining themselves in power and in countering parliamentary plots against them. The political parties were diffused organizations having no regular party dues and no agendas for or minutes of meetings. The party machines in the absence of elections atrophied as politics was continually dominated by a few personalities in Khartoum. All the Cabinets were party coalitions in the midst of continuous inter- and intraparty wranglings. Sadiq el-Mahdi, who held the position of the Prime Minister for a year, described the parliamentary scene thus:

> Outstanding leaders go about with parliamentary baskets in which they collect Members of Parliament. When one has collected the right number, he becomes the Prime Minister. When some of the MPs jump out, he ceases to be Prime Minister.[61]

This was an honest description of the way in which both Sadiq himself and Mahgoub of the Umma Party competed against each other in Parliament for the office of the Prime Minister. Indeed, as Sadiq put it, "each government was always about to fall, or a Cabinet reshuffle was always imminent."[62]

The parliamentary governments failed to bring about a settlement of the North-South conflict or to approve a constitution for the country. Pressures for an Islamic constitution increased and party politics was rendered impotent as the political leaders faced a dilemma as to whether their parties should or should not support such a proposal. The constitutional issue proved divisive as Islam also became a part of the debate.[63]

However, in early 1969, a new situation developed within the Ansar and the Umma party which might have stabilized parliamentary politics for a while. Sadiq el-Mahdi and his uncle, Imam el-Hadi, resolved their differences and agreed that Sadiq would support his uncle in a forthcoming presidential election, and that el-Hadi in return would back Sadiq in Parliament to head the Umma Party. The armed forces had, however, seen enough of the squabbles for leadership in Khartoum and of the decay of the governmental machinery. Hence, once again, it stepped in and captured power in a bloodless coup on May 25, 1969. The coup was led by the then Colonel Gaafar Mohammed el-Nimiery. This time the Army was not invited to take over power as was the case in 1958. Parliamentary instability and political rivalries had created a leadership vacuum, and the Army decided to remove the politicians from the reins of power and save the country from an Islamic constitution.

Conclusion

During the period from October 1964 to May 1969, raw power struggles ensued, mainly as a result of the absence of stable institutions for channeling and ordering politics. The Sudan witnessed not only the lack of bases for authority and legitimacy but also the breakdown of elite unity. Political leadership was so divided that it failed to give form to governmental institutions.

A situation similar to that of a praetorian society has since developed. The country appears to be more politicized than it is precisely because of "the absence of effective political institutions capable of mediating, refining, and moderating group political action."[64] As is the case in all praetorian societies, groups in the Sudan grapple directly for power. Social forces in such a polity, of course

> confront each other nakedly; no political institutions, no corps of professional political leaders are recognized or accepted as the legitimate intermediaries to moderate group conflict. Equally important, no agreement exists among the groups as to the legitimate and authoritative methods for resolving conflict.[65]

Mediating institutions often splinter or become ineffectual. In the Sudan, the loss of governmental capacity engendered a loss of legitimacy, and the diminished legitimacy of government invited intervention by one of the most politically important groups in the country: the armed forces.

Lack of viable and cohesive institutionalized polity to provide procedures to be used for resolution of political disputes and to provide a fair means for political participation in the Sudan produced much frustration among the elites. This led to a high incidence of political instability. The elite frustration, coupled with excessive lust for power, was manifested by both the civilian and the military elites in various attempts to capture power.

The traditional "old guard" politicians failed to provide the Sudan with a constitution—a viable system of government that would be responsive to mass needs and demands—or with a solution to the Southern question, which was in fact exacerbated by attendant repression in the South. Once again, the military intervened and removed the ineffectual politicians from power.

confront each other nakedly; no political institutions, no corps of professional

PART III

The African-Arab Conflict in the Sudan and the International Community

CHAPTER VII

External Involvement

International involvement in the African-Arab war in the Sudan was present from the beginning of the conflict. Hence, to a large extent, the character, the length, and the conduct of the war were dependent upon the resources which the international community made available to the contestants in the war. The nature of the involvement, however, varied from country to country, from organization to organization, and from time to time. As the war progressed, more parties became involved and the external dimensions of the conflict became broader. An examination of the involvement of each external party would make too extended a story to relate here. For our purposes, it will be more useful simply to identify the types of international involvement, both formal and informal, and some of the factors which shaped the roles played by various groups. The most important formal involvements relate to the recognition or nonrecognition of the competing parties, official government involvement in the supply of war materials and in relief operations, and efforts at formal mediation of the conflict.

It is clear in examining the pattern of international involvement in the Sudan war that the broadest and fullest formal support was for the Northern Sudan which controlled the state government in Khartoum. The Southern Sudan received no formal support as Biafra had, and the degree of informal support it was able to generate was dismally insignificant compared to that generated by the North through its formal channels. There were at least three factors which had given the North the advantages it had in its relations to the international community and in shaping the particular pattern of international attitudes and roles. These factors were, namely: First, the Sudan government was (and is) the bearer of recognized sovereignty and it enjoyed (and still enjoys) international legal standing. Second, the organization of African Unity (OAU) and the Arab League—two important regional organizations of which the Sudan is a member—and their respective members supported the territorial unity of African states and the maintenance of present African boundaries. Hence, they backed the Sudan government in the war against the Southern

Sudanese secessionists. Third, the attitude and role of the major powers (permanent members of the United Nations Security Council) bolstered the position of the Sudan government. These three factors made the United Nations quiescent on the Sudan war and also on the Nigerian-Biafran conflict. We shall try to explore the various aspects of each of these three factors and how they on the whole reinforced the position of the Sudan government in the war between the North and the South.

The Sudan as a Bearer of Recognized Sovereignty

The Sudan government was the bearer of recognized sovereignty: it had international legal standing throughout the duration of the war from 1955 to 1972. It carried on diplomatic relationships with foreign powers, held seats in international bodies—the U.N., the OAU, and the Arab League—all of which the Sudan is a member. Therefore, the Sudan government could claim the same access to markets and to the sources of military supplies which it could have claimed if there had been no war and which other independent countries could claim. The Northern Sudanese through the Sudan government were thus the beneficiaries of any status quo in relations with foreign powers. Those countries which did not wish to be actively involved in the conflict did not withdraw their recognition of the Sudan government. Hence, to do nothing meant to continue relations with the Sudan government substantially on the same basis as they had been before the war intensified. For, indeed, as George Modelski has pointed out, there is no internal war without international intervention:

> Even though a country may decide not to act at all, to do nothing and to say nothing, then by this very fact it, too, helps—sometimes unwittingly—to mould the outcome of the process: for by refusing to act, it helps the stronger party to suppress the weaker, irrespective of the merits of the case. This is the meaning of Talleyrand's celebrated definition of non-intervention: a mysterious word that signifies roughly the same thing as intervention.[1]

The international recognition of the Sudan, on the one hand, as a sovereign state carried very profound advantages for the Northern Sudan, while on the other hand, the characterization of the Southern Sudan as a rebel and secessionist party had real political and diplomatic disadvantages. The claim by the Sudan government (of the North, by the North, and for the North) that the problem was an "internal affair" became a convenient reason for foreign powers not to become involved against the Sudan government and thus not to change the basis of their diplomatic relations with the Sudan. Therefore, the international status of the Sudan as a recognized independent sovereign state was itself a significant factor in shaping the roles of other countries and external actors in the North-South War.

Africa, the Arab World, and the Sudan War

Undoubtedly, a major factor in the diplomatic isolation of Southern Sudan was the success of the Sudan government in winning a commitment from the African and Arab states, and from the OAU and the Arab League on the maintenance of the so-called territorial integrity of the Sudan. In a diplomatic sense, the African-Arab conflict in the Sudan was viewed, first, as an "internal affair" of the Sudan and, second, whereas the sub-Saharan African group of states treated it as an African affair not dissimilar to other internal conflicts in the continent, the Arab states of the OAU (and others) looked at the Southern Sudan as a strategically important area for Arab acculturation and Islamization and as a stepping stone for Arab influence into the heart of Africa. Therefore, lack of a broad sympathy and formal support for the Southern Sudanese cause from black African states made non-African states uneasy in providing formal recognition and, especially, material support. That is, the attitude of the African states was centrally crucial to the diplomatic position of the conflict. But, what is the basis of the fear of African states to secessionist movements?

Among African states, there exists the notion that self-determination operates only within the context of decolonization and that it is something which justifies independence from colonial powers.[2] They argue that self-determination has no relevance in the relations between free, independent sovereign states, and it does not justify the division of independent African states into smaller units. In other words, the principle of self-determination is seen by African states as having relevance where "foreign domination is the issue, and it has no relevance where the issue is perceived to be territorial disintegration by dissident citizens."[3] Secession is seen as being detrimental to African interests because it is considered to be incompatible with the goal of African unity. Any successful secession is viewed to set a precedent that could lead to further "Balkanization" of the continent.[4] Thus, the international legal order of independent Africa as embodied in the OAU Treaty accepted the boundaries of the inherited political order, thereby making secession illegitimate. As Bowett has pointed out, the OAU members view as unacceptable the notion that the equitable readjustments of colonial boundaries can be made by the application of the principle of self-determination.

> Indeed, the reaction has been so strong as to prompt resolutions at the OAU Summit Conference and the Non-Aligned Conference in 1964 designed to affirm the validity of all frontiers as they existed at the date of independence. Thus, while the last vestiges of colonialism in the political, economic, and cultural spheres are ruthlessly and sometimes possibly unwisely removed, this one particular remnant of colonialism, the frontier, is zealously safeguarded. This apparent contradiction has been justified, within the debates of the Organization of African Unity, by the arguments that any general movement

towards the revision of frontiers would create havoc and endless interstate strife amongst African nations; that movements for secession run contrary to the aims of these states to create a free, multiracial society which will cut across religious, ethnic, and linguistic barriers; and that self-determination is confined to the birth of a free nation and does not justify the partition of a nation into fragments having no political or economic viability.[5]

The arguments against secession as presented and articulated by the OAU and member states, and their advocates, in the academic community may sound good for political consumption, but under closer scrutiny, these arguments lose their intellectual persuasion. First, the right to self-determination is an inalienable right of "a people"[6] and there is no specific time and period in history for it to be denied to them. Second, the presupposition of strife between groups of peoples is not of itself "a consequence of the principle of self-determination but the reflection of a desire to resist it."[7] For indeed,

> . . . if the states involved are prepared to accept a result based on self-determination, then there is no reason to presuppose violence will ensue, no more than it did over the Saar in 1955, or the British-administered Togoland in 1956, or the Cameroons in 1961. Indeed, there is evidence to suggest that resistance to a plea for self-determination, especially in the form of a demand for secession, will often lead the state into a situation of continuing internal strife in the form of "liberation movements" and that this is ultimately as harmful and costly, in economic terms, as any international strife. The experience of the colonial Powers indeed suggests, further, that in the long run it is usually impossible to win this kind of armed contest against a determined, indigenous population.[8]

The fear of secession reflects the fact that it is internal rather than external conflicts which pose the greatest threat not only to the states concerned but to African stability generally. Therefore, it only seems sensible that African leaders should address themselves to these internal conflicts by examining relevant solutions for containing the grievances of specific afflicted groups in order to stabilize their regimes for social and economic development.

We now come to the third argument, which is that self-determination need not necessarily produce political and economic fragmentation. For it is unlikely that secession of a group of people in one country will cause a chain reaction resulting in fragmentation of African states. It is doubtful that other secessionist movements would have risen to imitate the Southern Sudan or Biafra, precisely because such movements must have local sources of conflict if they are to attract wide support. The Eritreans and the Moslem Chadians are unlikely to have been strengthened in their resolution to fight by knowledge of the Southern Sudanese secessionist movement.

The fear of "Balkanization" of Africa is unfounded for it does not rest on solid ground and common sense. In the case of the Sudan, the argument about "Balkanization" of Africa does not apply for the Sudan is the largest country on the continent (about one million square miles) and the secession of the Southern region would not reduce it to a tiny country. If anything, it would make it easier to administer. On the other hand, the Southern region has a greater area and a larger population than many independent African countries. To illustrate the point at issue, Table V shows some comparisons of Southern Sudan with ten independent African countries in area, population, and economy.

In terms of area only, the Southern Sudan is much larger than many independent African countries not shown in the table (to mention a few: Cameroon, Tunisia, Uganda, Kenya, Niger, and Lesotho). As Richard West rightly asked: "if Balkanization has not been bad for the Balkans, why then should it be bad for Africa?"[9] The exercise of the right to self-determination by the Southern Sudanese or the Biafrans would not have led to disintegration of other African states. For Africans more likely than not, "have more sense than to allow self-determination to dissolve Africa into anarchy."[10] The right to self-determination in some cases makes political and economic good sense.

The fourth argument is that if African unity is conceived to be a union of African peoples within the framework of a common political system, then it is difficult to see how a secession of a viable group of people can be regarded as an impediment to the achievement of such a union. It is equally dif-

TABLE V

The Southern Sudan Compared with Ten Independent African Countries

Country	*Area (sq. mi.)*	*Population*	*Economy*
The Southern Sudan (Region)	254,000	over 4,000,000	Cotton, sugar, rice, sesame, coffee, groundnuts, cattle, fish, timber, tobacco, copper, hides
Botswana	220,000	629,000	Diamonds, manganese, cattle
Burundi	10,747	3,475,000	Coffee, cotton
Central African Republic	238,000	1,518,000	Cotton, coffee, diamonds, groundnuts
Dahomey	44,913	2,640,000	Palm oil, cotton, groundnuts
Gabon	102,317	485,000	Timber, rich in minerals
Gambia	4,000	360,000	Groundnuts
Guinea (Conakry)	96,865	3,890,000	Coffee, bananas, diamonds, aluminum, iron ore
Rwanda	10,169	3,500,000	Coffee, tin ore
Senegal	77,814	3,980,000	Phosphates, groundnuts
Togo	21,895	2,000,000	Coffee, cocoa, phosphates, palm oil, cotton

Source: Africa Independent: A Study of Political Development, *Kessings Research Report*, 6 (New York: Charles Scribner's Sons, 1972).

ficult to see how African unity is consistent with the forceful coercion of minorities by their own governments.

The fifth argument against hostility to the exercise of the right to self-determination and secession in postcolonial Africa is that African boundaries are neither sacred nor inviolable, for it must be remembered that these boundaries were "originally drawn to suit the balance of power rather than to fit ethnographic realities in Africa."[11]

> In the final analysis, in arguments against secession, one comes face to face not with arguments of economic and political good sense, but with arguments based upon political pride and a theory of statehood which attaches territory to the state rather than to the inhabitants of the territory. One is left with the very basic question, what is the purpose of the state? It has at that stage ceased to be promotion of the well-being of the people of the territory according to their own freely expressed desires.[12]

The Southern Sudanese secessionist movement did not receive official recognition or sympathy from the black African states. The attitude of the Uganda government under Milton Obote illustrates in many ways the position of most black African states on the African-Arab War in the Sudan. Therefore, a discussion of the relations between the Uganda government of the First Republic[13] and the Southern Sudan secessionist movement, on the one hand, and between the former and the present Khartoum government, on the other, will be in order.

Although Milton Obote might have been expected to support the Southern Sudanese in their cause because many of them are ethnically linked with Northern Ugandans (the Lango people of whom Obote is a member, the Acholis, the Madi, the Lugbara, and the Kawka), he consistently took a sympathetic view of the Khartoum government and remained hostile toward the Southern Sudanese politicians. There are a number of explanations for Obote's policy toward the Sudan War. The newly independent government of Uganda inherited a policy toward the Southern Sudanese from the British colonial days—a policy that was governed by the Alien Refugees Ordinance. The main features of this policy became Uganda's policy toward the Southern Sudanese refugees. Its main elements were fourfold:[14] (1) continued good relations with the Sudan government as the cornerstone of the policy; (2) an open door policy to the refugees fleeing from the Sudan in accordance with the ordinance; (3) the undesirability of permitting the refugees to indulge in political activity and to use Uganda as a base of operations against Sudan in accordance also with the International Convention on Refugees; and, accordingly; (4) the desirability of removing refugees from the Sudan borders.

These elements of Uganda policy, however, in their execution worked considerably more against the Southern Sudanese than the Northern Sudanese. Relations between the Khartoum and Uganda governments were extremely cordial. The Uganda authorities at various times took vigorous and punitive action against Southern Sudanese political leaders in Uganda for allegedly indulging in political activities injurious to the neighborly good relations between Uganda and the Sudan. A number of Southern Sudanese politicians were thus either imprisoned or detained by the Obote regime.[15]

The policy of the Obote regime was continually disillusioning to the Southern Sudanese and even to some Uganda Members of Parliament, particularly those from the Nilotic areas of Northern Uganda. In January 1966, the leader of the Uganda Parliamentary Opposition Party, Alexander Latim, was so upset by the actions of the Obote government that he had to say in sympathy with the Southern Sudanese: "The Arab Sudanese go out to the Arab World and call for help, and the Arab World does help them in their problem of the Southern Sudan as to how they should suppress that part of the black world, but when the Southern Sudanese appeal to the black world, and show them that this is inhuman, they just laugh."[16]

It was interesting though that Uganda did not pursue the same consistent policy toward the wars in the neighboring states of Zaire (then Congo-Kinshasa) and the Sudan. The Obote regime took a more sympathetic attitude toward the Congolese who fought against the Central Congolese authority than toward the Southern Sudanese. As both Tandon and Gingyera-Pinycwa have argued, the policy of the Uganda government seemed to others incomprehensible:

> In the Congo, it was covertly assisting an African rebel force to topple the authority of a government which was also African, whereas in the case of the Sudan it was prepared to accept with equanimity the rule of an Arab central authority over fellow black Africans in the south. Secondly, whereas both in the Sudan and in Congo, the so-called rebels were resisting the central authority, in the Sudan they were fighting for their fundamental rights as human beings who asked to be treated with at least as much respect for their languages and religion as enjoyed by the Arabs in the north. In the Congo they were fighting more because of their disagreement with the system of Government in Leopoldville and their political aversion to one or two characters—like Tshombe—who occupied the seat of Government. It is at least defensible on moral grounds to argue that they should spare them for those who were fighting for their basic human rights than for those who were fighting to change the character and composition of a regime.[17]

However, some Ugandan Members of Parliament did not turn blind eyes to the differential treatment by the Uganda government of the Congolese and Sudanese cases. They were disturbed by both the "apparent lack of sympathy of the Government for the Southern Sudanese, and also by the apparent inability of the Government to take strong action against the Khartoum Government consequent upon frequent violations of the territorial integrity of Uganda by the Arab Sudanese forces, whereas the same government had made vitriolic verbal attacks on the Tshombe Government of the Congo following the 1965 incidents at Goli and Paidha (in which Congolese air force bombed Uganda villages)."[18]

There were at least two pertinent reasons why the Obote regime was hostile toward the Southern Sudanese political movement. First, the Southern Sudanese politicians befriended members of Uganda's Opposition Party (the Democratic Party), most of whom were Catholics. Some of the Southern Sudanese politicians such as Joseph H. Oduho and Fr. Saturnino Lohure were Catholics and had cordial relations with the Catholic Church in Uganda, which was closely identified with the Opposition Party. It so happened that the critics of the Uganda policy toward the Southern Sudanese cause were mainly Opposition Members of Parliament (particularly from Northern Uganda, and who have ethnic connections with the Southern Sudanese). The Obote government was not happy about the association of the Southern Sudanese politicians with its critics and with the Catholic Church. Perhaps more important is the second reason, that the Sudan government through its embassy in Kampala, Uganda, was able to use substantial amounts of money for bribing some members of the Obote regime.[19] The Southern Sudanese did not have the resources to buy support. They thought—incorrectly—that the mere facts of their case would generate some sympathy for them. Instead, however, the Obote regime supported the Sudan government and even at times engaged the Ugandan Army in the war in concert with the Arab Sudanese soldiers against the Anya-Nya.

Unlike the Southern Sudanese, the Congolese rebels, the Simbas-Lumumbists, had the necessary resources (money, gold, and ivory) with which to gain the support of influential Ugandan politicians.[20] Indeed, the Simba rebellion in 1965 gained momentum and won the support of African and Arab governments because its leaders were shrewd enough to use the enormous amounts of material which they had for bribing heads of states. As Tshombe began to use the same countermeasures, the Simba leaders were soon declared undesirable elements in some African capitals.[21]

The Sudan gave sanctuary and training to both Chadian and Eritrean dissidents, and it allowed arms shipments to the Eritreans and the Simbas against both the Addis Ababa and Kinshasa governments, respectively, but neither the Chadian nor the Kinshasa (except during the Tshombe regime) government took any serious punitive steps against the Sudan. One also would have expected the Ethiopian government to support the Southern Sudanese secession, at least in retaliation for the material support that the Khartoum government has been able to give to the pro-Arab Eritrean Liberation Front (ELF). The ELF has been trained by the Palestinian El Fatah and some members of the Arab League and has received financial support from them through the Sudan; all the military supplies for the Eritreans have passed through the Sudan. The late Emperor Haile Selassie, however, did not retaliate against the Khartoum government. Indeed, Ethiopia granted refuge to the Southern Sudanese but it refused them arms. Perhaps, more than anything else, it was the Ethiopian position as the headquarters of the OAU that prevented the former Imperial government from giving recognition to the Southern Sudanese cause. Although, of course, it must be remembered that Ethiopia was not only ready to, but did give military training to the Arab Northern Sudanese regardless of the use of such technical skill against Southern Sudanese.

The Southern Sudan, unlike Biafra, did not receive formal recognition from any of the black African OAU member states.[22] Although President Julius K. Nyerere of Tanzania, in recognizing Biafra, was ready to argue that "unity can only be based on a general consent of the people involved,"[23] he was not ready to extend the same rationalization to support the Southern Sudanese cause. Yet, the philosophical basis of Nyerere's argument was applicable not only to the Biafrans but to the Southern Sudanese as well:

> Surely when a people is rejected by a majority of the State in which they live, they must have the right to live under a different kind of arrangement which does secure their existence. . . . States are made to serve people; governments are established to protect the citizens of a State against external enemies and internal wrong-doers. It is on these grounds that people surrender their right and power of self-defence to the Government of the State in which they live. But when the machinery of the State, and the powers of the government are turned against a whole group of the society on the grounds of racial, tribal, or religious prejudice, then the victims have the right to take back the powers they have surrendered and to defend themselves.[24]

But if the African states withheld support to the Southern Sudanese secession, what about the collective and individual attitude of the members of the Arab League toward the Sudan conflict? Did the Arab world help the Arab Sudanese in the war or did it pretend that it was an internal affair of the Sudan and that outside involvement would be inappropriate?

The Sudan is a member of the Arab League, but the attachment of Northern Sudan to the Arab world goes much deeper than mere membership in the Arab League; Northern Sudan has its roots in the Arab heritage of the Arab Sudanese. The predominantly Arab-Islamic orientation of the Khartoum governments, therefore, was successful in generating strong support—both material and moral—from the Arab world. We shall select the particular example of Egypt, the Sudan's northerly neighbor and the headquarters of the Arab League, to illustrate the concern for the Arab Sudanese by the Arab world in contrast to the African neglect of the African Sudanese as shown by the behavior of the Uganda government under Obote. We shall explain briefly the basis of the Egyptian involvement in the Sudan War.

Egypt was a colonial partner with Britain in the Sudan, but because its role was more nominal than actual, the Northern Sudanese do not hold a grudge against her people. Moreover, Egypt has been and still is the Sudan's natural link to the Arab world. Additionally, cultural and economic ties are so close between the Northern Sudanese and the Egyptians, and Egypt's position in the Arab world is so dominant, that the Arab Sudanese have looked to their Northern neighbor for ideological inspiration and political guidance, particularly during the Nasser years. For Egypt, its primary objective in its policy in the Sudan is to safeguard its strategic interests and the most vital concern by far, of course, the River Nile.[25] The Sudan, after all, does control the sources of the River Nile and it is the country in which the Blue and White Niles meet to form the Great Nile. The location of the Sudan in the heart of Africa is also considered strategically important: the Sudan is the meeting point of the African and Arab worlds, and it could control the important lines of communication that run to and from tropical Africa. Besides the geopolitical factors, there are also vital economic and commercial considerations influencing Egypt's policy in the Sudan.

For all these reasons, Egypt unhesitatingly backed the Arab Sudanese in the War against the Africans in the Southern region. Also, the Egyptian government solicited on behalf of the Sudan government some material support from other members of the Arab League, mainly Algeria, Libya, and Saudi Arabia.[26] Egyptian soldiers and MIG fighter pilots were actively involved in the war. Financial aid to the Khartoum governments for the execution of the war came from Saudi Arabia and Libya. Algeria gave military and material supplies. On the whole, the Arab states either individually or collectively through the Arab League, did not make any pretense about their involvement in the Sudan War; they were committed morally, physically, and financially to help the North defeat the South.

The Attitude and the Role of the Major Powers

The attitude of the major powers was important in connection with the role of the international community in the African-Arab War in the Sudan. The Soviet Union defied the Leninist policy of self-determination for nationalities and supported the hegemony of the Arab Sudanese over the Africans in the South. It is not, of course, unusual these days for the Soviet Union to subordinate self-determination to what it considers legitimate intervention in internal conflicts, particularly when the protection or promotion of socialism or communism is involved. But in the Sudan, promotion of socialism was nonexistent. Therefore, the Soviet involvement was predicated upon its national interests in the Arab World. Indeed, it seems that the Soviet Union followed the Egyptians into the Sudan, just as it followed them into Yemen and Aden.

The nature and the extent of the Soviet involvement in the Sudan war was extremely substantial.[27] Soviet military pilots ferried military supplies in from Egypt in Antonov transports. The Russians also gave the Sudan MI-8 civilian helicopters converted with armor-plating and rocket-launchers, more than 100 T-55 heavy tanks, as well as howitzers, artillery, and ground rockets. More than 1000 Soviet Army advisers, helicopter and jet pilots, and ground crews went to the Sudan. Of these, more than 100 were reported to have served with the Arab Sudanese combat units in the Southern Sudan.

Most of the Soviet aid went to the Sudan following the 1967 Arab-Israeli War when the Sudan government, in changing its policy toward the West, broke diplomatic relations with the United States in accordance with an Arab League policy. Thereafter, the Sudan accepted large quantities of military aid from the Soviet Union, Czechoslovakia, and Yugoslavia. The Soviet support alone amounted to $150 million. Both Soviet and Czech contributions included tanks, armored personnel carriers, artillery, and jet aircraft, as well as training missions. After the 1969 coup in the Sudan, the Soviet Union became increasingly more involved both militarily and materially, undoubtedly as a result of the militant voice of the new government headed by Colonel Gaafar Mohammed el-Nimiery. Nimiery's successful coup was welcomed by the Sudan Communist Party, some of whose central executive members became cabinet ministers.

The Western countries of Europe and North America seem to place undue emphasis on economic development and the importance of large states and national unity for development. They regard African countries as being composed of loose ethnic coalitions and regard support for secessionist movements as leading to their fragmentation. The integral entity of African countries is also beneficial for the operations of Western multinational corporations, since these companies would prefer to deal with larger units. Hence, all the major Western powers, just like the countries of the Eastern bloc, placed more value on the unity of Sudan.

In the case of the United States, its position on the issue of secession in Africa was graphically summarized by the then Assistant Secretary of State for African Affairs, Joseph Palmer, Jr., in a reference to Biafra in the following words:

> When I speak about self-determination, I am talking about those areas of Africa that still remain under foreign control. I think it will be an unfortunate precedent for the rest of Africa, if groups, no matter how legitimate their grievances are, will try to fractionalize the continent any further.[28]

Since the Congo crisis of the 1960s, the U.S. public policy toward internal conflicts in independent African states seems to be that the Africans must sort out their own problems. In private, however, the United States supported the central governments of Nigeria, the Sudan, and continues to back the Addis Ababa government against the Eritreans. In the case of the Sudan, the United States provided the Khartoum governments with economic and military aid totaling $101.7 million between 1958 and 1967. About $2.2 million of this sum was purely for military assistance.[29] The United States also provided military training to Northern Sudanese officers.[30]

Britain, the main colonial power in the Sudan, did not even attempt to mediate the conflict which it had played a major role in creating. In fact, the British decision to unite the North and the South of the Sudan on the eve of their departure amounted to the handover of the South to the North. Throughout the seventeen years of war, all British governments, Conservative and Labor, supported Arab control over the peoples of the Southern Sudan, and relations between London and Khartoum remained extremely cordial.[31] Britain provided both military supplies and financial aid to the Sudan.

All in all, the Sudan government received the following:[32] (1) Air training for its army in Britain, Egypt, Yugoslavia, and West Germany; Aircraft from Britain, the Netherlands, Egypt, Switzerland, and the Soviet Union; (2) Military training from Britain, the United States, Ethiopia, Pakistan, and India; small arms, artillery, and vehicles purchased from West Germany and armored cars from Britain and the United States; and (3) Naval training in Britain and Yugoslavia. But despite all this massive military and financial aid to the Northern Sudanese, their army was not able to crush the Anya-Nya forces in the South. A stalemate prevailed despite the deployment of two-thirds of the Northern Sudanese Army, consisting of 40,000 men, in the South. We shall now explore the sources of external support received by the Southern Sudanese.

External Aid for the Southern Sudan

When the African-Arab confrontation in the Sudan flared into open violence in 1955, the neighboring African countries were still in colonial bondage. The Northern Sudanese with the help of the British Royal Air Force were able to airlift troops to the South. Thereafter, the Southern Equatorial Corps scattered, most going to the neighboring countries for refuge and others forming armed groups so as to continue to harass the Northern troops. These armed groups became the nucleus of the Anya-Nya. Those Southerners who sought refuge in Uganda, Kenya, and Zaire had to surrender their arms to the then colonial authorities in these countries and their arms eventually were handed over to the Khartoum government. Hence, right from the beginning of the Sudan war, the South was at a disadvantage: it did not receive any formal or informal military, material, or moral support from the colonial authorities in control of East Africa and Zaire. The Anya-Nya forces were for a long time poorly armed[33] but their will and determination kept them fighting until eventually they were able to capture weapons from the inexperienced Northern Sudanese troops, who found it extremely difficult to confront the Anya-Nya in their own environment. More often than not, the morale of the Northern Sudanese soldiers was so low that they threw their guns away during Anya-Nya pursuit and ran to their army trucks.

As the war continued, the Anya-Nya gradually were able to buy arms from black markets in the neighboring countries of Zaire, Uganda, Kenya, and Ethiopia, but their real luck came with the turn of events in Zaire between 1964 and 1966. By late 1964, a steady stream of arms from Eastern Europe, the Soviet Union, China, Algeria, and Egypt were being flown to Khartoum and thence to Juba en route to the Zairean rebels (Simbas) across the Southern Sudan border with Zaire.[34] The arms shipments, however, reached the Simbas at the time when they were falling back in disarray before the Zairean central government forces. The Simbas were defeated. Completely demoralized, and on the verge of starvation, they were ever ready to trade their new weapons for money, clothing, food, or alcohol. The Anya-Nya were happy to find this sudden influx of weapons and bought large quantities of them. Thus the Simbas sold their arms because of the necessity of circumstances not because of a desire to help the Anya-Nya. In fact, relations between the two groups were bad before the defeat of the Simbas. The bad relations existed because the Simbas received their military and other material supplies through the Sudan and in order to reciprocate for the help rendered to them, the Simbas cooperated with the Khartoum government against the Anya-Nya.[35]

In retaliation against the Sudan government for its active and massive support of the Simbas, the Zairean authorities turned a blind eye to the Anya-Nya activities within Zaire at the border with the Sudan. For the first time, the Anya-Nya found an African government which was indifferent about its territory being used as a springboard for attacks against the Northern Sudanese forces. On the whole, the Civil War in Zaire became an excellent opportunity for the Anya-Nya to replenish their stocks, which until that time had been low.

In 1965, Khartoum became a center of Chadian, Zairean, and Eritean exiles. All these exiles were fighting (and some are still fighting) their central governments. The interesting point here is that whereas the Northern Sudanese politicians were ready to support secessionist movements in neighboring countries, they were thoroughly unsympathetic with the Southern Sudanese grievances, which were not dissimilar to those of other secessionists, if not even more fundamental and justified.[36] At any rate, the late President Tombalbye of Chad was angered by articles printed in Khartoum newspapers, apparently written by Chadian exiles. He publicly threatened retaliation against Northern Sudanese citizens in Chad and added that "if the Sudan does not return those adventurers in Khartoum who call themselves the Government of the Islamic Republic of Chad in exile, the Sudan can no longer count on Chad to practice good neighbourliness towards it."[37] Although Tombalbye made broad hints that his government might open its borders to the Anya-Nya, he did not do so. The Chad government refused to render any military or material support to the Southern Sudanese secessionist movement. However, it did eventually harass Northern Sudanese living in Chad.

The only head of state in Africa who publicly condemned the Sudan Government for its repressive policies against the African population in the

South was President Kamuzu Banda of Malawi. He also criticized other African governments for their silence on the African-Arab conflict in the Sudan. Speaking in the Malawi National Assembly, he put it bluntly that:

> If Malawi needs to be sending mercenaries to fight any other country, she must send them to the Sudan where Arabs are butchering our own African kind. Arabs in the Sudan are obliterating African villages. While they are doing that, they are keeping their mouths wide open shouting about Rhodesia and South Africa. Worse than that some African leaders posing as champions of African unity kept mute at the OAU about the Sudan. They have even made state visits there. The Arabs in the Sudan are shooting Africans indiscriminately there now. Not only that, the Arabs enslaved our people for centuries. The trouble is that we have too many ignorant, immature, and inexperienced people in Africa.[38]

However, Malawi was too far away to give sanctuary to the Anya-Nya and too poor to render any material support. Nonetheless, Banda's brave and lonely stand was well received by the Southern Sudanese.

If governments were unsympathetic to the Southern Sudanese cause, scattered individuals and some organizations were compassionate enough to help it though not necessarily directly. The churches were a case in point. The mass expulsion of missionaries from the Southern Sudan by the Khartoum government in 1964 enraged the churches. Some of them eventually gave material help in the form of food and medicine to the Southern Sudanese refugees in neighboring countries, but some of these supplies got into the hands of the Anya-Nya. International relief agencies such as the International Red Cross, Caritas Catholic International Charity Organization, and Oxfam carried on direct negotiations with both sides regarding supply of food and medicine. The World Council of Churches through its branches was also involved in this humanitarian effort. A Norwegian Association for the Southern Sudan was launched and it raised funds for the Southern Sudanese refugees in the Scandinavian countries.

The activities of these organizations raise interesting questions regarding the role of international agencies in such situations. In some instances, as in the Biafran war, it was extremely difficult for them to remain impartial. However, in the case of Southern Sudan, they did not involve themselves in any massive support for the Anya-Nya. Nor did they recruit mercenaries for the Anya-Nya. There was only one mercenary, a certain Rolf Steiner, allegedly recruited for the Anya-Nya by religious and charitable groups in West Germany.[39] The church organizations, though, did perform a very important service to the Southern Sudanese movement: they provided publicity for the war in their campaigns to raise funds for the refugees. Also some of the publicity was conducted by individual Christians particularly those who worked in the Sudan as missionaries and either were expelled in 1964 or left. The most active vitriolic publicity against the policies and actions of the Khartoum governments toward the South came from the Catholic church.[40]

One important result of the Northern Sudanese's close ties with the Arab

World is the official position of the Sudanese Governments on the Arab-Israeli conflict. The Sudan maintained a firm anti-Israeli posture. As is common among leaders to blame their internal problems, rightly or wrongly, on external actors, the Khartoum governments, since the days of the Abboud military junta, blamed Israel and Zionism for the Southern Sudanese uprising. In fact, the Sudan government advertised the war for the Southern Sudanese for a long time. Israel listened to the accusations made against her by the Sudan governments for a long time before actually intervening. Indeed, Israel was the last of the four outside powers eventually involved in the Middle East to intervene in the Sudan war (following Egypt, the United States, and the Soviet Union, all three of whom supported the Northern Sudanese with supplies of military and material aid). All the Israel military aid went to the Anya-Nya after the Six-Day War of June 1967. Following that war, the Sudan government sent some regiments to serve in the Suez Canal Zone, and Israel resented it, but even then, the Israeli aid to the Anya-Nya was not substantial. It was only after the ascent to power in 1969 of the relatively militant Nimiery regime, particularly vis-à-vis Israel, that Israeli sympathy for the Southern Sudanese cause was translated into military supplies for the Anya-Nya.

The Israelis used DC-3s to parachute arms to the Anya-Nya. Their supplies included heavy machine guns, hand grenades, 303 World War II rifles, and old mines of Russian and British origin. Almost all these arms were captured by the Israelis from the Arabs during the 1967 war. Most of the arms, bearing Arab labels, were captured from the Northern Sudanese soldiers—so boasted the Anya-Nya. The Israelis also trained some of the Anya-Nya military forces. This military help bolstered the morale of the Anya-Nya and served to improve their performance to such an extent that they were able to control the countryside and render the Northern Sudanese soldiers ineffective. Thus, two-thirds of the Northern Sudanese Army, along with Egyptian equipment and reinforcements, was effectively diverted from Israeli targets. This maneuver served the main interest of Israel in the Sudan conflict.[41]

There is one important factor which shapes the pattern of international involvement in a conflict like that in the Sudan: the perception by external actors of who is most likely to win. No one is ready to support a losing side and, therefore, for the weaker side to gain outside help, it must be seen to be fighting well and capturing ground. In the Sudan conflict, the Southern Sudanese did not receive massive material and military support from the international community, and, consequently, the odds against their winning the war were considerable. They were unable to mount as successful a propaganda effort as the Biafrans, lacking the propaganda machinery to bolster their position. There were neither many educated persons in the movement outside the Sudan nor were there any Southerners of the international standing and caliber of many Biafrans.[42] Generally, the Southern Sudanese had poor political leadership; most of their politicians in exile were not only inept but also lacked radicalism often presumed to be necessary for any successful guerrilla movement. Also, unlike Biafra, the Southern Sudan lacks available mineral resources (it is not known whether minerals exist since the region has not been explored). Therefore, outsiders did not see any economic potential in the South Sudan.

Not much was heard in the outside world about the war, although, by the time a peace agreement was reached, it had been the first and the longest secessionist war in Africa. Publicity was sparse because individual outside reporters were not enthusiastic about entering the Sudan, and also there was no systematic and sustained effort to cover the progress and effects of the war from both the Northern and Southern sides. The Khartoum governments at any rate did not want any publicity on the war lest it arouse public opinion in the North against its futile policies. On the whole, the Northern Sudan was perceived to be winning which to some extent affected possible support for the Southern Sudan.

Conclusion

Although external involvement was present in the Sudan war, the overall picture remains, on balance, that of a conflict which did not draw much international attention. This was partly because most of the external military and financial aid went to the Northern Sudanese who controlled the Khartoum government, and, as would be expected, had international connections and legitimacy. The nature of the international system is such that it reinforces the legitimacy of those in charge of the machinery of the state and isolates and discourages rebels, depriving them of international respectability, whatever their cause may be. If the Anya-Nya had received the same amount of military aid that the Sudan government was able to obtain, there possibly would have been more interest in the war shown by the international press.

The other reason for the relative obscurity of the Sudan war was the lack of a serious clash of interests in the Sudan among the major powers.[43] For instance, although the United States was not involved to the same degree as the Soviet Union, it accepted the unity of the Sudan and the holding together physically of a territory which psychologically was never one.

From the point of view of the African states, however rational a secessionist move might be for the Southern Sudan (or Biafra), and however consistent it might be with the historical evolution of the various component political communities of the Sudan, it nonetheless was a threatening precedent to them. This is so because territorial unity in Africa appears as the panacea for survival and development. The doctrine of "an internal affair" was beneficial to the Sudan government as it permitted her an open role in international discussions while inhibiting the Southern Sudanese potential to obtain systematic, organized, open international consideration and action in coping with their crisis.

Whatever the arguments for the doctrine of an "internal affair," it must be remembered that a war of secession in which two parties are involved in de facto control of substantial parts of their national territory and population, and in which thousands of refugees have fled into neighboring countries, does not, intuitively at least, seem to fit neatly into this doctrine. As George Modelski reminds us, "all structures of internal war have international components. Only in the limiting or 'polar' case or a totally isolated political system—conceptually on a level with a 'Robinson Crusoe' model of the analytical economists—can we conceive of an internal war without components of an international (or 'external') kind."[44]

The roles of both the U.N. and the OAU in the African-Arab conflict in the Sudan was total support for the Sudan government. Despite the existence of OAU's Commission of Mediation, Conciliation, and Arbitration, it regarded its "noninterference" provision in domestic affairs of member states as applicable here. It did not, therefore, assume the role of a mediator as it pretended to do in the Nigerian-Biafran conflict. This peaceful role was gradually assumed successfully by a transnational organization: the World Council of Churches (WCC).

CHAPTER VIII

From Confrontation to Accommodation: The World Council of Churches in Conflict Mediation

In this chapter, we shall trace and analyze the gradual involvement of the World Council of Churches (WCC) and its member council, the All Africa Council of Churches (AACC), as mediators in the African-Arab war in the Sudan. We shall highlight only the important stages in their approach to the whole issue of North-South reconciliation. An attempt will be made to assess the forces at work that enabled the WCC and the AACC to play such a crucial mediating role in that intriguing conflict. In other words, the whole discussion will be carried out in the context of understanding the dynamics of the change of leadership and the attitude of the protagonists, from intransigence to reconciliation.

The WCC and the AACC in Mediatory Contacts

The WCC for many years was concerned about the suffering of people and the alienation of fellow Christians in the Southern Sudan. This concern was expressed in a number of ways, including support through relief assistance and supply of personnel both within the Sudan and among Southern Sudanese refugees in neighboring countries, scholarship aid to student refugees, pastoral activity among the refugees, and visits to the churches in the Sudan, accompanied often by talks with government officials. These visits to the Sudan increased after the reorganization of the Sudan Council of Churches and after its affiliation with the AACC and the WCC. One year after the expulsion of all the foreign missionaries from the Southern Sudan in 1965, the WCC sent a representative to find out what the WCC could do in the light of the continuing conflict. The result of this visit was a WCC appeal for increased aid to refugees, for scholarships, and for the intercessions of Christians around the globe.

In 1966 the central committee of the WCC urged its Commission of the Churches of International Affairs (CCIA) in consultation with the AACC "to continue to take all appropriate steps, including approaches to governments, so that an end may be put to the suffering of the population in the Southern Sudan and the exercise of religious freedom be ensured."[2] The concept "religious freedom" was highly suspected and unwelcomed by the Moslem Sudan government, which was as we have seen, strongly committed to Islamization and Arabization of the South. The WCC resolution was therefore unfavorably received by the Sudan government. This did not, however, discourage the WCC and the AACC from making more contacts with the Sudan government. Unlike the Roman Catholic Church, the WCC did not openly criticize the Sudan government on the expulsion of foreign missionaries from the Sudan, and it was also more restrained in its comments on the situation in the Southern Sudan. In the same year (1966) that the WCC passed its resolution on "religious freedom" in the Sudan, it was successful in arranging a good-will mission from the AACC to visit the Sudan at the invitation of the Sudan government, extended through its Ambassador to Kenya. The purpose of this visit was to assess the situation in the Sudan and to enable the AACC to offer its services for peace negotiations.

The AACC delegation met with government and church leaders in the Sudan. Upon its return, it issued a report in which it stated that it was convinced of: (1) the desire of Southern Sudanese for a greater share in governing the Sudan; (2) the need for a constitution guaranteeing religious freedom; (3) the need for reconciliation to avoid military operations; and (4) the need for a revision of the 1962 Missionary Act to permit outside help to strengthen the Sudanese churches.[3] The Sudan government agreed that African missionaries from other African countries would be accepted, but the AACC report was contested in some quarters, especially among ex-missionary groups to the Sudan such as the Verona Fathers and the Southern Sudanese politicians in exile. Those who disputed the AACC report argued that its mission had completely ignored evidence submitted by Southern Sudanese refugees and representatives of the Anya-Nya. In fact, the AACC delegates did not seek to learn anything about the Anya-Nya and their point of view. The report was substantially adverse to the Southern Sudanese secessionist movement.

It must, of course, be remembered that the AACC was committed to the OAU policies of noninterference in the internal affairs of member states and of acceptance of the belief that internal dissension in postcolonial Africa is usually the result of neoimperialist plots.[4] Not long after the AACC visit to the Sudan, the Church Missionary Society (Anglican Church) in the Sudan adopted a policy of cooperation with the government of Sadiq el-Mahdi (1967–1968) and appealed to Southern Sudanese refugees in East Africa to return home and work with Prime Minister Sadiq el-Mahdi to reach a compromise. The Anglican Bishop of the Sudan endorsed the

AACC report and made a visit to East Africa for the purpose of persuading Southern politicians to return. The Bishop's mission proved disastrous and the image of his role as a Christian missionary was damaged among the Southern Sudanese refugees, especially those who were Christian converts.

The AACC seemed to have taken well the criticisms of its report by the Southern Sudanese exiles. It did not give up its efforts to find a way to alleviate the sufferings of fellow Christians and potential converts in the Southern Sudan. Hence, in the face of international silence on the war in the Sudan and similar situations in Africa, the AACC and the WCC began to address themselves to three pertinent questions, namely: (1) How, in the face of oppressive policies and practices in Africa, can the churches fulfill their "appointed task" of reconciliation? (2) Should the churches pretend that the situations do not exist and therefore do nothing about them? (3) If the churches are anxious to take the Gospel seriously, what must they do to make it relevant?[6] After conferring over these questions, the WCC and the AACC resolved to take an active role as mediators in the Sudan war. The situation was made easier for the WCC/AACC's initiative by the coming to power of General Gaafar Mohammed el-Nimiery who announced a policy of regional autonomy for the South. Before the resumption of discussion of the WCC/AACC's role in the achievement of peace, we will examine the policy of the Nimiery regime toward the South in the context of the political forces and events within the Sudan and the Southern Sudanese exiles' reactions to them.

The Nimiery Regime and the Policy of Regional Autonomy for the South

When the Sudanese people awoke on the morning of May 25, 1969, they found that they had a new government: once again, the soldiers were in power.[7] The Army officers who staged the coup were revolutionaries of the Nasser–Egyptian type. They gave the impression that they were a group determined to see the Sudan transformed, Arab unity pursued, corruption rooted out, and socialism introduced. Radicals of leftist political persuasion, and communists supposedly uncorrupted by previous access to power, were co-opted by the members of the May Revolutionary Council into their regime to serve as Cabinet Ministers.

Fortunately, the leader of the May Revolutionary Council, then Colonel Gaafar Mohammed el-Nimiery, served in the South and he personally knew well how intractable the problem had become. Also not of less importance was the presence of members of the Communist Party in the government. The communists, for a long time, recognized the Southern question and urged autonomy for the Southern region. One of the two Southerners appointed to the government, the late Joseph Garang, was an avowed communist and a member of the central committee of the Sudan Communist Party. The other Southerner in the cabinet, Abel Alier, was a man of different ideological persuasion from Garang. Alier was the Secretary General of the Southern Front Party at the time of the coup, and before joining the Nimiery regime, he extracted a guarantee that a policy of regional autonomy for the South would be pursued. These three factors were crucial: (1) General Nimiery's knowledge of the war situation in the South; (2) the presence of communists in the government (long supporters of a policy of autonomy for the South); and (3) the appointment to the Cabinet of Abel Alier, who would not take an oath of office unless there was an undertaking for the new regime to solve the Southern problem—this position influenced the new regime to announce a positive policy toward the South.

On June 9, Nimiery announced his government's intention to grant "Regional Autonomy to the Southern Sudan Provinces within the framework of a new integral socialist Sudan."[8] Nimiery's policy statement on the Southern question recognized the cultural, racial, religious, economic, and social differences between the North and the South, accepted the basic grievances of the Southern Sudanese, blamed past governments for their failure to solve the Southern problem, and then prescribed "regional autonomy" for the South as a solution for the North-South confrontation. A four-point program was announced at the same time: (1) promulgation of an amnesty law for Southern Sudanese refugees; (2) economic, social, and cultural development of the South; (3) appointment of a Minister for Southern Affairs; and (4) training of personnel.[9] The statement did not, however, define the nature of the regional autonomy. That was left for future discussions. Point (3) was implemented immediately: Jospeh Garang was appointed Minister of State for Southern Affairs.

There were mixed reactions to the announcement of policy of regional autonomy for the South. In the North, the right-wing groups vehemently opposed it, while the moderates, though not opposed to it, emphasized that it must not be a sellout. The communists and the socialists applauded it as much as the Southerners within the Sudan. There were at least three different reactions from the Southerners in exile: First, the Nile Provisional Government (NPG) remained unconvinced. It argued that the Nimiery statement was not much different from previous Sudan government promises. Moreover according to the NPG, the solution of regional autonomy was one-sided in that it was not reached after a meeting of Southerners and Northerners—it was imposed by the latter. The second view, from the Anya-Nya, was that the activities of the Northern Sudanese soldiers in the South did not change and, therefore, the announcement of regional autonomy was a trick to make Southerners surrender. The Anya-Nya certainly could not accept the policy of a government which continued to refer to them as "rebels and outlaws." The third view was held by the Southern Sudanese students, particularly those in Makerere University (Kampala).[10] Their view was that Southerners should not remain obstinate and intransigent, but should try to test the sincerity of the Nimiery government by accepting in principle the statement on regional autonomy. This school of thought contended that whereas the Anya-Nya should continue to fight, all the Southern politicians in exile should dissolve their small factions, unite under one movement and establish a line of communication with Southerners such as Abel Alier and others within the Sudan, and that all the Southern politicians should ask the Nimiery government for a conference of representatives from both the North and the South to discuss the fundamental principles and details of the policy of regional autonomy. The Southern Sudanese students at Makerere University were so convinced of this strategy that they sent a delegation to the Sudan to assess the situation from within and particularly to ascertain the extent to which the policy of regional autonomy was popular among Southerners.[11] The Southern Sudanese Makerere student delegation to the Sudan tried to open a line of communication between Southern politicians inside and outside the Sudan. Their report was widely acclaimed for its objectivity.[12]

Unfortunately, no consensus emerged among Southerns either outside or inside the country. The appointment of Joseph Garang as Minister for Southern Affairs also hardened the attitude of the Southerners. For many of them, Garang's appointment meant nothing because he had no political base in the South, having three times lost his deposit in elections. Garang had a different perspective on the Southern problem from his fellow Southerners. He believed that the cause of the Southern problem was the inequality which existed between North and South by reason of an uneven economic, social, and cultural development and that all the ills in South-North relations sprang from this situation.[13] Consequently, for Garang the solution was development and the elimination of disparity. He was firmly opposed to negotiations with Southerners outside the Sudan including the Anya-Nya. In fact, he called Southern politicians in exile "reactionaries and stooges of imperialism." He also accused the Anya-Nya of being fronts for Zionism. Such rhetoric by Garang could hardly win the confidence of Southerners outside and much less those inside the Sudan.

Unfortunately, some influential members of the Nimiery Government supported Garang's position and some even opposed autonomy for the South for two basic reasons: religion and ideology. Radical Northern Sudanese elites—communists and Arab socialists—accused Southerners of being accomplices of imperialism, and of being conduits for Israeli penetration into the Southern flank of Arab Africa. Thus during Garang's control of the Ministry for Southern Affairs, the full implementation of regional autonomy was impeded, partly because its details had not been spelled out, and partly because of his first preference of building a political base for the Communist Party rather than a constitutional settlement.[14] Northerners who had misgivings about the policy of regional autonomy were happy to see Garang in charge of the Ministry for Southern Affairs because in him they found an obstacle to execution of the policy. Garang's argument that the building of a "socialist democratic movement" in the South was a prerequisite for the implementation of regional autonomy did not make sense to Southerners.[15] It is difficult to understand how a political movement could be built in the South before the state of emergency was lifted, or, in the final analysis, before the full definition and implementation of the policy of regional autonomy with the cooperation of Southern politicans and the Anya-Nya. In actuality, one could not talk of the building of a political movement before a peace agreement was reached between the antagonists. The lack of serious concern on the part of the government to implement its policy toward the South prompted the Southern Youth and Students Organization in Khartoum in November 1970 to send a memorandum to President Nimiery in which they pointed out that:

> . . . the process of the solution is almost static, the details of the regional self-rule are not yet out, which makes us feel that the Declaration of regional self rule will be but ink on paper. In fact, apart from a few steps taken in promotion and appointment of Southerners, the political programme of the Government towards the South is largely unclear. The share of the South in the Five-Year Development Plan is less than one-eighth of the whole budget, a step which is even more discouraging. The Ministry of State for Southern Affairs, which was supposed to hurry up with the implementation of the solution, is still a ministry without powers.[16]

Vocal criticism of the slowness in implementing the regional autonomy policy was expressed not only by the youth and the students but also by the Southern politicians in Khartoum who grouped under the umbrella of "the Southern Sudan Intellectuals Association." They all accepted the new policy but they were disappointed with the lack of desire to implement it. Of no less concern to Southerners was the regime's enthusiastic pursuit of the dream of Arab unity. They were apprehensive of the Tripoli Agreement signed by Egypt, Libya, and the Sudan in 1970 to form a federation. Furthermore, President Nimiery's statement in Cairo in November 1970 that, "Libya, Egypt, and the Sudan could possible struggle in Africa to defend the Arab civilization which is being encircled and hampered by imperialism in an attempt to stop its flux into the heart of Africa."[17] produced suspicions among Southerners of the government policy. The President's Cairo statement was offensive to the South, for in it he also said that the people in the South had no culture of their own. The government's new educational policy which abolished village schools and declared Arabic as the only medium of instruction up to secondary level in the South seemed to reinforce the President's Cairo statement. Of course, both this statement and his government's new educational policy contradicted the 9th of June Declaration of Regional Autonomy for the Southern Provinces. Indeed, the rhetoric of the government and its actions between July 1969 and July 1971 seemed to confirm the feeling that its announcement of regional autonomy was merely for political consumption and that there was no genuineness in the desire to reach an accord with the South through peaceful means.

In the North, the Nimiery regime faced difficult challenges, first from the

Mahdists and reactionary forces and, second, from the communists. The leader of the Ansar sect (Mahdists) Imam Abdel Rahman el-Hadi retreated to Aba Island, south of Khartoum, when Nimiery and his colleagues staged their coup. He did not recognize the government and continued to issue threats to it until finally a military confrontation flared up between his forces and those of the government. Thousands of people died, including the Imam who succumbed to bullets fired by the security patrols at the Sudan-Ethiopian border while he was trying to flee to Ethiopia.[18] Even today the scars remain as the Ansar supporters continue to play prominent roles in attempts to overthrow the government.[19] The second threat to the government came from the orthodox wing of the Communist Party. The alliances in the government among the secular nationalists, communists, and pan-Arabists were weakening.[20] An open conflict eventually came to the surface between the Communist Party and the government and this led to the dismissal from the government of all orthodox communists except Joseph Garang. A period of political tension and uncertainty ended with the abortive communist coup on July 19, 1971. General Nimiery lost power for seventy-two hours but was back in office after a successful countercoup. All the communists allegedly involved in the coup, including Garang, were unfortunately executed.

After the communist failure, the posture of the Nimiery regime changed radically. President Nimiery surrounded himself with pragmatic men of some intellectual sophistication.[21] He began to react to events cautiously and from a Sudanese context as he gradually eschewed ideology—particularly pan-Arabism and Arab socialism. The Soviet Union and its client states were discredited and were regarded with suspicion after the abortive communist coup; and overtures were immediately made to the West. It was soon realized in the corridors of power in Khartoum that Arab unity did not in practice hold any charm. Not long after, it became obvious that pursuit of Arabism and closer alliances with the Arab world were incompatible with the attainment of a solution with the Southern Sudanese. Indeed, Nimiery and his advisers were now persuaded more than before to accept the grievances and suspicions of the South as genuine and deeply rooted and to see that the need for real concessions was imperative.[22] Abel Alier, who played a significant role in Southern politics and in whom all Southerners within and outside the Sudan had great confidence, was named the new Minister of State for Southern Affairs and later became one of the three vice presidents following a plebiscite in which General Nimiery was overwhelmingly confirmed President.[23]

The appointment of Abel Alier to the Ministry for Southern Affairs and a Vice President indicated to Southerners outside and within the Sudan that the government was now moving in a positive direction toward the South. Alier moved swiftly: he reorganized the Ministry for Southern Affairs and appointed a group of prominent Southerners in Khartoum to draw up a document setting out a concrete plan for the implementation of the policy of regional autonomy.[24] This group produced a document which was circulated to various Southern Sudanese groups outside the Sudan. The Anya-Nya leadership also received a copy. It needs to be pointed out here that by the summer of 1970 then Colonel Joseph Lagu had successfully tightened his grip on the Anya-Nya, and the politicians seemed to have accepted his leadership and united behind him. By 1971, he realized that he had clearly emerged as the dominant Southern leader in exile and head of the Anya-Nya and, therefore. he allowed the formation of the Southern Sudan Liberation Movement (SSLM) under the aegis of the Anya-Nya armed forces. Representatives of SSLM were appointed in East Africa and in Europe.[25]

President Nimiery was persuaded by Vice President Abel Alier to recognize that the Anya-Nya must be a party to whatever settlement was reached between the North and the South. This point was explicitly stated in East Africa by Peter Gatkwoth, who was then serving as Deputy Minister in the Ministry for Southern Affairs: "The Anya-Nya are a part of the problem, and in prescribing a solution for the problem, we would like to associate them—firstly as Southern Sudanese, and secondly as people who have left the country for a cause. This is a Sudanese problem, and we must involve everyone who has contributed either negatively or positively to it."[26] This new kind of attitude was refreshing to Southerners in exile: the approach to the problem by the new team of Southerners under Abel Alier was, indeed, remarkably different from that of the late Joseph Garang. It facilitated contacts between representatives of the SSLM and those of the Ministry for Southern Affairs. The WCC and the AACC proved to be good intermediaries between the Sudan Government and the SSLM.

We now resume our discussion of the initial moves by both the WCC and the AACC to work for peace in the Sudan. The change of events and attitude in the Sudan, more than ever before, produced a possibility for peace between the feuding sides.

Steps Toward a Negotiated Settlement: The WCC and the AACC in an Intermediary Role

When stresses and strains began to crystallize into a confrontation between the Sudan Communist Party and President Nimiery, he turned to Abel Alier who was then Minister of Works for advice on the Southern Question and African affairs. Alier gave his advice when it was sought, but he carefully avoided upstaging Joseph Garang at the Ministry for Southern Affairs. In early 1971, Nimiery sent Alier on an extensive tour of Western Europe to explain to organizations that were helping Southern Sudanese refugees in neighboring African countries, and also allegedly helping the Anya-Nya, the intentions of his government to reach a peaceful solution with the South on the war. Alier's trip was very successful in that he was able to renew contacts with fellow Southerners such as Mading de Garang and Lawrence Wol Wol, both of whom were important SSLM representatives in Europe.[27] Also, Alier had an audience with Pope Paul VI at the Vatican and the news of it was well received by the Catholic groups which were concerned with the suffering of fellow Christians in the South. It was a good gesture on the part of the Sudan government to send one of its ministers to explain to His Holiness the policy of regional autonomy for the Southern provinces.[28] The representatives of the organizations which had an interest in the Sudan, as well as the SSLM representatives in Europe, were very impressed with Abel Alier, who not only was ready to admit the previous mistakes in the approach of the Nimiery policy toward the South, but also emphasized candidly the need for a conference between the government and the SSLM to discuss the nature of regional autonomy for the Southern provinces. On his return to the Sudan, Abel Alier persuaded the government to accept a joint WCC/AACC delegation to the Sudan.

The WCC/AACC delegation flew to Khartoum in May 1971. The aims of the delegation were three-fold: (1) to discuss with the government of the Sudan and Church leaders in the country the type of aid to be given to the people in the Southern Sudan; (2) to assess the possibilities of and ways toward reconciliation; and (3) to ask the Sudan government to allow aid from the WCC/AACC to the Southern Sudan through Khartoum in the North.[29] By now, the WCC was already convinced of the necessity for some settlement as a precondition for effective relief and development programs in the Southern region. Such a possibility for peace was thought to exist following the announcement of the policy of regional autonomy. Also, the attitude and approach of Abel Alier toward the problem was impressive and promising to the WCC. Hence, before visiting the Sudan, the WCC did some preliminary thinking concerning the way in which it could play a role in the resolution of the conflict. It decided that if it could not arrange talks between the North and the South, it could at least: (1) approach two or three heads of state in Africa, in whom the Sudan government had respect and confidence, to discuss the situation in the Sudan and the churches' concerns for a settlement which could eventually provide a climate for effective relief and development programs; (2) inform the Sudan government of the interest of the churches to bring about peace, possibly through the intermediation of some African governments between the Sudan government and the Anya-Nya fighters; and (3) appeal to the Anya-Nya to accept any invitation the Sudan government, through the churches, might extend to them for discussions at any time.[30] In this connection it would be essential to make formal contact with the Anya-Nya and keep them informed of the WCC/AACC thinking in this regard. While the WCC and the AACC were both aware that the Sudan is an independent, sovereign state, they trusted that it would at least pay attention to the voices and views of other African leaders. It was for this reason that they recommended the good offices of respected African governments as a way to bring about peace negotiations.

The meeting between the WCC/AACC delegation, representatives of the Sudan government, and the Sudan Council of Churches took place on May

15, 1971. Two main issues were discussed: relief aid to the victims of the war in the South through Khartoum, and reconciliation between the Sudan government and the SSLM. The issue of relief was discussed in detail and the Sudan government was willing to allow aid to the South but only through Khartoum. It was, however, realized at the meeting that if reconciliation could be reached, then the issue of relief aid would be easy to handle. Hence, the discussion was eventually centered on ways and means of establishing direct contact between the protagonists which could lead to peace negotiations. The WCC/AACC delegation later reported that six points were agreed upon at the meeting, namely, that: (1) the Sudan government was in favor of the WCC/AACC delegation making direct contact contracts with representatives from the South with a view to establishing direct contact for talks on reconciliation; (2) the groups to be represented were those which had influence on people in the South and among the refugees; (3) the talks could take place anywhere; (4) the Sudan government would agree to a "cooling-off" period if no security danger was involved; (5) the details of regional autonomy within one Sudan would be discussed; and (6) the question of under whose auspices the talks would take place would be discussed later.[31]

The Sudan government agreed with the report of the WCC/AACC delegation and encouraged both church organizations to contact the Southern leaders. These transnational organizations proceeded to make contacts with Southern leaders in Africa and with the SSLM representatives in Europe. To effect their decision, they drew up a plan of action: (1) that the AACC delegation would meet with whatever groups were available in their area; (2) that the WCC should endeavor to identify all groups and individual Southern Sudanese who had interest and influence in the Southern situation; and (3) that the general secretary of the Sudan Council of Churches, with the authority of the WCC/AACC delegation, would visit and talk to groups and individuals in Ethiopia.

In June 1971, the WCC approached one of the European SSLM representatives based in London, Mading de Garang, and gave him a copy of the WCC/AACC delegation's report on its visit to the Sudan the previous month. The SSLM reacted favorably to the report and its reply indicated a considerable change of attitude toward reconciliation:

> 1. We welcome the use of your good offices in attempting to establish direct contacts between the representatives of the Sudan government and South Sudan with a view to holding talks on negotiations.
>
> 2. . . . As a result of the prevailing unity among the Anya-Nya and the Southerners outside control of the Sudan government, the only competent and organized body which you can contact, and which will eventually nominate the delegates to the proposed talks, is the Southern Sudan Liberation Movement (SSLM). We would also like to point out (that) those under control of Khartoum, share the same view with regard to the Southern case. . . . It will . . . be a gesture of goodwill on the part of the Sudan government to allow some of the Southern

> Sudanese under their control to leave the country to join us in the negotiations. . . .
>
> 3. The willingness expressed by the Sudan government that the proposed talks can take place anywhere is both acceptable and appreciated. We ourselves propose either the headquarters of the OAU at Addis Ababa or the Zambian capital, Lusaka. Choice shall be made jointly by both sides.
>
> 4. The conditional proposal made by the Sudan government that they "agree to a cooling off" period taking place, if there is no danger to security, should be clarified. The main purpose of a "cooling-off" period is to remove the danger to security on both sides. . . . We propose a definite cease-fire instead of a "cooling-off" period. The terms of a cease-fire could be worked out during the pre-negotiation talk.
>
> 5. Discussion of the "details of Regional Autonomy within one Sudan" as a proposal of the Sudan government for solving the Southern problem is welcome. Since the main issue is to find a lasting mutually acceptable solution to the Southern problem, we feel the Sudan government's offer of the regional autonomy is a good starting point for discussion of other problems. The question will be whether the extent of the substance and the spirit of regional autonomy shall satisfy and guarantee the particular interest of the South as well as the interest of the Sudan (as a whole).
>
> 6. We agree that the question of under whose auspices the talks are to be held should be left until a later date. However, when that time comes the choice shall be made jointly by both sides.[32]

The abortive Communist coup in July 1971 brought the progress of the WCC/AACC peace efforts to a standstill. But the appointment of Abel Alier as Minister for Southern Affairs to replace the late Joseph Garang sped up the reconciliatory process. As mentioned earlier, Abel Alier set up a political committee to help him define in detail the meaning of regional autonomy for the South. Simultaneously, Dr. Gaafar Ali Bakheit, the Minister of Local Government, also set out to produce a document describing what he felt regional autonomy should mean. At first some Southerners thought Dr. Bekheit's efforts were an attempt to sabotage what the Ministry for Southern Affairs under Alier was trying to do. It seemed that Abel Alier intervened to see that no conflict arose between his political committee and the humble efforts of Dr. Bakheit. Instead, he enlisted the support of Dr. Bakheit within the government and worked closely with him. Consequently, what emerged as the final government document on the nature of regional autonomy for the South was a conflation of the documents produced by the Ministry for Southern Affairs and Dr. Bakheit's committee. While those documents were being worked out, the WCC was directed to proceed with its contacts with the representatives of the SSLM.

Henceforth, the WCC decided that to facilitate adequate discussions among the Southern leaders, it would be worthwhile for the SSLM representatives in Europe to travel to Africa to confer with their colleagues. The spirit of the WCC's motives, plans, and strategies in the resolution of the Sudan conflict was clearly contained in a letter from the office of the

Commission of the Churches on International Affairs to the Southern representatives in Europe:

> We are pleased that following several conversations with you as the delegated representatives of the Anya-Nya in Europe, during which you informed us of the present situation of your movement; and following the visit of a joint World Council of Churches/All Africa Conference of Churches mission to Khartoum, where we were given the Sudan government's position on reconciliation and relief, we are now able to help make your journey to Africa possible. This we do out of our sincere interest that a peace be established in the Sudan which will make possible a creative use of the relief assistance to the suffering Sudanese which the churches stand ready to give as soon as it can be determined that such assistance can be properly supervised and distributed.
>
> You have been fully informed about our visit to Khartoum, where we were asked to enter into conversations with you which might lead to negotiations between the two parties in the conflict. It is our understanding that, despite the events which have occurred in the interim, these positions remain firm and can be considered those of the Khartoum government. We have a standing invitation to return to Khartoum for further discussions in which we would hopefully be able to faithfully represent the views of the Southern Sudanese leadership. We therefore look forward to having a report of your visit on your return. We hope that it will include (a) the reaction of your leadership to the positions stated by the Khartoum Government; (b) the obtaining of a list of Southerners whom Anya-Nya leaders would want to be involved in any negotiations; and (c) the obtaining of letters of credence stating whom in fact Col. Lagu wishes to authorize to deal with the WCC/AACC on behalf of the Anya-Nya. Allow me to repeat that the WCC has offered its services to you and to the Khartoum Government as a politically disinterested international humanitarian organization. Our sole motive is to best serve the people of Sudan, North and South, for which we understand that a lasting peace is indispensable. Please convey our greetings to Col. Lagu and the other leaders of the Southern Sudan.[33]

The SSLM representatives in Europe, Mading de Garang and Lawrence Wol Wol, set out in August 1971 to travel to four African countries: Ethiopia, Kenya, Uganda, and Zaire. The purpose of their trip, as defined in the letter from the WCC (CCIA), was to sound out the opinion of some selected Southern Sudanese living in exile on the issue of negotiations with the Nimiery regime. Although there was a substantial feeling among those who aired their views that federation was a better and preferred solution to regional autonomy, there was a wide consensus that the SSLM should proceed to hold talks with the Sudan government. The Commander of the Anya-Nya and head of the SSLM, Major General Joseph Lagu, put the view explicitly: "We welcome the idea to prepare for talks because we are not just troublemakers, we are a people struggling for a cause, and if that can be achieved by talking we see no reason why we do not accept to talk."[34]

With regard to the plans by relief agencies to provide aid through Khartoum to the victims of the war, the SSLM leadership was not satisfied and rejected the proposal for three reasons. First, it was thought the aid would not reach the majority of Southerners who were outside the control of the Sudan government. Second, it was feared that if the aid went to the South through Khartoum, it might be interfered with. Third, it was argued that the Sudan government might use the aid as a means to infiltrate the Anya-Nya security lines.[35] Mading de Garang and Lawrence Wol Wol prepared a comprehensive report about their findings, which they communicated to the WCC and the AACC. It was now concluded by all parties that both the SSLM and the Sudan government agreed on a negotiated settlement. Henceforth, the scene was set for the final rounds of contact to begin.

Once again, the WCC and the AACC revived their idea of revisiting the Sudan for further talks with the Khartoum government on the issue of delivery of aid to the Southern Sudanese victims of the war. The joint WCC/AACC delegation was well received by the Sudan government, and the issue of negotiations with the SSLM was raised and discussed. The Sudan government responded positively to the SSLM position as communicated by the WCC/AACC delegation. It was finally agreed that preliminary talks would take place in Addis Ababa, Ethiopia, on November 9, 1971.

To ensure the success of the preliminary talks, President Nimiery launched a diplomatic offensive—he paid a state visit to Ethiopia from November 6 to 8, immediately before the preliminary talks began. He won the support of Emperor Haile Selassie who paid a return visit to the Sudan at the beginning of January 1972. Both Ethiopia and the Sudan reaffirmed their public policy to cease giving assistance to each other's secessionists and both set up a joint boundary commission.

The preliminary talks began in Addis Ababa as scheduled. The press was not allowed to cover the proceedings and every development was kept secret. The Sudan government was represented by Vice President Abel Alier, who was then also the Minister for Southern Affairs, and Major General Mohammed el Baghir Ahmed, then Minister of the Interior. On the SSLM side were Mading de Garang, Lawrence Wol Wol, Elisapana Mula, and Job Adier.[36] Both the WCC and the AACC acted in a mediatory capacity and were represented by Dr. Leopoldo Niilus—Director of the WCC's Commission of the Churches on International Affairs, the Rev. Kodwo Ankrah—the Refugee Secretary for the WCC, Canon Burgess Carr—Secretary General of the AACC based in Nairobi, Kenya, and Samuel Bwogo—of the Sudan Council of Churches. The SSLM and the Sudan government both decided to dispense with their observers when the talks began.

The Sudan government delegation argued that formal talks should take place within the framework of one Sudan, but that the Southern Provinces should become regionally autonomous in a newly defined constitutional structure for the Sudan. The SSLM delegation on the other hand, contended that there was no unity in the Sudan and to talk of one Sudan was farfetched and presumptuous. The concept of regional autonomy was also disputed by the SSLM delegation. However, it was eventually agreed at this informal meeting that both parties to the war were sincere in wanting to record a negotiated settlement, and the Sudan government delegation handed the SSLM representatives a document containing proposals to study for the formal negotiations. Tentatively, it was agreed that under specified conditions formal negotiations could be carried out within the idea of one Sudan.[37] The formal talks were scheduled for January 20, 1972.

In informal conversations among the delegates, Vice President Abel Alier seized the opportunity to convince both Mading de Garang and Lawrence Wol Wol that: (1) President Nimiery was genuinely committed to a negotiated settlement with the SSLM and to a full implementation of whatever would be agreed upon; (2) there was a better chance to reach a peaceful settlement with President Nimiery than with any other future leader in the North; (3) the need for a quick peace agreement without necessarily sacrificing the basic grievances of the South was imperative; and (4) it would be foolish for Southerners to live in the illusion of believing that the rest of the world was going to support them in their struggle for a military victory which was not in sight. Vice President Abel Alier is a reserved and low-keyed gentleman and is known to use his lawyer's training and gifts of persuasion to move people gently through a process of reason, sometimes to conclusions they had previously resisted. Unlike most Sudanese politicians, he is a cool and an unflappable person and has great capacity to size up people. He knew both Mading de Garang and Lawrence Wol Wol personally, and the former was his client before leaving the Sudan.[38] He calculated that since both men were responsible for giving publicity to the SSLM in Europe and were also instrumental in securing financial, material, and moral support for the Southern cause, they must have gained Major General Joseph Lagu's confidence and trust. Hence, once both of them agreed to a negotiated settlement within a united Sudan, it would not be very difficult to persuade the Anya-Nya command to accept it. Later events proved Vice President Abel Alier's calculations correct.

The two delegations reported back to their respective superiors that the Anya-Nya leadership was happy and that it was ready to authorize formal negotiations. Major General Joseph Lagu nominated eight persons representing various shades of SSLM opinion to participate in the formal talks. In Khartoum, President Nimiery was also pleased with the outcome of the informal talks and authorized Vice President Abel Alier, who did not need any encouragement, to use all the tact and intellect at his command to reach a negotiated settlement with his fellow Southerners.

But soon after the informal talks, differences began to emerge among the Southern Sudanese exiles. There were disagreements as to who should go to the formal talks. Some of the veteran politicians began to reappear once again and started in earnest to exert pressure on General Lagu to include them in the delegation to the formal talks lest they not accept any settlement to which they were not a party. General Lagu was able to withstand such pressures and appointed a team that was on the whole acceptable to most Southerners.

The most divisive issue was, however, the nature of the peace agreement that might be concluded at the formal talks. While some Southerners agreed that regional autonomy was good enough to be a basis for discussion, others argued that the SSLM delegates should not accept anything less than a federation. Yet another group concluded that the North was then willing to negotiate because its military position was weakening in the South and that, therefore, the SSLM delegation should press for secession and nothing less than that.[39]

The news of the differences building up among Southern Sudanese exiles soon reached the ears of Vice President Abel Alier. Thereafter, he launched a three-frontal diplomatic offensive. First, he sent his Deputy Minister for Southern Affairs, Peter Gatkwoth, to Europe to try to continue contacts with the aid agencies which were interested in the resettlement and rehabilitation of Southern Sudanese refugees. These agencies were invited to a much larger and more publicized conference than the previous one in Khartoum. This conference was scheduled to take place at the same time that the formal talks would take place at Addis Ababa.[40] Second, Alier sent four groups of emissaries to meet with Southerners in exile in an effort to avert any splits in the SSLM. These emissaries went to Ethiopia, East Africa, Zaire, and England (all of them were Southerners and they were to meet fellow Southerners who were living outside the Sudan). The group which went to London was composed of close political associates and friends of Alier and, at the time of their assignment, they were outside the Sudan.[41] A meeting was successfully arranged with the SSLM's European representatives, Mading de Garang and Lawrence Wol Wol. Peter Gatkwoth was in London at the time, but he kept in the background. The SSLM representatives presented a four-state proposal for a federation in the Sudan (North, South, West, and East federal regions). The Alier emissaries rejected this proposal as both naive and unacceptable. The four-state proposal was then withdrawn and replaced by a two-state proposal for a confederal constitutional structure between North and South of the Sudan with a center in Khartoum. There was a heated discussion, but finally the SSLM document was substantially revised, and both groups produced a joint document entitled: "Revised (and Amended) Recommendations for a New Constitution for the Republic of the Sudan." This London meeting between the SSLM representatives and the Alier emissaries helped both sides to iron out major disagreements on the concept of Regional Autonomy and it also enabled each side to know what the other would and would not accept. Peter Gatkwoth reported the outcome of the London deliberations to Alier in Khartoum; Mading de Garang flew to Uganda and thence to the Anya-Nya headquarters in South Sudan to brief the Anya-Nya high command on what transpired in London.

In East Africa, the Alier emissaries were finding enormous difficulties. Most Southern politicians refused to meet them on grounds that they must have been agents of the Sudan government since they were receiving their allowances from the Sudan embassies. That they had been fraternizing with members of the Sudan diplomatic missions was viewed as more than enough proof that they were spies for the Sudan government rather than personal emissaries of Alier.[42] Also tribalism began to reemerge among the exiles: the Dinkas were accused of monopolizing the scene of the secret contacts between the Sudan government and the SSLM. This was a clear reference to Mading de Garang and Lawrence Wol Wol, both of whom happened to be Dinka. The author anticipated the possibility of such a problem arising and, therefore, suggested to Alier's emissaries in London that they should dispatch a respected Southern Sudanese who must be a non-Dinka to East Africa to explain to the exiles there what was happening up to that time and what was going to take place soon in Addis Ababa.[43] This suggestion was accepted and Henry Bagu (a former treasurer of the Southern Front Party and an ex-seminarian who was attending a course in London) was sent to East Africa immediately to help to avert a clash between the veteran politicians from Equatoria and the Dinka.

Meanwhile in Khartoum, Alier adopted his third strategy: he cultivated and enlisted the full support and help of Foreign Minister Dr. Mansour Khalid.[44] Alier persuaded Khalid to recall all Sudanese Ambassadors abroad to Khartoum for briefing about what had been taking place and what was about to take place between the Sudan government and the SSLM. This was important and necessary in that the Sudan embassies had to stop their propaganda against the SSLM and the Anya-Nya in the foreign press. A change in attitude on the part of the Ambassadors was more than necessary for they had helped facilitate contacts that were going on with the SSLM leadership.

Finally, the delegations of the Sudan government and the SSLM arrived in Addis Ababa in early February 1972 for the formal negotiations. Initially, both sides thought that Emperor Haile Selassie would chair the plenary sessions. The Emperor, however, changed his mind because the Ethiopian government reasoned that if he chaired the negotiations and if the Southern Sudanese won substantial autonomous status, then the Eritreans might press for a similar position, which the Imperial regime had no intention of granting to them. Therefore the Emperor stayed in the background but, of course, he was represented at the talks and was kept informed of their progress.[45] The WCC and the AACC representatives who sat in the talks as observers were asked by both sides—the Sudan government and the SSLM—to provide a chairman. They chose Canon Burgess Carr, the Secretary General of the AACC, to act as a moderator for the meetings.[46]

After two weeks of hard negotiations, the two sides produced a peace settlement: "The Addis Ababa Agreement on the Problem of South Sudan." Soon after the signing ceremony, a reception was held at the OAU headquarters for the negotiators and the witnesses to celebrate the peace agreement, thereby giving it a measure of international recognition.

The Addis Ababa Agreement on the Problem of South Sudan

According to the Addis Ababa Agreement, the Southern Region becomes a self-governing unit within the Republic of the Sudan.[47] Thus previous extreme positions held by the protagonists were dropped—insistence on maintenance of the *status quo* (centralized administration dominated by the North), and separation of the Southern region from the rest of the Sudan—were abandoned. The territorial unity of the Sudan is preserved, but at the same time, the wishes of the South are met in that its indigenous citizens have been given the power to run their own local affairs and services, and Arab hegemony in their area has been legally curtailed. In what follows, we shall describe and analyze the main aspects of the agreement: divisions of functions and power and the military agreement.

The division of functions between the central and regional governments are explicitly described in Chapters IV and V of the Addis Ababa Agreement. Article 7 defines the functions which are exclusively a preserve of the national government and are therefore outside the jurisdiction of both the People's Regional Assembly and the High Executive Council (HEC).[48] On the other hand, Article 11 specifies the functions granted to the Southern region: "The People's Regional Assembly shall legislate for the preservation of public order, internal security, efficient administration and the development of the Southern Region in cultural, economic, and social fields. . . ." In the same Article 11, twenty areas which reflect regional value preferences are rendered to the South, but, although legislative authority has been granted to the region in a number of important areas such as education, police, traditional law, and custom, regional legislation is supposed to conform with national plans.[49] Such a provision may in some cases act as a constraint on the performances of the People's Regional Assembly.

With regard to the division of political power, the existence of the regional government is guaranteed in the organic law and it cannot be unilaterally altered by the central government: "This law shall be issued as an organic law which cannot be amended except by a three-quarters majority of the People's National Assembly and confirmed by a two-thirds majority in referendum held in the three Southern Provinces of the Sudan."[50] This provision gives constitutional guarantees and legal protection to the regional government. Its effect virtually creates a federal status for the South although the word "federation" is not used. It explicitly distinguishes the Southern regional government from a merely decentralized government whose local organs can be altered at will by the central government.

The Addis Ababa Agreement provides the regional government with enough sources of tax revenue so as to establish its own financial autonomy to a degree sufficient to maintain its existence.[51] The financial arrangement permits the regional government to behave independently on matters important to its existence. However, although the region can impose internal taxes, in the short run, the tax base is so small that for practical purposes it will be dependent on subsidies from the national treasury and on external assistance.

The regional president and members of the High Executive Council are answerable to two authorities: the national President and the People's Regional Assembly.[52] The powers of the People's Regional Assembly are to some extent balanced by the national President's retention of veto powers over regional legislation and also by his authority to appoint both the members and the President of the HEC. In case of the latter, he is appointed on the recommendation of the national President. The structure of the regional government appears to be quite weak here given its multiple executive which will tend to constrain decisive action and which may become alienated from the people and legislature because of the nature of its origin. Even though there is obviously a very complex balancing of regional and central forces in the appointment and removal of the HEC, the role of the national President is both a highly significant one and a serious intrusion by the central branch into the fundamental affairs of the Southern region.

It is somehow unusual that a regional government is established only in one part of a country. For there is not really a full layer of regional governments to balance out the central government. However, in the practical administration of the Sudan, and by virtue of the operation of the organic law for regional self-government for the South, the North is treated as a separate entity. The central powers rest with the national President and he regulates the relationship between the HEC and the central ministries.[53]

The agreement stipulated that there should be a southern command of an Army to be composed of twelve thousand officers and men, half of whom would originate in the South and the other half of whom would come from elsewhere in the Sudan. Most of the troops from the South were expected to be drawn from the former Anya-Nya Army. There was, however, a provision that there should be integration between the two halves; that is, each unit of Southern soldiers would receive elements from the old Sudan government forces in the form of an officer, to act as second in command, and various technical and administrative personnel.

On the whole, the Addis Ababa Agreement appears to be a hybrid of federal and nonfederal features which are narrowly adapted to the specific circumstances of the Sudanese situation. On balance, it is more than a simple decentralized arrangement subject to the unilateral whim of the central government (the substantive guarantees of regional autonomy assume that) and yet less than a full-fledged federal structure (along the lines of the

United States model) given the degree of control of internal affairs of the Southern Region by the national President. There is therefore the danger that if the national President interprets the document at will, the written guarantees may be rendered meaningless. It is unlikely that President Nimiery will do that, but it is uncertain what another Northern Sudanese of different political persuasion might do.

Ratification of and International Response to the Addis Ababa Agreement

It was agreed by the negotiators at Addis Ababa that the peace settlement would be ratified at noon on March 12, 1972. However, it soon proved that whereas the interval between signing and ratification of the agreement was too long for the Sudan government, it was too short for the SSLM. The SSLM leadership had enormous difficulties in communicating the news of the peace settlement to the Southern exiles, the Anya-Nya, and to those Southerners living in the forests away from the main roads in fear of government soldiers. By the time of the peace settlement, most of the roads in the South were out of repair and had been mined by the Anya-Nya Army.

Hence, despite the broadcasts by foreign radios of the news of the Sudan peace accord, a great deal of explanation and reassurance was needed among the Southerners. After all, many of them were taken by surprise: they had become accustomed to despair and found it difficult to believe the good news of the peace settlement. It was inconceivable to many of them that a negotiated settlement could ever be reached with their traditional enemies, the Arabs and the Arabized peoples of the Sudan. It had to be explained carefully and at length to the Southerners that, indeed, a peace agreement was reached as a result of a change of attitude of the leadership in the North. It was obvious that the SSLM leaders would need more time before ratification, so the Sudan government promptly acceded to a request for a later date.[54]

However, both President Nimiery and Vice President Alier were worried that, in the meantime, something might happen to upset things and possibly make the SSLM leadership change its mind. Indeed, there was a basis for such a fear: the Sudan embassies in the neighboring countries of Ethiopia, Kenya, Uganda, and Zaire were sending reports to Khartoum that pressure was being exerted on Joseph Lagu, the SSLM leader, by the SSLM's foreign supporters and by a few Southern hardliners not to ratify the Addis Ababa Agreement until certain changes were made in it.[55] Henceforth, President Nimiery decided to forestall such dangers and went ahead and ratified the agreement in a public rally at Wad Nubawai, Omdurman.[56] He also signed a decree by which the agreement was made into a law: "The Southern Provinces Regional Self-Government Act." He declared a cease-fire on March 12 and ordered the Sudan Army stationed in the South to end hostilities immediately. To ensure that his order was complied with by the Army, President Nimiery in the company of Vice President Abel Alier flew to the South to explain to the Army commanders and to the people at large what was accomplished at Addis Ababa.

The swift actions of President Nimiery meant that the Addis Ababa Agreement was treated as a fait accompli: the SSLM had no better alternative than to follow his example. The Anya-Nya leader, Joseph Lagu, personally went to ratify the Agreement at Addis Ababa.[57] The then Sudan Foreign Minister, Dr. Mansour Khalid, signed it on behalf of President Nimiery at the same ceremony.

Thereafter, the Addis Ababa Agreement on the problem of South Sudan was accepted by both sides and became a legal document. The organic law that organized regional self-government in the Southern provinces has since been incorporated into the country's permanent constitution which was approved by a partly elected and partly appointed People's National Assembly in the middle of 1972.

There was an atmosphere of considerable euphoria in the Sudan, particularly in the Southern region, after the ratification of the Addis Ababa Agreement. Both President Nimiery and the Anya-Nya leader, Joseph Lagu, received congratulatory messages from the international community. They were praised throughout Africa for their wisdom and applauded in many world newspapers as well as in the OAU headquarters in Addis Ababa and in the corridors of the U.N.[58] Although some Arab leaders were not happy with the agreement because they mistakenly thought that the Nimiery regime had given too many concessions to a region of the Sudan which was fundamentally opposed to the Sudan's Arab orientation, the Arab League resolved to offer help to the Sudan government in the form of financial aid and equipment for use in social and economic development.[59]

World organizations, both regional and international, praised the achievement of a negotiated settlement as a positive contribution to the principles of peace, security, and order. For President Senghor of Senegal, the Sudan peace agreement constituted an event of much larger historical dimensions than might perhaps be realized at first glance.[60] A Kenya newspaper tended to concur: "the agreement will perhaps become one of the biggest achievements by Africa."[61] Generally, the agreement was viewed as a rare example of what is lacking in so many places all over the world. Whether or not a solution similar to that employed in the Sudan would be appropriate to the wars now taking place in Ethiopia (Eritrea) and Chad remains to be seen.

The praise of the Addis Ababa Agreement by the international press and the congratulatory messages received by the Sudan government and the SSLM leadership, many of which were followed by offers of help in cash and services, must have in a way helped the Sudanese people in both regions to accept the negotiated arrangement as the most reasonable settlement of their conflict. The Sudan government began to implement the agreement in earnest and made appeals to the international community for help in its reconstruction projects in the Southern region.

Conclusion

It is rare to find a negotiated settlement of a secessionist effort, especially in independent Africa. Usually, as in the case of Katanga and Biafra, the secessionists are beaten into submission.[62] However, in the Sudan, after many years of fighting each other, the protagonists were able to agree to sit down, discuss their differences, and arrive at a compromise solution. They were brought to the negotiating table by the efforts of transnational organizations—the World Council of Churches and its member Council, and the All African Council of Churches. The success of the peace talks revealed the potential of the WCC (and its affiliate member councils) as a reconciling force in Africa.

The question that arises is: why did the Sudan government, after a period of bitter conflict in which it had invested considerable resources, change its policy and agree to terminate the wars on terms which throughout the period of fighting it had deemed unacceptable? What factors of interplay, both internal and external, brought about the change from confrontation to accommodation and facilitated the WCC and the AACC to assume the mediation role? There seemed to be at least seven mutually reinforcing factors which enabled peace negotiations to move forward at that particular time.

First, both parties in the war realized that neither side could win nor lose the war: they had reached a military stalemate. The Sudanese government troops controlled the towns in the South, while the Anya-Nya Army was in effective control of the countryside, making the former's movements between the towns extremely difficult. Both the Sudan government and the SSLM realized that a military victory for either side was not possible and were able to accept the fact that they could not continue in that situation indefinitely.

Second, the war was a drain on the meager resources of the Sudan government. Moreover, as long as the war continued, any regime in power would be perpetually unstable. Although there was a general approval in the North of the war against the South, the constant increase in the death toll among the Northern Sudanese soldiers serving in the South gradually generated antigovernment feeling for its failure to defeat the Anya-Nya Army. The instability of governments in Khartoum made it difficult for the Sudan to attract foreign investments and borrow funds from international financial institutions such as the World Bank. The Nimiery regime came to realize that the enormous amount of borrowed money spent on sustaining the war could be used beneficially in social and economic development, to which it was committed. A solution ought therefore be found to end the war.

Third, the policy of regional autonomy for the South stated in the June 9, 1969, declaration by President Nimiery found support among Southern Sudanese elites within the Sudan. Although some of them had reservations about the policy of regional autonomy, they reasoned that it should be given a fair chance. Hence, they called for a comprehensive definition of the institutional and power relationships between the central government and the Southern region. They united under the "Association of Southern Intellectuals," and maintained a reconcilatory attitude with the regime even though it showed some indecisiveness on implementing its Southern policy. When Abel Alier became the Minister for Southern Affairs, the Association of Southern Intellectuals gave him full support and its leaders helped him both to define the nature of regional autonomy for the South and to sell the policy to the rest of Southerners at large.

Fourth, the abortive coup d'état of July 1971, and the dramatic return to power of General Nimiery, led him to a reordering of priorities. He changed his foreign and domestic policy orientations. At home he became more convinced than before that he must reach an accommodation with the South. And he soon realized that the pursuit of federation with the Arab nations of Libya, Egypt, and Syria was incompatible with the pursuit of reconciliation with the Africans in the South Sudan because they are not predisposed to Arabism. Now, after the abortive communist coup d'état, President Nimiery's relations with the Soviet Union, which was then the main arms supplier to the Sudan, deteriorated. He turned to the Western world for aid and loans, and he received a sympathetic ear. The prospective donors were interested in stability and, privately, they encouraged President Nimiery's government to reach a peace settlement on the Southern question. The traditional Western European friends of the Sudan, such as the United Kingdom, now agreed that the Sudan government could not win the war in the South against the Anya-Nya Army and they encouraged negotiations. The Sudan government could not possibly ignore that advice at a time it wanted aid and loans.

Fifth, the appointment of Abel Alier as Minister for Southern Affairs and Vice President paved the way for a speedy implementation of the policy of regional autonomy. Vice President Abel Alier enjoyed the trust and confidence of Southerners both inside and outside the Sudan, and he was also widely respected by many Northern Sudanese elites. For a long time, Alier had advocated negotiations with the Anya-Nya Army leadership and the Southern exiles. But his colleague in the cabinet, Joseph Garang, disagreed and advised the government to pursue a nonnegotiations policy. Once Alier was in charge of Southern affairs, he persuaded President Nimiery to seek a negotiated settlement with the SSLM, and he began in earnest to make contacts with the Southern exiles. After the peace agreement was reached,

President Nimiery complimented Alier for his efforts in the search for peace and in carrying out his Southern policy. At the same time he blamed Alier's predecessor for systematically sabotaging his policy of regional autonomy:

> The 9th of June Declaration, issued when the Revolution was only a month old, offered regional autonomy to the South within the Unified Sudan. . . . But the treachery of those entrusted with the implementation of the policy in the South, as well as their "comrades" in the North, has impeded the progress of regional autonomy plan. Those people, well-known to you, have used their official positions to further their selfish partisan interests; obstructing in the process of revolutionary policies towards the South. The sabotage acquired such dimensions that our Southern brothers started to doubt the sincerity of our intentions and thought we were just feeding them with promises. But the revolutionary tide that swept the country after the failure of the perfidious Communist coup and which accompanied the plebiscite campaign, has opened new avenues for the country. A settlement preserving the unity of the country and satisfying the aspiration of the South, as become possible.
>
> The Ministry for Southern Affairs recommended its efforts, this time under the guidance of Brother Abel Alier, Vice President of the Republic. He is a man whom I have known for about three years and I admire his tolerance, his tact and his sincerity and was my right arm on all matters pertaining to that dear part of our country, the South.[63]

Indeed, Vice President Abel Alier worked diligently to convince the SSLM leadership to trust President Nimiery and accept negotiations for a settlement of the Southern question under a united Sudan. That was not an easy task. It required tact and political astuteness, as well as a thorough understanding of the Southern problem and of its psychological manifestations.

Sixth, the Uganda coup d'état and the change of leadership from President Obote to General Amin worked in favor of the SSLM. Obote had consistently supported governments in Khartoum against the SSLM, but his Army commander gradually became resentful of such a policy, particularly when it involved the Uganda Army fighting on one side with the Sudan government soldiers against the Anya-Nya Army at the Sudan-Uganda border. When Obote was overthrown, he commuted between Dar es Salaam (Tanzania) and Khartoum (Sudan). He persuaded the Sudan to assist in preparation for an invasion of Uganda. General Amin soon learned of the active military and material support Obote was receiving from the Sudan government. In retaliation against the Sudan government for its support of Obote, General Amin became an enthusiastic supporter of the Southern Sudanese cause. Henceforth, Amin and Nimiery began to engage in many verbal salvos.[64] President Amin threatened to give military support to the Anya-Nya Army if the Sudan government continued to train Obote's supporters. The Nimiery regime was frightened by President Amin's threat. The Israeli presence in Uganda at that time was also frightening to the Sudan government in that Israel had begun to give military aid to the Anya-

Nya Army. Events in Uganda eventually persuaded President Nimiery to reassess his military position and finally he decided that a peace settlement needed to be reached with the SSLM without delay. Moreover, the longer the war continued, the more perilous his political position would become. This point was continuously emphasized to President Nimiery by Dr. Gaafar Bakheit who was then his Minister of Local Government and a very close adviser.

Seventh, the role of Emperor Haile Selassie was of no less importance at the crucial time when preliminary contacts were going on between the Sudan government and the SSLM. The emperor used his good offices to persuade both sides to agree to meet in Addis Ababa. He also played an influential role in convincing the negotiators to accept a nominee of the WCC and the AACC to chair the talks. Once the talks were underway, the emperor took personal interest in their progress, intervening a number of times to keep them going when major disagreements developed.[65]

The interplay of these seven factors provided the groundwork for reconciliation in the Sudan. The WCC and the AACC intervened at the most opportune time to play the mediating role.[66] But why did the Sudan government and the SSLM accept the WCC and not other organizations or international actors to play such a crucial role? First, both the OAU and the Arab League precluded themselves by their charters, and more so by their consistent support of the Sudan government, to play active roles in mediation. Second, the "doctrine of an internal affair" made the international community uninterested in intervening as an impartial body. Therefore, a transnational humanitarian organization such as the WCC had a better chance of playing an impartial mediatory role. Moreover, the WCC left an impressive record in its rehabilitation scheme in Nigeria following the surrender of Biafra. It was felt in the Sudan that the WCC might play the same role if it was associated with the peace settlement.[67] Thus the WCC's record as a genuine humanitarian organization enabled it to be accepted by both the SSLM and the Sudan government as a mediator.

The Sudan government respected the WCC because, unlike the Roman Catholic Church, the WCC restrained its criticisms during the Civil War. Also, the WCC's stand against racism, its grants to liberation movements through its program to combat racism, and its continued assistance to refugees (the victims of racial and political persecution in Southern Africa) won the WCC a favorable image in Africa. Its "Addis Ababa Declaration on Unity and Human Rights in Africa" was well received by the SSLM and the Sudan government and, indeed, by Africa as a whole because it supported the unity of Africa, called for respect for human rights in Africa, and condemned oppression and foreign interference in the continent.[68] It contained something palatable to those who are against secession and to those who fight against internal oppression in African countries. Such a stand made the WCC acceptable to both the Sudan government and the SSLM.

In order to perform the task of promoting justice and peace in serving the people through programs designed to advance human dignity, the WCC realized since its founding that it should never align itself with any particular government in power to the extent that it is branded as a partner. To do so would make it difficult for churches to admonish governments and to exercise reconciling influence among "feuding" parties. This does not mean that the WCC and its member churches are immune from politics, for churches throughout history have been involved in politics.

In the Sudan, the history of hostility between the peoples of North and South made them suspicious of each other, and this, in turn, made it difficult for them to try to understand each other's point of view and work toward a common goal for the benefit of all. The WCC, by its transnational character and outlook, was able to grasp the complexity of the situation and persuaded both sides in the conflict to engage in peace negotiations.[69]

PART IV
Vision for the Future

CHAPTER IX

Toward a New Political System

The conclusion of the peace agreement in the Sudan ushered in a new era of relations between its two historically antagonistic peoples. An opportunity has at present been created for development of viable institutional structures. In what follows, an attempt will be made to evaluate the implementation of the agreement and the problems arising therefrom. We shall also suggest policy considerations for territorial autonomy in the form of a federal arrangement which will regulate the potentially conflictual African-Arab cleavages along the Nile Valley.

Following the ratification of the Addis Ababa Agreement,[1] President Nimiery promulgated the Southern Provinces Regional Self-Government Act of 1972. This act defined the powers of the Southern region's executive and legislative branches, and outlined other matters of principle. A month later, it was followed by a series of Presidential orders which (1) provided for the appointment of a Provisional High Executive Council to act as the regional government for a period of eighteen months until elections could take place; (2) defined the revenue from taxes and duties to be allocated to the Southern Region; and (3) established a special fund to meet the expenses of repatriation, resettlement, relief, and rehabilitation of refugees.

Repatriation, Resettlement, Relief, and Rehabilitation

Presidential Order No. 44 established a commission for the resettlement, relief, and rehabilitation of Southern Sudanese refugees. It set up its headquarters in Juba in May 1972 with a membership drawn largely from prominent members of the Southern political exiles. The main function of the commission was to

> effect a two-stage operation providing reception for the returning people, their transportation to their old villages or to new resettlement areas, and ensuring that they had supplies of tools, seeds and food adequate to carry them through to their first harvest. This done, the people they were caring for would come

> within the more normal framework of a second phase, a phase of reconstruction and development across the whole social and economic spectrum of the Southern Region, for which, under the guidance and control of the Central Government in Khartoum, the Provisional High Executive Council, as the regional government of the South, would be primarily responsible.[2]

To facilitate the work of the Resettlement, Relief, and Rehabilitation Commission, Presidential Order No. 45 provided for the setting up of an additional four commissions "for the repatriation of the Southern Sudanese refugees now residing in the neighboring countries." One commission was assigned to each of the main asylum countries: Central African Republic, Ethiopia, Uganda, and Zaire. These commissions were charged:

> With the cooperation of the governments of the countries of asylum and of UNHCR, with preparing a timetable for the repatriation of the expatriate refugees. This involved touring the refugee settlements, registering the identities, profession, trade, age and original homes of their inhabitants; and calculating their needs for food, accommodation, tools and work implements, means of transportation and education. The membership of the Commissions included prominent representatives of the former Anya-Nya and in their work were closely associated with the UNHCR Representatives in the countries of asylum, since this representation in both cases, being known to and trusted by the refugees, would assure them of the genuineness of the cease-fire. UNHCR also provided the funds for the movement of the returning refugees to the reception centers within the Sudan; though in the case of Zaire this assistance was channelled through the medium of the International Organisation for Rural Development (IORD) which, prior to the cease-fire had acted as UNHCR's operating agency in the settlement there of Sudanese and other refugees. It was also the function of the Commissions to advise these refugees to delay their return to the Sudan until such time as the problem of the internal returnees was on the way to solution and until adequate preparations for their own reception and resettlement might be established.[3]

Various international agencies played a crucial role in resettlement, relief, and rehabilitation work in the Southern region. The WCC launched an extensive international fund-raising campaign and created a commission for relief and rehabilitation. Five other voluntary organizations—the African Medical Research Foundation International, the International Organization for Rural Development, the International University Exchange Fund, the Norwegian Refugee Council, and Oxfam—joined the WCC and consolidated themselves into the International Agency for Cooperation in Development, which undertook plans for short- and long-term projects of assistance such as rebuilding schools and dispensaries.

The United Nations High Commission for Refugees (UNHCR) was mandated by the U.N. to coordinate the immediate relief program. Through an international appeal the agency collected $16.6 million in cash and services.[4] Although a few countries, such as the Netherlands, launched direct assistance programs for the Southern region, most countries preferred to contribute through the UNHCR. The contributions made to the UNHCR by the international community in response to the U.N. appeal for relief operation in the Southern Sudan were insubstantial, but other U.N. agencies, such as the United Nations Development Program (UNDP), also became involved in formulating development plans. The World Bank approved a $10.7 million loan for agricultural development.[5]

Although the international response for help in repatriation, resettlement, relief, and rehabilitation was not too bad, the war had shattered the flimsy structures of modernization in the Southern Sudan to such an extent that aid in the form of a Marshall Plan was needed to overcome the constraints of communications and transport and the lack of economic and social infrastructure. Unfortunately, that was not forthcoming and human conditions in the area remain unsatisfactory.

Military and Political Aspects

Under the terms of the peace accord, the Southern command of the Sudanese armed forces is to consist of 6000 officers and men from the Southern region and the same number from outside the Region.[6] Hence, the agreement preserves the armed strength of both sides until mutual trust can be restored. So far, the ceasefire has been surprisingly respected by both sides and this has paved the way for the smooth implementation of the other aspects of the Addis Ababa Agreement.[7] The integration of the Anya-Nya soldiers with other Sudanese Army units went better than anyone expected: 6200 of them were taken into the People's Armed Forces (national army) and 3116 and 545 into the Regional Police and Prison forces, respectively.[8] As the number of the Anya-Nya soldiers who turned up for interviews came to about 20,000, all of them could not be taken into the regular national armed forces.[9] Those who were medically unfit were absorbed into various civil departments of the regional government. Pensions were given to eleven officers who previously served both in the Southern Corps during the Colonial period and in the Anya-Nya armed forces.[10]

The work of integration of the Anya-Nya and the Sudan Army is being carried out by a Joint Military Commission established by a presidential decree in April 1972. In one of its reports, the commission found that the Anya-Nya "showed complete enthusiasm for the Agreement and determination to implement it."[11] However, despite such enthusiasm on the part of the Anya-Nya, special precautionary measures were taken to avoid any military confrontation between the former combatants.

Vice President Abel Alier was appointed by President Nimiery to head the provisional HEC, which reflected a balance of the various Southern Sudanese political factions.[12] Those who campaigned for Southern rights within the Sudan and those who worked outside in the different organizations of the Southern Liberation Movement were represented in the regional administration. The Anya-Nya Army Commander, Joseph Lagu, decided to remain a soldier and he became a Major General in the Sudan Army and chose then not to play an active role in politics.

The regional administration of the South is a ministerial system in which each ministry has a number of specializing departments under its aegis. An elaborate system of local government continued within those areas under the control of the central government and formed the basis for the new administrative infrastructure, while undergoing examination for adaptations consonant with the new regional government's structure and philosophy.[13] Nonetheless, the operation of the People's Local Government system brought into the open the overlapping of powers between the central and the regional governments. For example, the Provincial Commissioners (PCs) report directly to the national President even though their work necessarily concerns matters the Addis Ababa Agreement assigns to the region.[14] Worse still, the PCs have appointed Assistant Provincial Commissioners (APCs) to specialize in fields such as education, agriculture, and the like. These APCs tend to function as inspectors for particular regional ministries. Yet their superiors, the PCs, report directly to Khartoum. Such reports are seen as potential threats to the policy-making discretion of the directors of those regional ministries concerned.[15]

Another related issue of overlapping of powers is the Police Service in the South, which is supposed to be administered by the regional government. Yet the Assistant Commissioner of Police, who is the highest ranking official of the police forces in the South, reports to the Commissioner in Khartoum. Although such reports may be termed only routine, since they do not encroach upon the powers of the regional government in that the security affairs of the region are technically under the control of the President of the HEC (on behalf of the national President), the position of the Police Chief in the Southern Region is required to be firmly accommodated within the governmental structure based on the Addis Ababa Agreement.

As the Addis Ababa Agreement stipulated,[16] elections were held in the Southern region eighteen months after the establishment of the provisional HEC. They were organized and successfully conducted under the auspices of the Sudan Socialist Union (SSU) which is the only legal political party operating in the country. Based on the Election Law of 1973, the People's Regional Assembly consists of sixty members, of whom thirty represent the geographical areas, twenty-one represent the alliances of the people's working forces, and nine represent the administrative units. The elections were held in November 1973 by a direct secret ballot.[17] Despite the problems of registration and the short time available to organize the elections, all went well. No hidden conflicts emerged between the politicians who remained inside and those who were outside the Sudan during the war. All but five of the former Ministers of the provisional HEC were returned.[18] Abel Alier did not offer himself for election and he refused to promote his own candidacy for the post of the Presidency of the HEC.

The agreement calls for the People's Regional Assembly to "recommend" someone of its choice to the national President for appointment to the office of President of the HEC.[19] But after the elections of November 1973, President Nimiery, in an effort to make sure that Vice President Abel Alier retained the position, nominated him for the post before the People's Regional Assembly made its choice. President Nimiery rationalized his action on the grounds that: (1) the nominee for the post must be a member of the SSU and therefore he should be nominated by the SSU; and (2) that President Nimiery nominated Vice President Abel Alier for the position of the Regional Presidency in his capacity as Chairman and Secretary General of the SSU. However, President Nimiery's action was seen as a mistake by some members of the People's Regional Assembly, who argued that it showed the continuation of Northern Sudanese interference in an exclusively Southern affair. Certainly, President Nimiery's intervention was unnecessary, for even without it, there was no doubt that Vice President Abel Alier would have received a majority support in the People's Regional Assembly for the office of the President of the HEC. The incident did not, however, cost President Nimiery any of his wide popularity in the Southern region.

The provision concerning language in the Addis Ababa Agreement is somewhat ambiguous. Article 5 states that "Arabic shall be the official language of the Sudan and English the principal language for the Southern Region." Although this implies that the language of communication in the South would be English, post-war policy on education has put more emphasis on the teaching of Arabic in schools—a continuation of the previous policy. The disproportionate weight placed on Arabic in schools in the South is resented by many Southerners. However, there is at present an explicit acceptance in both the Addis Ababa Agreement and in the permanent constitution by the North that the Sudan will not project itself as an Islamic and Arabic state. This understanding is of vital importance to the South for it recognizes that to provide a basis for freedom and bring about a nondiscriminatory system, peoples of diverse cultures living within one state such as the Sudan, must be allowed to pursue their religious, spiritual, and philosophical beliefs without hindrance. Arabization and Islamization policies toward the South were abandoned as being both culturally imperialistic and dangerous to the maintenance of peace and stability. This is not to say that all is perfect with the present set-up.

The Southern region is not proportionately and effectively represented at the national level (in the central government). For example, there are at present no Southerners (at the time of writing) in the central cabinet. But since Vice President Abel Alier spends most of his time in the South (quite rightly), he rarely attends cabinet meetings in Khartoum. Of course, it could be argued that the central cabinet is not an important locus of power and decision-making in the Sudan in contrast to the Politbureau of the SSU.[20]

Nevertheless, it still does play some crucial role in shaping and, more so, in the implementation of policy. At present, the Northern region has exclusive monopoly and control of the areas of the critical decision making process in the country.[21] That has pleased the Northern Sudanese critics of the Addis Ababa Agreement, who think that it gives "too much" power to the South. Equally, the present imbalance at the center has made the South too dependent on President Nimiery and particularly on his personal relationship with Abel Alier, the Vice President and President of the HEC. It is with such problems in mind that we shall now explore the possibility of an improvement of the present constitutional and political relationship between the North and South of the Sudan in the form of a federal arrangement.

Political Integration and Federalism

One of the most overriding concerns of leaders of the new states of Africa is the problem of political integration. Like most concepts in the literature of social sciences, the term "political integration," although widely discussed, is often loosely defined so as to cover an extraordinarily broad range of political phenomena. Myron Weiner suggests that there are at least five uses of the term:[22]

1. *National integration*, or the creation of a sense of territorial nationality (among diverse groups) which overshadows or eliminates subordinate parochial loyalties.
2. *Territorial integration*, or the process of establishing national central authority over subordinate political units, or regions which may or may not coincide with distinct cultural or social groups.
3. *Elite-mass integration*, which refers to the process of bringing together the governors and the governed.
4. *Value integration*, or the creation of a value consensus necessary to maintain a social order.
5. *Integrative behavior*, or the capacity of people in society to organize for a common purpose.

It can thus be seen that the concept of "integration," covers a vast range of human relationships and attitudes. But as Weiner contends, these diverse definitions are united by a common thread: "they are all attempts to define *what it is which holds a* society and a political system together (emphasis mine)."[23]

The proposition that minorities should consent to the abandonment of the ethnic, cultural, and linguistic characteristics which distinguish them from the national majorities with whom they live, and to merge into nationally uniform communities with the majorities, is not plausible. For such an assimilationist version of society is counterproductive to development of a stable plural society. It is not through assimilation but through modernization that peaceful group integration may take place. This relationship between modernization and group integration is succinctly brought out by Huntington:

> Modernization means that all groups, old as well as new, traditional as well as modern, become increasingly aware of themselves as groups and of their interests and claims in relation to other groups. One of the most striking phenomena of modernization, indeed, is the increased consciousness, coherence, organization, and action which it produces in many social forces which existed on a much lower level of conscious identity and organization in traditional society.[24]

But then, what institutional mechanism can be used to facilitate the desired goals of one or another form of integration? In other words, what political arrangement in the case of the Sudan can provide regulatory processes, institutions, and practices which will continuously avert as well as cope with the causes and manifestations of conflict between the South and the North?

The unitary structures of government in the Sudan established by the departing colonial regime did not foster swift decision making, neither did they facilitate administration nor contribute to political integration. Waste, duplication, inefficiencies, and overlapping responsibilities were in abundance. The unitary system of government was inapplicable to the Sudan's circumstances because it lacked the capacity to reconcile the country's diversities. Moreover, such a unified administrative system implied ultimate central authority and this meant the subordination of the South to the North.

So far, the indications are that schemes of administrative decentralization within a unitary system are not by all means sufficient safeguards of territorial interests. Therefore, what the Sudan needs is a division of power which guarantees effective rather than limited autonomy. That is, since centralized administration failed, and regional autonomy for the South alone has inherent problems which do not satisfy the country's requirements of stability and equitable distribution of resources and political power, the investigation of new forms of statecraft is essential. It is time for innovation such as the formation of institutional structures. As one political scientist put it, if the politicians fear the unknown and shrink from commitments on a broad scale, logic requires that political analysts search out a variety of alternatives which will reduce integration load factors.[25]

In our search for a durable political arrangement, we must remember that (1) the Sudan is an artificial mosaic of two groups with radically different social and cultural backgrounds; (2) there exists some disparity in levels of economic development between the Southern and Northern regions; and (3) the two communal conflict groups are geographically concentrated. In such circumstances as exist in the Sudan, *territorial autonomy in the form of federation would perhaps be a viable conflict regulatory system.*

Like political integration, federalism lacks a consistent definition. Hence, because there is so much disagreement and confusion over what constitutes federalism, it will be necessary here to give a brief summary of each of the three dominant schools of thought which have crystallized since the Second World War.

I. *The institutional approach*. This approach to federalism is best illustrated in a classic publication by K. S. Wheare.[26] He postulates a strict division of functions between two independent and coordinate levels of government with each level sovereign within its functional sphere. For Wheare, the division in powers and functions of such two co-equal units form the basis of a federal classification. This definition of federalism is so restrictive that Wheare was able to identify only four genuinely federal governments: the United States, Australia, Switzerland, and Canada. In the case of Canada, Wheare argues that it lacks even a fully federal constitution because it allots too much power to the federal government. But he concluded that Canada is a federal government in practice because the provinces have in fact coopted much real power and functions. The main criticism of this approach has been focused on its legalistic character.[27] The Sudan, in its present constitutional arrangement, would not constitute a federation by this definition.

II. *Federalism as a process*. This school of thought views federalism as a process rather than as a static pattern of government. A. H. Birch, a proponent of this view, defines federation as "a union of groups, united by one or more common objectives, but retaining their distinctive group character for other purposes."[28] This approach attempts to identify factors which induce integration and those which impede it and encourage differentiation in a variety of situations. The main shortcoming in this school of thought is that the factors most commonly identified as creating the conditions for federal integration are the expectation of economic advantage and the existence of social and cultural bonds which generate a feeling of community.[29] It ignores the necessary political circumstances under which the political elites are likely to act to create a federation.

III. *The realist school*. This approach tends to treat federalism as a bargain. It holds that federal structures are essentially meaningless in themselves and that what is really important is the social cleavage structure which lies beneath the federal institutions and which establishes the real balance of power involved. As the main proponent of this view, Riker seeks to answer two fundamental questions: (1) what conditions should be regarded as necessary for the creation of the federal bargain? and (2) what conditions are necessary for the maintenance of a federal system?[30] Riker defines a federal constitution as one which provides for two levels of government, each of which has at least one area of action in which it is autonomous, and each of which has "some guarantee (even though merely a statement in the constitution) of its contained authority within its sphere."[31] This type of constitution, Riker argues, is always the result of political bargaining within a given and usually unique historical circumstance. He posits two conditions as necessary to strike the federal bargain: first, the existence of politicians who wish to expand the area of territorial control without the use of force; and, second, the willingness of assenting politicians to surrender part of their independence either because "they desire protection from an external threat" or because "they desire to participate in the potential aggression of the federation."[32] Riker concludes that the maintenance of a federal system depends on the nature of the political party system that develops.

The realist school puts so little importance on constitutions that it is content to assume a very broad definition of federalism and thus labels every tendency toward decentralization a case of federalism. The present political arrangement in the Sudan would be a federation according to this view. The advantage of such a perspective is that it encourages one to look beyond legal documents and to account for social forces. Thus it holds that a country with a feeble federal constitution may well come to operate a genuinely federal government because of the magnitude of centrifugal social forces.[33] Alternatively, a country with a distinctively federal constitution may yet operate a fully centralized government.[34] Although this approach is all very useful, it tends to become oversimplified, and it fails to account for the influence and behavioral incentives and constraints imposed by institutions themselves once established.

It is therefore clear that the basic elements deemed necessary to constitute a federal structure differ despite a few overlappings. However, on the whole, one is in the main stream of the field if one uses the criteria of at least some elements of functional differentiation between the levels of government combined with sufficient power in both the central and regional governments to defend their autonomy from unilateral action by the other which seriously affects the federal balance.

In the case of the Sudan, some variation of the federal principle under the special conditions of the country must be utilized to achieve an integrative revolution thereby making possible the political normalization of regional sentiment and identity. It requires only a little political surgery to modify the present constitutional arrangement by creating a layer of regional government in the North to parallel that in the South. Khartoum must still remain the seat of federal power to which there are many advantages.

Federation can provide a workable balancing mechanism between the extremes of centralism and separatism. An adequate, geographically based diffusion of power between the South and the North in the Sudan is a prerequisite to the maintenance of a lasting equilibrium. The extensive social diversity in the Sudan will buttress the formal spreading of power, and it will lay the foundation for an enduring dispersion of authority within the single state structure.

Federation should be seen as a means of spreading political power and of inhibiting the advent of majoritarian tyranny. As James Madison observed in his call for federation following the American War of Independence:

"extend the sphere and you take in a greater variety of parties and interests; you make it less probable that a majority of the whole will have a common motive to invade the rights of other citizens; or if such a common motive exists, it will be more difficult for all who feel it to discover their own strength, and to act in unison with each other."[35]

The federal structure we are suggesting should act as a means of attaining a national identity among the Sudan's diverse social and cultural groups and, also, for establishing some variant of central control over subordinate units of authority. It should provide a means for institutionalizing integrative behavior.

Such a federal arrangement as envisaged must not be viewed as a transitionary stage on the way to unitary forms, but rather as a means of dispersing power on a long-term basis. The competency of the central government should be limited to questions of general interest, and central authorities should be prohibited from intervening in regional matters except within the limits of coordination at the national level.

Federalism is certainly not the only answer to the complex problems of integration in the Sudan. But it can be used as an institutional mechanism to facilitate the desired goals of one or another form of political integration. Hence, all leaders of rational thinking should not shy away from such reconciliational institutions as federalism out of a fear that concessions to regionalism will inhibit modernization. The fact is that federalism does not necessarily impede modernization; instead, it brings government much closer to the people by facilitating more participation in public affairs and in development projects. For, by multiplying the number of actors in the polity, the salience of communal disputes may be reduced, coalitions may be fostered, and cross-cutting cleavages may emerge. Indeed, a large socially pluralistic society such as the Sudan makes some form of decentralized structural mechanism along federal lines essential.

The success of federalism depends largely on the spirit with which it is operated. Hence, the role of the political elites is critically important. It is essential to have proper political leadership to run a federal system and to adapt it to the unique circumstances of the Sudan. Unscrupulous political opportunists, who are not few in the Sudan, would be destabilizing elements. What the Sudan requires to run such a system is a breed of politicians who combine enlightenment with courage and vigor, and who must consider the pluralism they are fated to work with as legitimate.

Political realism requires a search for a viable compromise in the broad area between the extremes of strong centralization and full autonomy for constituent units. The experience of the last two decades in the Sudan makes one point quite clear: a constitutional arrangement must be designed, as far as is practicable, to conform to the basic configurations of power in the country or they are not likely to endure the test of time. To miss this point is to tempt grave instability—and perhaps the destruction of the state itself.

We are not unaware of the centripetal implications of federalism. But we think the Sudan should risk experimenting with it particularly when what it has falls short of meeting the needs, desires, interests, and expectations of the masses of its people. Indeed, it is possible that the plunge into unity can be made less awesome in the Sudan if it experiments with and considers conflict regulatory practices and processes as dynamic relationships which should be predicated on the continuity and persistence of its pluralistic society.

The role of the Sudan Socialist Union (SSU) in the context of a federal system is important. It can perform at least six crucial functions. First, the SSU should be organized and developed as a party capable of managing conflicts by channeling them through its own mediating structures thereby reducing their intensity. Second, it should allow open expression of dissent and drain off systematic political strains. Third, it should act as a broker and buttress the new federal constitutional order in the face of significant dissension. Fourth, it should strengthen and maintain national communications between the two regions. Fifth, it should undertake recruitment and socialization functions, that is, provide new elites for the federal system and politically educate the Sudanese citizenry. Sixth, it should formulate a well-defined ideology worthy of dissemination but generally enough to encompass diverse regional interests. Such an ideology must have a reasonable degree of elasticity capable of allowing some disagreement over concrete policies and their implications. However, it must, on the other hand, be remembered that a diffuse ideology is invariably devoid of direction. What is suggested here is the abandonment of ideological rhetoric, which is essentially futile, in preference for ideological precision operated with an open and flexible mind for the good of societal transformation. The SSU must be truly the forum for and catalyst of territorial unity and integrative behavior, the formulator and disseminator of a relevant ideology. It should exphasize and stand for equality of opportunity and social justice in the production and distribution of the national resources and it should provide the channels for political participation.

Conclusion

The Addis Ababa Agreement ended the military confrontation between the North and South of the Sudan. The response to international appeals for financial aid and services for repatriation, resettlement, relief, and rehabilitation of Sudanese refugees of the Southern region was poor in that contributions in "cash and kind" were insubstantial. However, despite the enormous problems facing the new regional administration, a remarkable degree of harmony has prevailed since the cessation of hostilities between the two regions. The political leaders of both areas have worked together to maintain peace and stability, and the integration of the Anya-Nya Army with the rest of the Sudanese armed forces has progressed smoothly, much more so than expected. Elections were carried out successfully after the eighteen months of the interim period expired and the provisional HEC was replaced by one which enjoys the mandate of the people.

It would, however, be presumptuous to claim that the African-Arab conflict in the area has been resolved. Indeed, it remains potentially explosive. The memories of the deeply rooted hatred between the two peoples of the Sudan, coupled with the intensity of the seventeen years' war fought on the Southern soil, will linger for many years. The built-in inequality between the North and the South in many relevant dimensions of modernization remains intact. Much of the confidence of the Southern people in the regional arrangement depends largely on the personal survival of General Nimiery as President of the country. President Nimiery's good personal relationship with Abel Alier, the Vice President and President of the HEC, has contributed greatly to the present seemingly cordial understanding between the two regions, but the situation remains frighteningly uncertain should anything happen to President Nimiery.

Hitherto, we have suggested a modification of the present constitutional arrangement and argued for a territorial autonomy in the form of a federal system. We think that a regional layer of government should be created in the North to parallel the present one in the South.[36] The powers between the regions and the federal government should be defined in light of the power configurations and diversities in the country. Certainly, federalism is not the only viable conflict regulatory mechanism, but the Sudan should not shy away from experimenting with it. After all, it might prove a viable constitutional arrangement which can effectively mediate communal conflict in the circumstances existing in the Sudan, especially if it is committed to building institutions responsive to the idea of equality as one important aspect of a system designed to secure the well-being of all Sudanese people.

CHAPTER X
Conclusion

Most independent African states have experienced the agony of internal conflicts to varying degrees. Some of these conflicts arose from efforts by disenchanted groups either to seize power or to break away from the sphere of influence of the central authority. In the Sudan, the African-Arab conflict was complex and tragic. As the situation deteriorated, an accumulation of antagonisms and of deep-felt hatred between the people of the North and South surfaced. Many factors played a role in both its generation and outcome.

Within the Sudan, the people of the North are differentiated from those of the South not only by religious beliefs but by practically every other characteristic. Both peoples differ in their conception of the universe. The value incompatibilities of both groups became more pronounced as the Northerners attempted to use their monopoly of state power to impose their culture upon the Southerners. The Arabs despised the African cultures in the South and called the African blacks infidels and considered them as fit only to be converted to Islam and to be assimilated into the Arab fold by all conceivable means not excluding a jihad (religious war). The Southern Sudanese resented vehemently the policies of Arab acculturation and were determined to defend their identity.

Historically, in most areas of the world where Arab Moslems made their presence felt, Islamic hierarchies dealt with strangers in their midst either by holding them in tribute as a subject population or, alternatively, by converting them. In the Sudan, the invading Arabs from Saudi Arabia, across the Red Sea, and from Northern Africa, by way of Egypt, successfully imposed their religion on the indigenous people in the Northern Sudan and, through intermarriages, they eventually established their hegemony over the natives and culturally assimilated them into Arabism. They tried without success to extend their influence to the South in the precolonial times. Their slave raids into the region coupled with brutal attempts to establish their domain and to launch Islamization left unforgettable memories on the people of the South. There are no good shared memories between the North and the South, and there is no basis of a common nationality.

The Anglo-Egyptian Condominium regime refereed between the two historically antagonistic regions. But whereas the colonial government initiated some modernization projects in the North, it completely neglected the South. Surprisingly, although the colonial regime treated the two regions as distinctly different with separate administrations, in conformance with its usual colonial policies, the British colonial regime integrated the administrations of the two regions and unashamedly handed the South to the Northern political leadership. Realizing that it was to be left at the mercy of its traditional enemy, the South plunged into war to defend its integrity from what it considered a new colonial rule. Hence, unlike the rest of the separatist movements in Africa, the Southern Sudan launched its struggle for autonomy before the complete withdrawal of the colonial regime. Both Britain and Egypt—the colonial partners—agreed to support the North in establishing its hegemony over the South. The deep-rooted historical hostility and mutual distrust between the two regions accentuated the cleavages between them and, in fact, continued to punctuate their relationship.

Patterns of social and economic discrimination reinforced the minority status of the Southern Sudanese within the independent Republic of the Sudan. Their political weakness in turn reinforced their social and economic patterns. Indeed, it really did not matter which way the causal connections worked. The Southerners could bring no pressure to bear on the political system. Their day-to-day lives offered them little hope in a united Sudan. They perceived themselves to be socially and economically deprived in comparison with the North. And they suffered humiliation. It became increasingly clear to them that they confronted a unified, though not a monolithic, Northern Sudanese majority and that they were the victims of popular oppression. As the propensity of the North to engage in discrimination, oppression, and violence against the South increased, the Southerners felt that since there was no justice in the political system, there was no legitimate state and no obligation to obey. They wanted to go their own way—free from Arab domination.

The Sudan is a classic case of a praetorian state. It lacks effective political institutions capable of mediating, refining, and moderating group political action. Political leadership in the country has been so divided that it failed to give form to governmental institutions. For many years no agreement ever existed among the groups as to the legitimate and authoritative methods for resolving conflicts. Such lack of viable and cohesive institutionalized polity to provide procedures to be used for resolution of political disputes and to provide fair means of political participation in the Sudan has consequently produced great frustration among the elites. This has led to a high incidence of political instability. This elite frustration coupled with excessive lust for power has been manifested by both the civilian and military elites in various attempts to capture power. A summary analysis of major coups—successful, unsuccessful, attempted or planned—shows clearly the incidence of political instability in the Sudan and the character of its praetorianism (see Table VI).

The absence of an established political order and the perpetual crisis of leadership in the North drove it to excesses in the South. All channels for free expression of dissent were closed. Increasingly the inability of the government to penetrate the South and its failure to respond to basic grievances helped polarize African-Arab relations.

The Arab Sudanese power elites unanimously decided that in order to contain the situation in the South the inhabitants of the area must be converted to Islam and be assimilated into the Arab culture and identity. Pursuit of such an ideology of Arabism and Islam coupled with repression in the South worsened the relationship between the two regions. External actors in the form of sovereign states and international organizations encouraged the Northern Sudanese through the Sudan government to prosecute the war against the Southerners in the name of territorial unity.

The people of Southern Sudan felt frustrated in their imposed relationship with the North. The psychological fear of discrimination and of domination was too much to bear. The North indicated no intention of improving the situation: instead it consciously pursued policies which reinforced its political hegemony over the South, the uneven distribution of economic projects, the inequality of opportunity for education, and the constant threat to African traditional values. It was the genuine perception of Southerners that their frustrations had reached a point of no return and that their conditions would not improve in the future without a confrontation with the sources of their frustrations. Their psychological apprehension led them to deployment of extraconstitutional means to remedy the situation.

The Southern Sudanese secessionist effort raised a series of critical problems for the concept of self-determination and for its use as a principle governing the claims of people caught in the processes of political change. It has been argued that the concept of self-determination applies only to the process of decolonization, and that once independence has been attained, it is fulfilled and has no further application to subsequent political changes in former colonial areas. In the case of the Sudan, the Southerners were not involved in the process of decolonization and they had not exercised their right to self-determination. Indeed, their uprising on the eve of the colonial departure was to emphasize this point. Moreover, since the Northern and the Southern regions were treated as separate entities by the colonial regime (and rightly so), politicians in the North could not claim to have fought for the self-determination of the South as well. They pressured Britain, and successfully did so with the help of Egypt, to hand the South to them so that they could assume the role of a colonizer in the area. This was later confirmed by their actions and policies.

However, even if the Southerners had exercised their right to self-

TABLE VI

Incidence of Political Instability, 1955–1976

	Event and Date	*Description*	*Participants*	*Apparent Causes*
1.	Self-determination and independence as a separate state from the North, 17 August 1955.	A nationalist uprising of Southern Sudanese Corps at Torit broke out in two companies. It later spread over all the Southern region. The war against the Arab-Sudanese administration and military occupation in the South continued for 17 years (1955–72).	Most of the members of the former Equatoria Corps later joined by the bulk of the Southern Sudanese peasants, professional politicians, civil servants, students, and defectors from the Sudan defense force, police, and prisons. In September 1963, the freedom fighters' forces were named "Anya-Nya."	1. Traditional hostility caused by Arab slave-raiding in the South during the 19th century. 2. Discrimination against the South by the newly set up Northern government. The Northern policies of domination of the South were clearly shown in the "Sudanization policy of jobs" which heavily favored the North. 3. Declared government policies of Islamization and Arabicization of the South. 4. Persistent failures of Northern-dominated governments to accommodate Southern grievances in a workable arrangement. 5. The immediate cause of the 17 August 1955 event was the announcement of transfer of the Southern troops to the North and replacement by Northern troops.
2.	Attempted coup by the Army, 12 June 1957.	A conspiracy to overthrow the parlimentary government was uncovered.	Leaders of the plot were not identified but 9 members of the Armed Forces were subsequently arrested. The accused were sentenced to imprisonment ranging from 7 to 20 years.	1. Disillusionment with the professional politicians. There was a lot of political bickering and dissension within the political parties. 2. Corrupt and inactive government of Prime Minister Abdullah Bey Khalil.
3.	Army coup d'etat,	Over 4000 troops under the	Lt. General Ibrahim	1. The Army was invited to take over by the

	17 November 1958.	Commander-in-Chief of the armed forces, Lt. General Ibrahim Abboud, staged a successful bloodless coup against the Parliamentary regime.	Abboud, Major-General Ahmed Abdullah Wahhab, Brigadier Hassan Beshir Nasr, and several senior Army officers.	Prime Minister Bey Khalil in a move to forestall a new parliamentary alliance including pro-Egyptian elements; and to silence Parliament which was increasingly becoming hostile to his policies. According to the arrangement, the Army was to return to barracks after subduing Khalil's opponents and give back power to the politicians. Power, of course, was too sweet to be surrendered voluntarily. The Army had to be overthrown six years later by a civilian uprising.
4.	Coup attempt, 4–9 March 1959.	Two provincial military commanders massed troops on Khartoum, and after failure to grab power, demanded reshuffle of the Supreme Military Council.	Brigadiers Mohieddim al-Din Abdulla and Abdal-Kahim Shenan.	1. Protest against exclusion from the Supreme Military Council. Demand for reshuffle of the Supreme Military Council and Command. 2. Show of military strength to back demands for removal from the Supreme Council of two opponents: Major General Ahmed Abdal Wahhab, Defense Minister, and Brigadier Hassan Beshir Nasr, Deputy Commander-in-Chief and Minister of Cabinet Affairs. The former was relieved of his ministerial and military positions and retired with a lucrative pension.
5.	Coup attempt, 21–22 May 1959.	Supporters of Mohieddin al-Din marched troops on Khartoum.	Two platoons from the Eastern Command led by a member of the Supreme Council and several young officers.	1. Brigadiers (staunch NUP supporters) were unpopular within the Supreme Council after their inclusion. They wanted the removal of President Abboud's right hand man, Brigadier Hassan Beshir Nasr. Abboud refused to relieve

TABLE VI (continued)

Event and Date	*Description*	*Participants*	*Apparent Causes*
			Hassan Beshir, dismissed the two Brigadiers and court-martialed them after arresting their supporters.
6. Coup attempt, 9 November 1959.	Army mutiny at the Infantry School in Omdurman aimed at overthrowing the government. It failed, for support from the rest of the Army was not forthcoming.	Young Army officers and new recruits. Later in December, two Army officers and three former officers were executed following a court-martial trial.	1. Not ascertainable. Some of the participants were associated with either the fanatical Moslem Brotherhood organization or the leftist groups. Probably lust for power.
7. Civilian Coup/uprising, 26 October 1964.	Well-coordinated mass demonstrations in Khartoum against the military government.	Urban coalition of workers, students, civil servants, professional politicians, and young leftist Army officers. The young Army officers backed the uprising and threatened to bombard the Presidential palace.	1. The civil war in the Southern Sudan. 2. Deterioration of the economy. 3. Restriction of political participation. 4. Corruption and nepotism in high circles of government. 5. Mishandling of student demonstration by the Army junta. 6. Disenchantment with the military regime.
8. Coup attempt, 18 December 1966.	Following the High Court ruling against the unconstitutional exclusion of the Communist party from	300 trainees in Khartoum led by 2nd Lt. Khalid Hassan. Six other officers were later arrested; and the	1. To put an end to the political wrangling and ideological feud between the political parties and the sectarian groups; and to replace the aging politicians.

		the National Assembly there were mass demonstrations staged by the interested parties. The Army attempted a coup.	leaders of the Communist party were detained although no link was made between the coup attempt and their party.	
9.	Coup d'etat, 25 May 1969.	Members of the Free Officers Organization with 400 soldiers led by Col. Gaafar Mohammed el-Nimiery staged a successful coup against the inept civilian government. Only 2 parachute units, an infantry unit, and an armored unit were involved.	Young revolutionary officers belonging to the Free Officers Organization led by Lt. Col. Babiker el Nur, Majors Farouk Osman Hamadallah, Khalid Hassan, and other majors.	1. Failure to solve the Southern problem by the civilian governments which applied force. 2. Economic crises—inflation and economic stagnation. 3. Political ineptitude. 4. Corruption, favoritism, and nepotism. 5. Breakdown in the Civil Service Administration. 6. Lack of a coherent radical foreign policy.
10.	Plot, 20 July 1969.	90 persons were arrested in connection with a conspiracy to overthrow the Nimiery government.	Army officers, noncommissioned officers, and civilians. Many of them were from the Nuba area.	1. Antipathy toward continued dominance of governments by Arab Sudanese. 2. Lack of economic development projects in their regions. 3. Opposition to radical policies and to the critics of the defunct conservative parties.
11.	Plot, 13 December 1969.	An attempt to overthrow the government was uncovered.	Supporters of the Moslem Brotherhood.	1. Opposition to the revolutionary rhetoric of the regime and fear of communist influence in the Sudan.

TABLE VI (continued)

	Event and Date	*Description*	*Participants*	*Apparent Causes*
12.	Plot, 12 January 1970.	Authorities uncovered a plot within the armed forces to overthrow the regime.	Several noncommissioned officers were arrested, including their alleged leader, Brigadier Abdulla Mohammed Adam.	1. Ideological differences with the Nimiery regime.
13.	Armed rebellion, March 1970.	President Nimiery escaped an assassination attempt during a visit to the White Nile area. This was followed by an Ansar Insurrection aimed at liquidating the military regime. Most of the confrontation was in Aba Island, south of Khartoum, where the Iman had fled after the Nimiery coup.	Followers of the Ansar sect under their leader, the Imam el-Hadi. The insurrection was suppressed and the Iman was killed while trying to escape.	1. Banning of political parties and competitive politics and obsessive resentment of Army rule. The Iman was aspiring for high political office—the Presidency—before the coup.
14.	Plot, 19 November 1970.	A plot by "reactionary elements" to overthrow the regime was foiled.	Members of the Moslem Brotherhood.	1. An opposition to a military regime. 2. Desire to restore parliamentary politics and establish an Islamic state.
15.	Abortive coup, 21–23 July 1971.	Army officers sympathetic to the Communist Party	Former members of the Nimiery Revolutionary	1. Opposition to the government's decision to join Egypt and Libya in an Arab Federation.

		seized power for two days, and imprisoned President Nimiery and other members of the Cabinet. On 22 July, a successful countercoup brought Nimiery back to power.	Command Council: Lt. Colonel Babiker el-Nur, Majors Hashim el-Atta, and Farouk Osman Hamadallah. The military attack was led by Hashim el Atta while his other two colleagues were in London. All the coup leaders were executed, including key members of the Communist Party who supported the coup.	2. Hashim el Atta and Babiker el Nur were active members of the Communist Party and were not happy at their expulsion from the government in October 1970. They disagreed on many domestic policies, including the banning of the Communist Party (all political parties were banned).
16.	Coup plot, 22 July 1972.	Security forces foiled a coup plot.	Young officers in collaboration with former politicians, supporters of the traditional political parties.	1. Desire to restore parliamentary politics. 2. Opposition to radical posture of the regime.
17.	Coup plot, 25 January 1973.	A plot to overthrow the government and assassinate President Nimiery and other senior Army officers and government officials.	Arab Nationalists and Moslem Brotherhood (officers) led by Brig. (Rtd.) Abdal Rahim Shenan and fifteen others, including eleven noncommissioned officers, and the Brigadier's son, Mohammed Shenan.	1. In protest against the failure of the Nimiery regime to pass an Islamic Constitution. 2. Nimiery's shift from emphasis on an Arab Middle Eastern policy. 3. To put an end to the Southern Sudan regional autonomy.

TABLE VI (continued)

	Event and Date	*Description*	*Participants*	*Apparent Causes*
18.	Student demonstrations backed by the right-wing groups, 31 August, 1973.	Khartoum University students staged a demonstration against the government. No public support was given to the demonstration and the Army and police quickly restored order.	University students, mainly supporters of the banned Umma Party and Islamic Charter Front (Moslem Brothers). Leaders of these groups were behind the student demonstrations. They thought that when the students were in the streets, the public would join them. This did not happen and the events of October 1964 were not repeated.	
19.	Coup plot, 12 May 1974.	A plot to overthrow the Nimiery regime.	Right-wing political groups with the backing of the Libyan Government.	1. Ideological differences with the Nimiery regime.
20.	A coup plot by four army officers, 7 October 1974.	Preparation to overthrow the Nimiery regime.	Army officers supported by the outlawed National Front (a group of opposition parties banned after the 1969 coup).	1. Ideological differences and pursuit of power.

21.	A coup plot, 19 May 1975.	Coup plan failed.	Leftist Army officers.	1. Ideological differences.
22.	A coup attempt, 5 September 1975.	A group of right-wing Army officers captured the radio station but were soon overpowered.	Operations led by Major Hasan Hussain Othman. Other leaders included Captain Mohammed Mahmoud el-Tom, Lt. Abdel Rahman Shabi Nawai, and a former judge, Abdel Rahman Idris. Backed by Moslem Brotherhood organization and the National Front.	1. Persecution and torture. 2. Destruction of press freedom. 3. Closing of the Islamic University. 4. Curtailment of freedom at the Khartoum University. 5. Ideological differences.
23.	An abortive coup, 2 July 1976.	A group of Army officers backed by the National Front captured the radio station and some key spots in the capital. Most of the soldiers in the operation were trained and financed by the Libyan government.	The operations were led by Colonel Mohammed Nour Saad (retired) and Captain Bushra Abdullah. The civilian leaders were Sadiq el-Mahdi and Sharif Hussain el-Hindi (both in exile).	1. Ideological differences with the Nimiery regime. 2. Alleged injustice, oppression, and corruption. 3. Despotism.

Sources: Dateline Data, 1969–78 (Connecticut, U.S.A.); Arab Report and Record (London, U.K.), 1969–1977; *The Nile Mirror,* 1970–75 (Khartoum, Sudan); *News,* Ministry of Information and Culture (Khartoum, Sudan).

Note: This is not a complete list of plots and attempted coups against the Nimiery regime. It only covers those incidents that were announced by the government or reported in a foreign press.

determination, they could still resort to and evoke it, precisely because it provides a unilateral right. In other words, the right to self-determination of a sizeable group of people in a geographically concentrated area within a sovereign state does not end at the time of independence from a colonial regime—it is an inalienable right. The people of the Southern Sudan did not agree to accept independence with the Arab Sudanese in a single territorial state. Their consent was not even sought. Besides, the governments of independent Sudan made unification of the two regions unattractive and too expensive in human terms to the South. Hence the eruption of violent confrontation between them.

The war stalemated until a new leadership emerged in the North in 1969 which recognized that the North was virtually unable to govern the South by coercion and that indigenous elites had to be put in charge of the South. The present institutional arrangement gives the South autonomous political status within the framework of one Sudan. From the perspective of the South, the setup is not without flaws, but it represents a point of departure upon which viable consensual relationships can be built. It puts the Southern Sudan in a transition.

Notes

Introduction

1. The Southern Sudanese African religious beliefs were neither recognized by Europeans nor the Arabs: the former referred to them, as they did with the rest of black Africans everywhere, as pagans; and the latter called them infidels.

2. M. G. Smith, *Plural Society in The British West Indies* (Berkeley: University of California Press, 1965), p. 82.

3. Leo Kuper and M. G. Smith, eds. *Pluralism in Africa* (Berkeley: University of California Press, 1969), p. 27. For differing views of "pluralism," see Vera Rubin, "Social and Cultural Pluralism in the Caribbean," Annals of the *New York Academy of Sciences,* vol. 83, art. 5 (1960); Leo A. Despress, *Cultural Pluralism and Nationalist Politics in British Guiana* (Chicago: University Press, 1967); Floyd Dotson and Lillian O. Dotson, *The Indian Minority in Zambia, Rhodesia, and Malawi* (New Haven, Conn.: Yale University Press, 1968); and Pierre L. Van den Berghe, *South Africa: A Study in Conflict* (Middletown, Conn.: Wesleyan University Press, 1965), especially see p. 270.

4. Smith, *Plural Society,* p. 62.

5. Mehden, Anderson, and Young, *Issues of Political Development* (Englewood Cliffs, N.J.: Prentice-Hall, 1967), p. 26.

6. Ibid.

7. Kenneth W. Grundy, *Guerrilla Struggle in Africa: An Analysis and Preview* (New York: Grossman Publishers, 1971), p. 23. I have benefited greatly from Grundy's Model of Violence in Africa presented in this book. Professor Grundy was also kind enough to send me a copy of his unpublished paper on "Segmented Instability: An Exploration of the Problems of Comparative Analysis." For a similar analysis of elites and ethnicity in Africa, see, for example, Richard L. Sklar, "Political Science and National Integration: A Radical Approach," *Journal of Modern African Studies,* vol. 5, no. 1 (May 1967), pp. 1-11. Also see A. Smock, *Ibo Politics: The Role of Ethnic Unions in Eastern Nigeria* (Cambridge: Harvard University Press, 1971), p. 203.

8. In his definition of nationality, John Stuart Mill emphasizes the importance of shared historical experiences which lead to shared prejudices and shared emotional dispositions: "A portion of mankind may be said to constitute a nationality if they are united among themselves by common sympathies which do not exist between them and any others—which make them cooperate with each other more willingly than with other people, desire to be under the same government, and desire that they should be governed by themselves or a portion of themselves exclusively. This feeling of nationality may have been generated by various causes . . . but the strongest of all is identity of political antecedents; the possession of national history and conse-

quent community of recollections; collective pride and humiliation, pleasure and regret, connected with the same incidents in the past.'' See John Stuart Mill, *Representative Government* (1961; reprint ed., New York: Dutton, 1962), cited in Ali Mazrui, *Cultural Engineering and Nation-Building in East Africa* (Evanston, Ill.: Northwestern University Press, 1972), p. 289. I have benefited from Mazrui's intellectual insights into the issue which I discuss here.

9. Throughout this discussion I treat systemic frustration as an independent variable and the conditions that lead directly to it (cultural pluralism and value incompatibilities, historical hostilities; psychological fear and relative and economic deprivation; and right to self-determination) as dependent variables. The other factors that prompt or may prevent it (legitimacy or illegitimacy of the regime; governmental ineptitude and closed channels for dissent; ideology and external actors; and crisis of leadership) are treated as intervening variables. For a detailed discussion of preconditions and precipitants of internal conflicts, see Harry Eckstein, ''On the Causes of Internal Wars,'' in *Politics and Society,* ed. Eric Nordlinger (Englewood Cliffs, N.J.: Prentice-Hall, 1970), pp. 287–290. Also see Harry Eckstein, *History and Theory*, vol. 4, no. 2 (Wesleyan University Press, 1965), pp. 133–163; and Harry Eckstein, ''Toward the Theoretical Study of Internal War,'' in *Internal War*, ed. Harry Eckstein (London: The Free Press, 1963). Also see Milton J. Esman, ''The Management of Communal Conflict,'' *Public Policy*, vol. 21 (Winter 1973). Communal conflict and civil violence are here used interchangeably. In both cases one participant is always a government (in the African context). See S. P. Huntington, ''Civil Violence and the Process of Development,'' *Adelphi Papers no. 83* (London: The International Institute for Strategic Studies, 1972). See John Stuart Mill, *Representative Government* (1961; reprint ed., New York: Dutton, 1962), cited in Ali Mazrui, *Cultural Engineering and Nation-Building in East Africa* (Evanston, Ill.: Northwestern University Press, 1972), p. 289. I have benefited from Mazrui's intellectual insights into the issue which I discuss here.

10. Peter Russell and Storrs McCall, ''Can Secession Be Justified? The Case of the Southern Sudan'' in *The Southern Sudan: The Problem of National Integration*, ed. Dunstan M. Wai (London: Frank Cass, 1973), p. 93.

11. The phrase is used by Samuel P. Huntington and for a detailed study of the institutional approach of political development, see his book, *Political Order in Changing Societies*, (New Haven, Yale University Press, 1968), particularly chap. I.

Chapter I

1. Khartoum, Ministry of Information and Culture, *Facts About the Sudan* (1973), p. 8. Also see K. M. Barbour, *The Republic of the Sudan: A Regional Geography* (London: University of London Press, 1961), chaps. 1 and 2; K. M. Barbour, ''North and South in Sudan; A Study in Human Contrasts,'' *Annals of the Association of American Geographers*, vol. 54, no. 2 (June 1964), pp. 209–226.

2. Barbour, ''North and South in Sudan.'' Also see E. Evans-Pritchard, ''Ethnographic Survey of the Sudan,'' Oxford University. Mimeographed.

3. Northern Sudanese academics and politicians treat the Southern problem as similar to problems of national integration in other African countries. This view runs through all the literature on the North-South conflict.

4. Speech by Aggrey Jaden, Khartoum Conference on the Southern Sudan, March 1965 (Khartoum, March 1965), p. 4. Mimeographed.

5. Colin Legum, Introduction to *The Sudan: Crossroads to Africa*, by Beshire Mohammed Said (London: Bodley Head, 1965), p. 34.

6. Richard Gray, Introduction to *The Problem of the Southern Sudan*, Joseph Oduho and William Deng (London: Oxford University Press, 1963), p. 2.

7. Audrey Butt, *The Nilotes of the Anglo-Egyptian Sudan and Uganda* (London: International African Institute, 1952), p. 41.

8. Francis M. Deng, *Dynamics of Identification: A Basis for National Integration in the Sudan* (Khartoum: Khartoum University Press, 1973), p. 88.

9. John Middleton and David Tait, *Tribes Without Rulers: Studies in African Segmentary Systems* (London: Routledge and Kegan Paul, 1958), pp. 6–7.

10. Deng, *Dynamics of Identification*, p. 90.

11. Angelo L. Loiria, "Political Awakening in the Southern Sudan 1946–1955: Decolonization and the Problem of National Integration" (Ph.D. dissertation, University of California at Los Angeles, 1969), pp. 54–60.

12. Ibid., pp. 66–67.

13. Barbour, *The Republic of the Sudan*, p. 19.

14. This kind of feeling is well reflected in the literature produced by Southern Sudanese political leaders. See, for instance, Oduho and Deng, *The Problems of the Southern Sudan*; Oliver Albino, *The Sudan: A Southern Viewpoint* (London: Oxford University Press, 1970); and *Grass Curtain* [a newsmagazine produced by the Southern Sudanese Association in Great Britain, which ceased publication in 1972].

15. See Oluwadare Aguda, "Arabism and Pan-Africanism in Sudanese Politics," *Journal of Modern African Studies*, vol. 11, no. 2 (1973), p. 182.

16. Yusuf Fadl Hassan, "External Islamic Influences and the Progress of Islamization in the Eastern Sudan Between the Fifteenth and Nineteenth Centuries," in *Sudan in Africa*, ed. Yusuf Fadl Hassan (Khartoum: Khartoum University Press, 1971), p. 73.

17. Loiria, "Political Awakening in the Southern Sudan," pp. 30–48.

18. Harold MacMichael, *A History of the Arabs in the Sudan*, (New York: Barnes & Noble, 1967), p. 197.

19. See K. M. Barbour, "Tribal Administrative Framework," in Barbour, *The Republic of the Sudan*.

20. See Wendy James, "Social Assimilation and Changing Identity in the Southern Funj," in *Sudan in Africa*, ed. Hassan, Yusuf Fadl, p. 201.

21. Muddathir Abd al-Rahim tends to argue that the synthesis between Arabism and Africanism is so complete and thorough in the Northern Sudan and the people there can claim to be both Africans and Arabs at the same time without contradiction. See Muddathir Abd al-Rahim, "Arabism, Africanism, and Self-Identification in the Sudan," in *The Southern Sudan: The Problem of National Integration*, ed. Dunstan M. Wai (London: Frank Cass, 1973), pp. 29–45.

22. Sayed Saddiq el Mahdi, address to the Constituent Assembly in October 1966, *Proceedings of the Sudan Constituent Assembly* (October 1966), quoted in Abel Alier, "The Southern Sudan Question," in *The Southern Sudan*, ed. Wai, p. 24.

23. Cited in Alier, "The Southern Sudan Question," p. 24.

24. Arnold Toynbee, interview in *Playboy*, April 1968. Professor Toynbee also observed that "the Northern Sudanese are masters in the Southerner's house as well as in their own, they are trying to make up for lost time. They are trying to assimilate the Southern Sudanese to the Northern way of life—an attempt that they were debarred from making under the British regime. This northern Sudanese reaction is natural, but it is surely wrong, and this both politically and morally"; in Arnold Toynbee, *Between Niger and Nile* (London: Oxford University Press, 1965), pp. 5–6.

25. Aguda, "Arabism and Pan-Africanism," p. 188.

Chapter II

1. Robert O. Collins, *The Southern Sudan 1883–1898* (New Haven: Yale University Press, 1962), chap. 1, p. 2.
2. Ibid.
3. Richard Gray, *A History of the Southern Sudan 1839–1888,* (London: Oxford University Press, 1961), p. 21.
4. Robert O. Collins, *The Southern Sudan 1883–1898,* pp. 177–182.
5. Gray, *The Southern Sudan 1839–1889*, p. 21.
6. Ibid., p. 22.
7. Ibid., pp. 45–46.
8. Gray, *The Southern Sudan 1839–1889*, p. 46.
9. Ibid., pp. 46–47.
10. Ibid., p. 48.
11. Ibid.
12. Gray, *The Southern Sudan 1839–1889*, p. 51.
13. Ibid., p. 51, fn.
14. Ibid. pp. 51–52.
15. Sir Samuel Baker, quoted in W. W. Cash, *The Changing Sudan* (London: Church Missionary Society, 1930), p. 12.
16. Collins, *The Southern Sudan 1883–1898*, chap. 1, pp. 22–54.
17. Major Titherington, "The Raik Dinka" (Sudan Notes and Records, 10 [1927], pp. 159–60), cited in Deng, *Dynamics of Identification*, p. 42.
18. Collins, *The Southern Sudan 1883–1898*, pp. 177–181.
19. P. M. Holt, *The Mahdist State in the Sudan, 1881–1899: A Study of Its Origins, Development, and Overthrow* (Oxford: Clarendon Press, 1970), pp. 45–50.
20. Ibid., pp. 45–60.
21. The analogy is used by Collins.
22. See Mohammed Omer Beshir, "The Southern Sudan" (Khartoum: Khartoum University Press, 1972), pp. 2–3. (Pamphlet) Many Northern Sudanese politicians also tend to take this line of reasoning.
23. Collins, *The Southern Sudan 1883–1898*, p. 179.
24. Collins, *The Southern Sudan 1883–1898*, pp. 11–12.
25. Chief Giirdit (a Dinka Paramount Chief) in an interview with Francis M. Deng, quoted in Deng, *Dynamics of Identification*, October 16, 1976, p. 29.
26. Sayed Ismael el Azhari, President of the National Unionist Party, address to the Round Table Conference on the Problem of the Southern Sudan, 16 March 1965.

Chapter III

1. Abd El-Fattah Ibrahim El-Sayed Baddour, *Sudanese-Egyptian Relations: A Chronological and Analytical Study* (The Hague: Martinus Nijhoff, 1960), pp. 84–99.
2. For details of the Fashoda incident, see J. S. R. Duncan, *The Sudan: A Record of Achievement 1898–1947* (Edinburgh: William Blackwood and Sons, 1952), pp. 81–84.
3. Alier, "The Southern Sudan Question," p. 14.

4. The formation of the Equatorial Corps exclusively from the Southern Sudan was completed in 1917. An army was also built in the North also exclusively from that region. The two armies were kept separate in their respective regions until the eve of colonial withdrawal when the British officers in the South were replaced by Northern Arab Sudanese.

5. A native administration system based on the philosophy of indirect rule was established in the Sudan. For details, see Muddathir Abd al-Rahim, *Imperialism and Nationalism in the Sudan* (Oxford: Oxford University Press, 1969), sec. 3.

6. J. S. R. Duncan, *The Sudan's Path to Independence* (Edinburgh: William Blackwood and Sons, 1957), p. 61.

7. HMSO, *Colonial Annual Report for 1905*, Egypt, no. 1, 2817 (1906), p. 125.

8. The Southern Sudanese ethnic groups had their own different days of rest depending on performances of spiritual rituals. Eventually, Sunday was accepted as a day of rest even by non-Christians.

9. *Laws of the Sudan*, vol. 1:93, 1941 edition.

10. The Southerners who went to the North were mainly servants of British officials who were transferred from the South to the North.

11. Civil Secretary Sir Harold MacMichael to the governors of the three Southern provinces and directors of departments (25 January 1930), C.S./1.c.1, Government Archives, Khartoum.

12. Ibid.

13. Alier, "The Southern Sudan Question," p. 3.

14. This line of argument is found in all writings by Northern Sudanese on North-South relations. It runs through the following three books in particular: M. B. Said, *The Sudan: Crossroad of Africa* (Chester Springs, Pa.: Dufour Editions, Inc., 1965); Mohammed Omer Beshir, *The Southern Sudan: Background to Conflict* (London: C. Hurst, 1968); and Muddathir Abdal-Rahim, *Imperialism and Nationalism*. See also, Muddathir Abd al-Rahim's Introduction to *Fourteen Documents on the Problem of the Southern Sudan*.

15. J. S. R. Duncan, *The Sudan: A Record of Achievement 1898–1947* (Edinburgh: William Blackwood and Sons, 1952).

16. P. M. McLoughlin, "Economic Development and the Heritage of Slavery in the Sudan" (mimeograph). McLoughlin states that there were several main slave-supply sources: (1) Sudanic people of the Nuba Mountains (Kordofan Province); (2) Sudanic people of Western Sudan Mountainous districts (which in 1916 became Darfur Province); (3) Sudanic peoples in the Central-Eastern Sudan near the Ethiopian border; (4) Nilotic, Nilo-Hamitic, Negroid, and other Southern Sudan peoples; (5) Abyssinia (now Ethiopia); (6) Belgian Congo (now Zaire), French Equatorial Africa (Central African Republic), Kenya, Uganda (along the White Nile and Bahr el Arab, through Bahr el Ghazal and Equatorial Provinces, and over several main routes which entered North-Western Sudan); (7) The pilgrimage from West Africa to Mecca in Saudi Arabia.

17. HMSO, *Annual Report for 1904*, Egypt, no. 1, ed. 2409 (1950), p. 140.

18. The Central Office of Information, *Basic Facts About the Southern Provinces of the Sudan* (Khartoum: The Central Office of Information, 1964), p. 13. Also see *Sudan Government Gazette* no. 731 (1964).

19. Dispatch no. 89 (1945) to the British colonial government in the Sudan by Lord Killearn.

20. Duncan, *The Sudan: A Record of Achievement, 1898–1948,* pp. 13–14.

21. Mekki Abbas, *The Sudan Question* (London: Faber and Faber, Ltd., 1952), pp. 174–175.

22. The Graduate Congress was an alumni association of Northern Sudanese and became a politically active association. Later politicians such as Ismael el-Azhari and Mohammed Ahmed Mahgoub (both became Prime Ministers) were members of the Graduate Congress. The Congress entertained ideas of ruling the South as part of one Sudan with the North; and of expanding Islamic and Arab influences along the Nile Valley to the middle of Africa.

23. Duncan, *The Sudan's Path to Independence*, p. 213. Also see Civil Secretary to the Legal and Financial Secretaries, Directors of Departments, and Governors of the Southern Provinces (16 December 1946), C.S./1.c., Government Archives, Khartoum.

24. The British supported the Mahdi family through the Umma Party (heavily supported by the Ansars, who were followers of the rival of the Ansars. The Mahdi family wanted the Sudan to maintain close relations with Britain, rather than with Egypt, after independence.

25. Report of Sudan Administration Conference (Khartoum, the Governor's Palace, 23 April 1946). The report was published 31 March 1947.

26. Governor of Bahr el Ghazal Province to Governor of Equatoria Province (6 March 1947), no. 139a/SCR.C1, Government Archives, Khartoum.

27. This was the view of the Civil Secretary, Sir James W. Robertson.

28. The Civil Secretary to the Governors of the Southern Provinces (16 December 1946), quoted in Abdal-Rahim, *Fourteen Documents on the Problem of the Southern Sudan*, Introduction, p. 29.

29. This was the view of the British officials in Khartoum and of the Northern Sudanese politicians and the Egyptians.

30. Governor of Bahr el Ghazal Province to Governor of Equatoria Province (see fn. 26 supra).

31. Fabian Society, *The Sudan: The Road Ahead* (London: Faber and Faber, 1947), pp. 25–26.

32. The Central Office of Information, *Basic Facts About the Southern Provinces,* p. 16.

33. Letter from Richard Owen, Deputy Governor of Bahr el Ghazal Province to B. V. Maywood, Governor of Equatoria Province (6 January 1947), C.S./1.c.1, Government Archives, Khartoum.

34. Ibid.

35. Letter from British Administrators in the Southern Sudan to Civil Secretary in Khartoum (10 March 1947), C.S./1.c.1, Government Archives, Khartoum. Also see Abdal-Rahim, *Fourteen Documents on the Problems of the Southern Sudan*, p. 15.

36. Governor of Equatoria to Deputy Governor Bahr el Ghazal (30 April 1947), C.S./1.c.1, Government Archives, Khartoum.

37. Civil Secretary's Memorandum on Juba Conference (15 May 1947), C.S./1.c.1., Government Archives, Khartoum.

38. These are the arguments that were later put forward by Northern Sudanese writers and politicians. See Abdal-Rahim, *Fourteen Documents on the Problem of the Southern Sudan*, p. 16.

39. For a detailed analysis of the Juba Conference, see Alier, "The Southern Sudan Question," pp. 16–18.

40. This was the view put forward by the Southern Front, a political party founded by Southern Sudanese professionals after the overthrow of the military government of General Abboud. (Letter by the Southern Front Executive Committee to the OAU Summit in Accra, April 1965.)

41. Appendix III, "Minutes of the Preliminary Meeting of the Members Referring to Civil Secretary's Memorandum," in *The Southern Sudan*, ed. Wai, pp. 199, 201.

42. Ibid.

43. Ibid., pp. 194–195.

44. Ibid.

45. Cited in letter from the Southern Front to the OAU Summit in Accra (April 1965).

46. Draft of Self-Government Statute, Government Archives, Khartoum (1948).

47. The pro-Egyptian Northern Sudanese Ashigga Party led the attack against the safeguards

for the South and it boycotted the debate in the Legislative Assembly. The campaign against the provision giving the Governor-General special powers for the South took the line that it was an "imperialist government," "a gross interference in the internal affairs of our self-government," "a hidden scheme for partition of the Sudan." See Debates in the Legislative Assembly (1948), Government Archives, Khartoum.

48. Professor Vincent T. Harlow was Beit Professor of History of the British Empire, and Fellow of Balliol College, Oxford.

49. See Vincent T. Harlow, Appendix II, "Memorandum on the Projected Measures of Constitutional Reform in the Sudan," in *Report of the Work of the Constitutional Amendment Commission* (Khartoum: McCorquedale, 1952).

50. *Khartoum*, The Legislative Assembly, *Weekly Digest* (9 February 1952), pp. 104-105.

51. See the Anglo-Egyptian (and Northern Sudanese) Agreement of 1953 prior to the establishment of self-government in Abdal-Rahim, *Imperialism and Nationalism*, Appendix IX, pp. 257–260.

52. Baddour, *Sudanese-Egyptian Relations*, pp. 170–176.

53. The clause that embraced the North and South as one country was to formalize the Civil Secretary's unilateral declaration of the merger of North and South. It is this clause that made the two regions into the present Sudan.

54. See Mohammed Ahmed Mahgoub, *Democracy on Trial* (London: Andre Deutsch, 1974), chaps. 2 and 3.

55. For a detailed discussion of the Sudan's movement toward independence, see Abdal-Rahim, *Imperialism and Nationalism*, pp. 213–218.

56. Most of the data used is obtained from Karal Jozef Krotki, "Political Statistics in the Sudan," in *Population of the Sudan: Report on the Sixth Annual Conference of the Philosophical Society of the Sudan, 1958, Sudan Notes and Records*, vol. 40.

57. Ibid., p. 84.

58. Self-determination in the Sudan: Resume of Developments, *CMD9829* (London: HMSO, 1956).

59. Azhari did, however, reverse his party's policy of union with Egypt upon coming to power as Prime Minister and led the drive for full independence. The distribution of the election results in Parliament were as follows:

House of Representatives

National Unionist Party	51
Umma Party	22
Independents (North)	4
Socialist Republican Party	3
Southern Party	10
Southern Political Association	2
Front Against Colonization	1
Independents (South)	4
Total	97

	Elected	*Nominated*	*Total*
National Unionist Party	22	10	32
Umma Party	3	4	7
Socialist Republican Party	-	1	1
Southern Party	3	1	4
Independents (North)	1	2	3
Independents (South)	1	2	3
Total	30	20	50

This distribution of party strength in both Houses of Parliament resulted after a number of crossings on the floor took place. Before these floor crossings, the NUP won only five seats from the South, the rest of the South being won by independents, Southern Party, or the Southern Political Association. The NUP had five members from the South.

60. Y. Tandon and Gingyera-Pinycwa, "Uganda-Sudan Relations and Uganda-Congo Relations, 1962–1966: A Comparative Examination," paper for the Social Science Conference, University of East Africa, December 1966, pp. 1-3. (Unpublished.) Cited in Wai, *The Southern Sudan*, p. 2.

61. Baddour, *Sudanese-Egyptian Relations*, P. Baddour reports that Egypt always kept the doors of her universities and higher schools open for (Northern) Sudanese to enter any time they felt they could pursue such higher studies. In 1955, the following were the number of Northern Sudanese students in Egypt:

Al-Azhar University	2,156
Cairo University	443
Heliopolis (Ein Shams) University	146
Alexandra University	113
Higher Schools of Higher Studies	67
Secondary, Intermediate, and Technical Schools	796
Total	3,721

62. For a detailed analysis of processes of nation-building, see Mazrui, "Culture Engineering and Nation-Building in East Africa," p. 289.

Chapter IV

1. *Report of the Commission of Inquiry into the Disturbances in the Southern Sudan During August 1955* (Khartoum: McCorquedale, 1956). [Hereinafter referred to as *Report of the Commission of Inquiry*.]

2. Benjamin Lwoke is a Pojulo from Loka, Yei River District in Equatoria Province. He was a primary school teacher before he became involved in politics. Stanislaus Paysma is from Bahr el Ghazal Province and a Dinka by tribe. Buth Diu was from upper Nile province and a Nuer by tribe. He worked as a civil servant before becoming active in politics.

3. Personal clashes, pursuit of personal egos and parochial interests, disagreements over strategy, personal ambitions, and inability to work as a unified group—all these and others—became the main dysfunctional characteristics of Southern leaders throughout the years of the Civil War.

4. Cited in the *Report of the Commission of Inquiry*, pp. 112–113.

5. This was only about .75 percent of the jobs Sudanized.

6. There were some Southerners in the civil service who were much more qualified than Northerners who were promoted and taken to the South as replacements for the British colonial officers. Moreover, there were no attempts to accelerate training of personnel in the South. The Juba Training Center which used to train clerks, bookkeepers, and junior civil servants during the colonial period was closed down and was never reopened.

7. A letter from Gogrial, Bahr el Ghazal Province to a Southern Member of Parliament (30 August 1954). Author's name unknown.

8. Liberal party documents. I am indebted to a friend who prefers to remain anonymous for allowing me to examine his material on Southern politics in the 1950s.

9. The memories of the Arab slave plunders in the Southern Sudan have never been forgot-

ten. Such memories increasingly make it difficult for Southerners to trust the Northern Arab Sudanese whose actions also, more often than not, reinforce them.

10. See *Report of the Commission of Inquiry*, pp. 115–117.

11. The Southern MP was Dak Dei. He resigned because the NUP government did not fulfill its promises to the South.

12. The dismissed Southerner from the Cabinet was Bullen Allier de Bior.

13. See *Report of the Commission of Inquiry*, p. 87.

14. The Southern MP was Siricio Iro from the Mahdi area in Torit District, Eastern Equatoria Province. He later became a member of the Supreme Council between 1956–1958.

15. *Report of the Commission of Inquiry*, p. 82.

16. *Report of the Commission of Inquiry*, p. 88. Copies of the letter were sent to the Governor of Equatoria province, the District Commissioner, and the Assistant District Commissioner, Yambio.

17. Ibid., pp. 90–91.

18. Ibid., pp. 92–93.

19. The Avungara were the traditional warrior ruling chiefs among the Azande people.

20. *Report of the Commission of Inquiry*, p. 93.

21. Ibid., p. 94.

22. Relations between Northerners and Southerners deteriorated badly in the South and particularly in Zandeland and among the workers in Nzara where the newly appointed Northern managers showed cultural and racial arrogance and contempt for the Southerners.

23. The description is by the *Report of the Commission of Inquiry*, p. 96.

24. Ibid., p. 95.

25. Ibid.

26. Ibid., p. 96. Also see Criminal Court Circular no. 41, cited in ibid.

27. See J. W. A. Wyld, "The Zande Scheme," *Sudan Notes and Records*, vol. 30 (1949), pp. 47–58.

28. *Report of the Commission of Inquiry*, p. 97.

29. Ibid., p. 98.

30. Ibid.

31. Ibid.

32. Ibid.

33. Ibid., p. 102.

34. This view was expressed by the Governor of the Upper Nile Province in a letter to the Commander of the Armed Forces (Kaid), Khartoum (25 March 1955), *Report of the Commission of Inquiry*, p. 104.

35. *Report of the Commission of Inquiry*, p. 104: (i) the ill-feeling which will be felt by the local and real inhabitants of the district towards the immigrant troops coming from a different part of the country at this particular period; (ii) the drop of morale among the whole Equatorial Corps, caused by the unproved suspicion of their efficiency, loyalty and faithfulness without practical corroboration; (iii) the loss of cooperation between this single company (that is Nuba or Arab) and the rest of the Southern Corps in case of trouble; (iv) the complete ignorance of the ordinary Northern soldier to the habits of his comrade of the South and the different system of living and its effect on him; and (v) the homesickness will be felt by the other ranks who will be serving out their district areas throughout the whole period of their term of service.

36. The description and analysis that follows has benefited from the *Report of the Commission of Inquiry* and from various research interviews of Southern Sudanese participants in the events of the period.

37. See the *Report of the Commission of Inquiry*, op cit., pp. 117–125.

38. As events later showed, this was not just a mere army mutiny. It was the beginning of a nationalist uprising in the Southern Sudan.

39. J. Bowyer Bell, "The Conciliation of Insurgency: The Sudanese Experience," *Military Affairs*, vol. 39, no. 3 (October 1975), p. 106.

40. European missionaries who saved many Northern Sudanese in the South during the 1955 Southern uprising were subsequently deported from the Sudan in early 1964 allegedly for helping Southerners.

41. See the *Report of the Commission of Inquiry*, p. 40.

42. For example, the massacre of Yei policemen who had been assembled to receive their pay after returning for duty.

43. This was particularly true in the period of party politics between 1965–1969.

44. Interviews with some Southern Members of Parliament at the time.

45. Marquis of Reading, interview, *East Africa and Rhodesia* (10 November 1955), pp. 330–331.

46. *The Middle East Journal*, vol. 10 (1956), pp. 192–193. Sir Knox Helm returned to Britian on 16 December 1956.

47. See Mahgoub, *Democracy on Trial*, pp. 56–57.

48. Reported in *East Africa and Rhodesia* (December 12, 1955), p. 648.

49. Ibid.

50. See Mahgoub, *Democracy on Trial*, p. 57.

51. Sayed Babiker Awadalla later became Speaker of the House of Representatives, Chief Justice, and for a while Prime Minister and Vice President under General Gaafar Mohammed el-Nimiery.

52. Parliment was sitting as a Constituent Assembly.

53. See Oduho and Deng, *The Problem of the Southern Sudan,* p. 36.

54. *The Middle East Journal* 10 (1956):192–193.

55. The South was allocated only 26.6 percent of representation in Parliament while it had 30 percent of the population in the country.

56. These Southerners who joined the Northern parties did not necessarily disagree with the Liberal Party platform. They only thought that they would pursue Southern interests more successfully within the dominant Northern parties. They were wrong: nobody listened to them and nobody feared them since they were considered "soft voices" susceptible to manipulation.

57. For the concepts of primary and secondary, see Mazrui, *Cultural Engineering and Nation-Building*, p. 286.

58. *The Middle East Journal*, 13 (1959):94.

59. *Report of the Commission of Inquiry*.

60. *Report of the Commission of Inquiry*, p. 7.

61. Ibid., p. 6.

62. *Report of the Commission of Inquiry*, p. 117.

63. Ibid., p. 7.

Chapter V

1. There was a feeling among the informed members of the Northern elite group that what the Sudan needed at that time was a strong and effective leadership like those of Egypt and

Pakistan under Army officers: Colonel Gamal Abdul Nasser and General Ayub Khan, respectively.

2. General Abboud's only Southerner in his government was Mr. Santino Deng, a former member of Parliament, a Dinka by tribe from Yirol District, Bahr el Ghazal Province. He was Minister of Animal Resources.

3. The South remained under a state of emergency from August 1955 to March 1972, until after ratification of the Addis Ababa Peace Agreement.

4. Cited in Peter Kilner, "A Year of Military Rule in the Sudan," *The World Today* (November 1959), pp. 260–261.

5. General Abboud wanted to experiment with both President Nasser's system of local government and with General Ayub Khan's basic democracy in Pakistan.

6. *Report of the Commission on Coordination Between the Central and Local Government* (Khartoum, Sudan), p. 9. Also, for a comprehensive discussion of Abboud's efforts to institute a system of local government democracy, see B. S. Sharma, *Elections in the Sudan During the Military Regime, Parliamentary Affairs*, vol. 20, no. 3 (Summer 1967), pp. 274–280. Also see Sharma's similar article in *Political Studies*, vol. 15 (1967). I am indebted to these articles for some information.

7. This was the system of participatory government that General Ayub Khan initiated in Pakistan. It did not prove entirely successful.

8. P. S. Casanova, "Internal Colonialism and National Development," in *Studies in Comparative International Development* (St. Louis: Social Science Institute, Washington University, 1965), vol. 1, no. 4, p. 33.

9. *Documents on the War in Sudan*, compiled by the Southern Front Party. I am indebted to a former Executive Member of the Southern Front for allowing me to look at these documents.

10. See *Rai el Amm* (Khartoum), 18 April 1960.

11. See *Anba el Sudan* (Khartoum), 9 March 1960.

12. Robert O. Collins, *The Southern Sudan in Historical Perspective* (Tel Aviv: University of Tel Aviv, the Israel Press, 1975), p. 76.

13. Ibid., p. 75.

14. Cited in *Sudan Law Journal and Report* (1962), p. 83.

15. The Missionary Societies Act, 1962. The motive of the act, according to the government, was to regularize the work of the missions. For the missionaries' reply see the *Black Book of the Sudan* (1964). All references that follow are from the Missionary Societies Act, 1962.

16. On the expulsion of the missionaries, see Government of the Sudan Statement, *The Missionary Societies Act* (Khartoum: Government Printing Office Press, 1962), p. 11.

17. Ibid., p. 17.

18. Collins, *The Southern Sudan in Historical Perspective*, p. 77.

19. For details, see Albino, *The Sudan*, p. 100.

20. Collins, *The Southern Sudan in Historical Perspective*, p. 78.

21. Oduho, Rume, and Fr. Lohure were former members of the House of Representatives which was dissolved following the Army coup of November 1958.

22. It was true that the quality of food in schools in the South was poor. The author was a student in Rumbek where the first strike took place. In Rumbek the food, especially the quality of the bread and beans, was bad. But what frightened us most was the presence of soldiers around the school buildings and dormitories at night. No satisfactory explanation was given for their presence.

23. Anya-Nya declaration of war, cited in Beshir, "The Southern Sudan," p. 84.

24. Abel Alier, speech delivered at the Makerere Students' Guild Center, Kampala, Uganda, February 9, 1970.

25. The abortive attempt by the Anya-Nya to capture Wau was led by Barnadino Mau who was captured by the Sudan Army and subsequently executed.

26. Bowyer Bell, "The Conciliation of Insurgency," p. 107.

27. The Presidential Commission was composed of nineteen Northerners and thirteen Southerners with a Northerner as chairman.

28. Robert O. Collins, "The Sudan: Link to the North," *The Transformation of East Africa: Studies in Political Anthropology*, in Stanley Diamond and Fred G. Burke, eds. (New York: Basic Books, 1966), pp. 1–2.

Chapter VI

1. William Deng, who was a founder member of the Southern Sudan Liberation Movement in exile, spent most of his time outside the Sudan traveling in Europe, the Americas, and Australia explaining the African-Arab conflict in the Sudan to the international community. He did more to publicize the Civil War at the time than any of his colleagues. He did not want to be subjected to anybody's authority or accountable to the SACDNU President, which made it difficult to work with Deng in a group.

2. See Speech of Prime Minister Sir el Khatim el Khalifa in *Documents on the Round Table Conference on the Southern Sudan* (Khartoum: Sudan Information News Agency, 1965). [Hereinafter referred to as *Documents on the Round Table Conference.*]

3. The Northern and the Southern politicians could not agree on the state of emergency in the Sudan: the Southerners argued that the government should lift it before and while the Round Table Conference was on. The Northerners argued that their security would be endangered if the state of emergency was lifted; they also thought that relaxing the state of emergency would give the Anya-Nya an opportunity to regroup.

4. The Southern Front Party was formed by Southern professionals in Khartoum after the civilian coup of October 1964. It was registered as political and became the most militant Southern group inside the country. Its policy was "self-determination" for the South.

5. William Deng tried hard in vain to persuade his SANU colleagues to go and operate from within the Sudan after the downfall of the military regime. He was thoroughly disappointed by the reactions to his suggestion and by the labels attached to him by his colleagues.

6. Santino Deng's Unity Party and those parties formed by other Southerners, such as Philimon Majok, Buth Diu, and Stanislaus Paysma, were heavily financed by Northern Sudanese who did not want unity among Southerners. Indeed, schisms among Southerners developed and rendered them at times ineffective.

7. See *Documents on the Round Table Conference*, p. 120.

8. Both the speeches of the Chairman of the Round Table Conference and of the Prime Minister blamed British imperial policy for having "allegedly" promoted the differences between the North and the South. This was the traditional and confirmed Northern view which was shared by all Northern politicians.

9. *Documents on the Round Table Conference*, p. 76.

10. *Documents on the Round Table Conference*, p. 162.

11. Ibid, p. 12.

12. *Documents on the Round Table Conference*, see M. O. Beshir, Southern Sudan: Background to Conflict (C. Hurst, 1968), *Appendix*.

13. *Documents on the Round Table Conference*, pp. 203, 207.

14. Ibid, p. 204.

15. It remains beyond my comprehension how it was believed that the Peace Commission could restore "law and order" since the conference did not change the fundamental aspects of the "law" on security which the Anya-Nya was fighting against. The phrase to "campaign for restoration of law and order" was a face-saving one for the conferees; the conference had failed.

16. *Documents on the Round Table Conference*, pp. 220–223.

17. Collins, *The Southern Sudan in Historical Perspective*, p. 83.

18. Alier, "The Southern Sudan Question," p. 23.

19. Ambrose Wol is a Dinka from Gogrial. He was editor of the *Sudan News*, the mouthpiece of Abboud's military regime. He wrote critical articles against the Southern movement in exile and lost the respect of Southerners. Ezibon Mondiri is a Moru. He was a founder member of the Federal Party, a former member of Parliament, and was imprisoned during the entire period of Abboud's regime. Clement Mboro is a Belanda from Bahr el Ghazal Province. He was a member of the Juba Conference of 1948, and later a Deputy Commissioner for several years.

20. Compare with the Round Table Conference Resolutions and the recommendations of the twelve-man committee.

21. I am indebted to a number of Southern Sudanese politicians in Khartoum during the period of the transitional government for most of the information in this section.

22. Southerners went to the airport to wait and welcome Clement Mboro, then Minister of Interior, who was scheduled to return to Khartoum from the Southern Sudan. Clement Mboro's plane was late but there was no proper explanation from the airport authorities to the Southerners who gathered at the airport. It was assumed that something might have happened to Mboro's plane and so Southerners got angry and thereafter physical confrontation ensued between them and the Northerners at the airport. The rioting expanded into the city. Most Southerners were later shipped to the South.

23. *Documents on the Southern Problem Compiled by the Southern Front Party* (Khartoum: Southern Front Party, 1965), pp. 5–8. [Hereinafter referred to as *Southern Front Party Documents*.]

24. *Southern Front Party Documents*, p. 7.

25. *Southern Front Party Documents*, p. 6.

26. *Africa Independent: A Study of Political Developments*, Kwesing's Research Report., no. 6 (1972), pp. 77–87.

27. Despite the fact that the Northern political parties agreed with the Southern parties that elections would be held only in the North, they went on to encourage some Northern traders in the South to declare themselves "elected unopposed." This was a clear breach of understanding by the Northern politicians. They were not ashamed to declare Northerners representatives of the South in Parliament.

28. *Southern Front Party Documents*, p. 3.

29. The South was thus represented in the Constituent Assembly by Northerners. No Southerners were members of the assembly since the Southern parties did not contest the elections purely because of the state of emergency and also partly because the Northern parties had agreed that elections would only be held in the North.

30. Collins, *The Southern Sudan in Historical Perspective*, p. 84.

31. See Dunstan M. Wai, "Political Trends in the Sudan and the Future of the South," in *The Southern Sudan*, ed. Wai, p. 152.

32. Ibid., p. 153.

33. Mohammed Omer Beshir, *The Southern Sudan: From Conflict to Peace* (London: C. Hurst, 1975), p. 16.

34. Particularly members of the Umma Party and the NUP, see Beshir, *The Southern Sudan: From Conflict to Peace*, p. 17.

35. Sam C. Sarkesian, "The Southern Sudan: A Reassessment," paper presented at the African Studies Association Annual Meeting, Philadelphia. Pa., November 8–11, 1972, p. 13.

36. The reconciliation and merger between the ALF and the SALF was the work of Dr. Justo Muludiang, Dr. Lawrence Wol Wol and Mr. George M. Lomoro. All three Southerners were educated in Europe and had opposed the replacement of Joseph Oduho as President of SANU by Aggrey Jaden. They argued that continuity in leadership was essential for the Southern movement. All of them were supporters of Joseph Oduho.

37. Collins, *The Southern Sudan in Historical Perspective*, p. 40.

38. See Wai, "Political Trends in the Sudan," p. 164.

39. Joseph Oduho was arrested and detained by the Anya-Nya Commander for Eastern Equatoria province, the then Colonel Joseph Lagu (a Madi by tribe) who was a protégé of Fr. Saturnino Lohure.

40. For instance Jaden's political bureau consisted of: Jaden (Equatoria) as President; Camelio Dhol Kwat (Bahr el Ghazal) as Vice President; Francis Mayer (Bahr el Ghazal) as Attorney General; and Severino Fulli (Equatoria) as Minister of Presidential Affairs. Upper Nile Province was well represented in the Executive Council composed of:

Name	*Position*	*Province*	*Tribe*
Aggrey Jaden	President	Equatoria	Pojulu
Akot Atem	Defense	Upper Nile	Dinka
Elia Lupe	Interior	Equatoria	Kakwa
Gordon M. Mayen	Foreign Affairs	Bahr el Ghazal	Dinka
Othwan Dak	Education	Upper Nile	Shilluk
Gabriel Kao	Justice	Bahr el Ghazal	—
George Kwanai	Information	Upper Nile	Shilluk
Lawrence Wol Wol	Agriculture	Bahr el Ghazal	Dinka
Joseph Oduho	Communications	Equatoria	Latuko
Elia Duang	Animal and Natural Resources	Bahr el Ghazal	Dinka
David Kwak	Social Affairs and Refugees	Upper Nile	—
Tadio Pedit	Finance and Economics	Bahr el Ghazal	—

41. See Wai, "Political Trends in the Sudan," p. 164.

42. Aggrey Jaden's supporters and admirers who were behind the formation of the "Anyidi Government" were Eliyoba Surur and Sarafino Wani Swaka. The former is a Pojulu as is Jaden and the latter is a Bari from Juba District.

43. Sudan Azania was formed by Ezibon Mondiri and Alphonso Malek Parjokdit; Sue River Republic was an organization of the Azande led by Michael Tawil; and the Anya-Nya organization was led by the then Colonel Joseph Lagu.

44. Colonel Joseph Lagu and Major General Taffeng constantly disagreed. The former thought the latter was an old man and militarily unfit to lead a guerrilla movement. Taffeng on the other hand envied Lagu's military talents and thought he was arrogant. I am indebted to various Anya-Nya officers who prefer to remain anonymous.

45. Collins, *The Southern Sudan in Historical Perspective*, p. 90. Compare this with my own description in Wai, "Political Trends in the Sudan," p. 165.

46. Among the most able Southern politicians were Hilary P. Logali, Abel Alier, William Deng, Bona Malwal, Samuel Aru, and Henry Bagu.

47. Coincidentally, the U.S. Supreme Court declared the loyalty oath, under which com-

munists and communist sympathizers were deprived of employment in state and federal departments and agencies.

48. See *Joseph Garang and Others v. The Constituent Assembly, High Court*, 1965, Khartoum, Sudan.

49. The Supreme Council was a political body and it was not a surprise that its views were partial. See *Proceedings of the Sudan Constituent Assembly*, October 1966, cited by Alier, "The Southern Sudan Question," p. 26.

50. Cited in Alier, "The Southern Sudan Question," p. 24.

51. See the *Christian Science Monitor*, April 26, 1966.

52. Sadiq el-Mahdi's speeches on the Civil War are similar to those of European colonial officers against nationalist uprising.

53. Luigi Odwok of the Southern Front Party Executive disagreed with his colleagues and contested the elections successfully in his home area in Malakal. He was expelled from the Southern Front party.

54. Particularly in areas where fighting was heavy.

55. See Alier, "The Southern Sudan Question," p. 25.

56. This was the view of Ali Abdul Rahman, a former Minister of Interior. See *Parliamentary Proceedings: Second Sitting of the First Session of Parliament*, 1958, p. 3.

57. The Council of Ministers persuaded about 80 members to resign their seats in order to reduce the 210-person membership of the assembly below the two-thirds majority. This move was to reinforce the government's decision to dissolve the assembly for a general election.

58. The DUP came out strongly in the elections. The results were as follows:

Party	*Seats*
DUP	101
Umma (Sadiq)	36
Umma (Imam)	30
SANU	15
Southern Front	10
Islamic Charter Front	3
NUBA (GUN)	2
Beja	1
Socialists and Communists	2
Independents	10
Local Parties	6
Others	2
Total	218

59. William Deng continued to support the Anya-Nya in Bahr el Ghazal secretly, but this possibly became known to the authorities in view of the fact that he refused government escort during his campaign in the South.

60. See Wai, "Political Trends in the Sudan"; as Joseph Nye has argued, as much as corruption destroys the legitimacy of political structures in the eyes of those who have power to do something about the situation, corruption can contribute to instability and possibly to national disintegration. In the Sudan, corruption must have contributed to the aura of disillusion that preceded the coups of 1958 and 1969. See Joseph P. Nye, "Corruption and Political Development: A Cost-Benefit Analysis," *American Political Science Review*, vol. 11, no. 2 (June 1967).

61. See Sadiq el-Mahdi, "Reflections on Government and Politics in the Sudan: Our Experience in Office," paper delivered at Department of Political Science Staff Seminar, University of Khartoum, December 2, 1967, cited in Oluwadare Aguda, "The State and the Economy in the Sudan," *Journal of Developing Areas*, vol. 7, no. 3 (April 1973), p. 44.

62. Aguda, "The State and the Economy," p. 44.

63. See Sadiq el-Mahdi in interview reported in the *Christian Science Monitor*, April 26, 1966.

64. See Huntington, *Political Order in Changing Societies*, chap. 4.

65. Ibid.

Chapter VII

1. George Modelski, "The International Relations of Internal War," Research Monograph, no. 11, Center of International Studies, Woodrow Wilson School of Public and International Affairs (Princeton: Princeton University Press, May 1961), p. 9.

2. See D. W. Bowett, "Self-Determination and Political Rights in the Developing Countries," American Society of International Law, *Proceedings of Sixtieth Annual Meeting, 28–30 April 1966* (Washington, D.C., 1966), p. 129. I am indebted to this article for its intellectual resourcefulness.

3. This was the argument used by the Kenya delegation to the OAU [founding] Summit in 1963 against the Somalis of the Northern frontier district of Kenya who wanted to transfer their allegiance from Nairobi to Mogadishu. The Kenya statement became the basis of arguments against secessions in Africa. See Joseph P. Nye, *Pan-Africanism and East African Integration* (Cambridge: Harvard University Press, 1965), p. 40.

4. Balkanization meant the overthrow of empires in Europe and the setting up of new nations in the Balkans—Greece, Bulgaria, Yugoslavia, Albania, and Rumania. These countries have maintained their sovereign rights, but the small nations of Latvia, Lithuania, and Estonia were incorporated into the Soviet Union.

5. Bowett, "Self-Determination and Political Rights," p. 130.

6. The concept of "a people" is an illusive one. For some attempts at definition, see Rupert Emerson, "Self-Determination in the Era of Decolonization," an Occasional Paper, Center for International Affairs, Harvard University, 1964.

7. Bowett, "Self-Determination and Political Rights," p. 130.

8. Bowett, "Self-Determination and Political Rights," p. 130.

9. Richard West, "The Accusing Face of Young Biafra," *Sunday Times* (London), 1 June, 1969.

10. Bowett, "Self-Determination and Political Rights," p. 148.

11. Nye, *Pan-Africanism and East African Integration*, p. 40.

12. Bowett, "Self-Determination and Political Rights," p. 131.

13. Uganda became a republic in September 1967. The period in which Apollo Milton Obote was President is referred to as the First Republic. General Amin's Uganda is known as the Second Republic.

14. Tandon and Gingyera Pinycwa, "Uganda-Sudan Relations," p. 3.

15. For instance, Joseph H. Oduho, a founder member of the Southern Sudanese secessionist movement in exile, and Severino Fuli were imprisoned in February 1964 allegedly for organizing a rebel army against the Sudan. Lawrence Wol Wol, Justin Muludiang, and other prominent Southern Sudanese politicians living in Uganda in 1967 were detained by the Uganda government.

16. *Uganda Hansard,* 56 (January 13, 1966):469–470, cited in Gingyera, "Uganda-Sudan Relations," p. 4.

17. Tandon and Gingyera Pinycwa, "Uganda-Sudan Relations," pp. 10–11.

18. Tandon and Gingyera Pinycwa, "Uganda-Sudan Relations," p. 11. The opposition in the Uganda National Assembly introduced a motion of censure in January 1966 expressing "the deepest regret for the silence the Uganda government has displayed over the frequent violations by the Sudanese troops of our territorial integrity." *Uganda Hansard*, vol. 57 (January 21, 1966), cited in Tandon and Gingyera Pinycwa.

19. Interview with a member of the Sudanese Embassy in Kampala who participated in formulating the Sudanese government strategy in Uganda (1972).

20. Interview with a high-ranking official of the Simba rebellion who now lives in exile and prefers to remain anonymous (1973).

21. Ibid.

22. Biafra was recognized by four African states, namely, Tanzania, Zambia, Gabon, and Ivory Coast.

23. *Case for Recognition of Biafra, Tanzanian Statement*, April 13, 1968. The arguments and the style of that document were clearly from President Nyerere's pen. Cf. J. K. Nyerere, "The Nigerian/Biafra Crisis," Dar es Salaam (Tanzania) September 4, 1969 (memorandum for private circulation only).

24. Nyerere, "The Nigerian/Biafran Crisis."

25. For a good survey of Egyptian/Sudanese relations, see T. Y. Ismael, *The UAR in Africa: Egypt's Policy under Nasser* (Evanston, Ill.: Northwestern University Press, 1971), chap. 7.

26. This information is obtained from a variety of sources, see particularly the *Arab Report and Record* (published bimonthly) and *Africa Research Bulletin and Africa Confidential.*

27. For information on military aid to the Sudan, consult T. N. Dupuy and C. W. Blanchard, *The Almanac of World Military Power* (Dunn Lorgin, Va.: T. N. Dupuy Associates, 1972), pp. 259–61.

28. U.S. Information Services, *Bulletin, Press Conference in Yaounde*, Cameroon, September 19, 1968.

29. U.S. Department of State, *U.S. Aid: Economic, Military and Other, Prior to 1967, to the Republic of the Sudan* (unclassified material, 1976).

30. The current President of the Sudan, General Gaafar Mohammed el-Nimiery, was among Sudanese officers who received some training in the United States.

31. Some members of the Church of England and former colonial officials who worked in the Sudan, however, were staunch sympathizers with the Southern Sudanese cause.

32. See Dupuy and Blanchard, *The Almanac of World Military Power*, pp. 259–61.

33. When the Anya-Nya regrouped in October 1962, most of them were armed with long knives ("pangas"), spears, and sticks. Gradually, they began to get some old guns, mainly from Southern Sudanese defectors from either the Sudan Army or the Police.

34. Interview with a former Simba official, who coordinated his movements' demands with the Arab governments.

35. Ibid.

36. Of course, this is a matter of opinion. Cf. Tandon and Gingyera, "Uganda-Sudan Relations," pp. 10–12.

37. See John Howell and Beshir Hamid, "Sudan and the Outside World, 1964–1968," *African Affairs*, vol. 68, no. 273 (October 1969), p. 303.

38. See *Africa Digest*, vol. 15, no. 5 (October 1968), p. 100. Later in 1971, General Idi Amin of Uganda joined President Banda's denunciation of the Sudan government policies toward the Southern Sudan. The Sudan had given political asylum to Obote who was organizing an army in the Sudan to invade Uganda. Eventually Obote's forces invaded Uganda from the Tanzanian side. It was a disastrous operation.

39. *The Grass Curtain*, published under the auspices of the Southern Sudan Association Ltd. in London, carried an article in its October 1971 issue denouncing Rolf Steiner. The article

disclaimed Steiner's confession that he was recruited to fight for the Southern Sudanese cause. See *Grass Curtain*, vol. 2, no. 2 (October 1971), p. 2.

40. For instance, the Verona Fathers, expelled from the Sudan in 1964, published *The Black Book of the Sudan* (1965), in which they denied the charges against them point by point and criticized the Khartoum policies in the South.

41. It must, of course, be remembered that the Israeli aid to the Anya-Nya was not a new departure from her policy in the Middle East in that she accorded similar aid to the Yemeni royalists after an Egyptian-backed coup ousted the Yemeni royal family from power in 1962.

42. Biafra had many leaders of international standing, for example, to mention only a few: Dr. N. Azikiwe, Sir Louis Mbanefo, and Professor Kenneth O. Dike.

43. Also see A. G. G. Gingyera-Pinycwa, "The Border Implications of the Sudan Civil War: Possibilities for Intervention," in *The Southern Sudan*, ed. Wai, pp. 128–135. Cf. the Angolan Civil War, 1975–1976.

44. Moelski, "The International Relations of Internal War," p. 1.

Chapter VIII

1. The World Council of Churches (WCC) is formally international in control, multinational in personnel, and transnational in operations. It is a transnational organization in that its transnational interactions are institutionalized. For description of the structure, functions and activities of the WCC, see R. Rouse and S. C. Neill, ed., *A History of the Ecumenical Movement,* vol. 1 (London: Oxford University Press, 1967); N. Goodall, *Ecumenical Progress 1961–1971* (London: Oxford University Press, 1972); H. Fey, ed., *A History of the Ecumenical Movement,* vol. 2 (London: Oxford University Press, 1970).

2. Kodwo Ankrah, "In Pursuit of Peace in the Sudan," *Study Encounter*, vol. 8, no. 2 (1972), p. 4. For most of the information in this section, I am indebted to many Southern Sudanese politicians for allowing me to consult their files at various times.

3. Ankrah, "In Pursuit of Peace," p. 4. Also see AACC's *Confidential Memorandum: Mission to Sudan* (Nairobi, Kenya, 1966).

4. Although the AACC is critical of internal oppression in African countries, it publicly accepts the rhetoric of African leaders about neocolonial activities in the African continent.

5. The Rt. Rev. O. Allison, then Bishop of the Sudan, in an address to a group of people including some Southern exiles in the house of Dr. Tom Watson at Makerere University, sounded sympathetic toward the Sadiq el-Mahdi government and urged Southern Sudanese refugee students to return home. His advice was not well received.

6. The AACC met in Abidjan, Ivory Coast, in 1969 and discussed "The Christian Response to the African Revolution" and "the abuse by governments and individuals" of newly acquired power in Africa, and the role of the churches in their appointed task of reconciliation. The Nigeria-Biafra war and the African-Arab war in the Sudan influenced much of the agenda for discussions. Many questions on the role of the Church in Africa were raised at this Conference. Although it was a Regional Conference of the WCC (the AACC is affiliated to the WCC as a Regional Council Member), some delegates from the WCC member churches attended it. See *Proceedings of the AACC Conference in Abidjan, Ivory Coast*, 1969.

7. For details of the return of the soldiers to power in the Sudan, see Dunstan M. Wai, "Civilian-Military Regimes and the Crisis of Political Participation in the Sudan," in *The Search for Political Legitimacy in Africa* (forthcoming) ed. Dunstan M. Wai.

8. *Policy Statement on the Southern Question by President Nimiery, June 9, 1969* (Khartoum, Ministry of Information, 1969), p. 2.

9. Ibid.

10. I was President of the Southern Sudanese Makerere Students' Union at the time, and I participated in the formulation of this stand. At the beginning, it was an unpopular position, but gradually all the Southern Sudanese political factions, including the Anya-Nya Army leadership, came to accept it.

11. I was Secretary of the Southern Sudanese Makerere Students' Union delegation to the Sudan. The visit was sponsored by the Ministry for Southern Affairs, Khartoum, Sudan. All the details of the visit were finalized through the United Nations High Commission for Refugee's Office in Kampala, Uganda and the Uganda Ministry of Culture and Community Development which was in charge of refugees.

12. The report was comprehensive. It analyzes the reactions to the policy of regional autonomy and the attitude of Southerners towards the Nimiery regime. The military situation in the South was also described. The report was accepted as a good one by the Sudan government and Southern exiles. J. Garang, Minister for Southern Affairs (now deceased), told me in September 1970 that he was amazed by the verbatim accounts of various meetings he had with the members of the delegation embodied in the report and yet they were not taped.

13. Joseph U. Garang, "On Economics and Regional Autonomy," in *The Southern Sudan*, ed. Wai, pp. 83–92.

14. The slogan was the building of "a democratic movement" in the South, which meant the building of a branch of the Sudan Communist Party in the Southern region under the control of Joseph Garang. Garang was aware that he did not have a political base in the South and was therefore interested in building one before the full implementation of the policy of regional autonomy.

15. The Association of Southern Intellectuals in Khartoum criticized Garang for his emphasis on the building of a socialist democratic movement before the definition of regional autonomy. Most Southern elites became disenchanted with the Ministry for Southern Affairs under Garang.

16. Memorandum sent to President Gaafar M. Nimiery and members of the Revolutionary Command Council by Southern Sudanese Students and Youth Organization, Khartoum, November 19, 1970.

17. Speech by President Nimiery reported in *Al-Ahram* newspaper (Cairo), November 1970.

18. For details, see Wai, "Political Trends in the Sudan," pp. 157–159.

19. The abortive coups against the Nimiery regime in September 1975 and July 1976 were engineered and planned by the leader of the Mahdists (Ansars), Sadiq el-Mahdi.

20. There are four rival ideological groups in the Northern Sudan: (1) the secular nationalists, who favor a policy of closer friendships with their African rather than their Arab neighbors; this is now the largest group and it is supported by the Southern Sudanese; (2) the Muslim Brothers, who wish to turn the Sudan into a militant and purified Islamic state; (3) the communists, who are split between a pro-Moscow faction and one closer to Arab socialism; both basically share the same views as the nationalists about greater cooperation with non-Arab Africa; and (4) the pan-Arabists, possibly the smallest group, which gives high priority to the Arab cause and to active involvement against Israel. On coming to power, General Nimiery made alliances with groups (1), (3), and (4). He moved against (4), and is now largely backed by (1). He maintains an independent Arabist policy from group (4).

21. These were: Dr. Gaafar Bakheit, Minister of Local Government and the theoretician of the Sudan Socialist Union; Dr. Mansour Khalid, then Minister of Foreign Affairs and now Minister of Higher Education; Major General Mohammed el Baghir Ahmed, Vice President; Vice President Abel Alier, also President of HEC.

22. For a similar point of view, see J. Bowyer Bell, "The Sudan's African Policy Problems and Prospects," *Africa Today*, vol. 20, no. 3 (Summer 1973), pp. 93–121.

23. President Nimiery was the only candidate in the Presidential plebiscite.

24. The group of Southerners included Hilary P. Logali, Samuel Aru, Natale O. Akolawin, Andrew Wieu, Cleoto Hassan, Samuel Lupai, Moses Chol, and Buth Diu.

25. A few of the Southern politicians assumed the role of being representatives of the SSLM in East Africa and Europe without having been appointed. They were, however, eventually confirmed by the Anya-Nya Army leader, Joseph Lagu.

26. January 31, 1972.

27. Mading de Garang was based in London, and Lawrence Wol Wol lived at the time in France, where he devoted part of his time to doctoral studies.

28. The Roman Catholic Church was involved in the propagation of Christianity in the Southern Sudan for many years, and most of the missionaries expelled from the Sudan in 1964 were Catholic priests. The Catholic press at the Vatican carried articles on the sufferings of peoples in the Southern Sudan much against the liking of the Sudan government. The Catholic circles were certainly happy that Alier visited the Pope to brief him on the new policy toward the Southern region. This tactic placated some Southern exiles who were members of the Catholic Church.

29. Ankrah, "In Pursuit of Peace," p. 7.

30. Ibid.

31. Ibid, p. 8.

32. Letter from Mading de Garang and Lawrence Wol Wol to Dr. L. Niilus, Director of the WCC's CCIA, Geneva, June 28, 1971.

33. Letter from the CCIA to the SSLM's representatives in Europe, Mading de Garang and Lawrence Wol Wol.

34. Letter from Major General Lagu, the Anya-Nya Army Commander to Mading de Garang, cited in Ankrah, "In Pursuit of Peace," p. 6.

35. Letter from Lawrence Wol Wol and Mading de Garang to Dr. L. Niilus, Director, CCIA (August 30, 1971).

36. Elisapana Mula attended the meeting as a personal representative of Major General Lagu, but he was only an observer. As the preliminary talks progressed, all the observers were dispensed with, and Mading de Garang and Lawrence Wol Wol were the only two who represented the SSLM, while Abel Alier and Major General Mohammed el-Baghir Ahmed represented the Sudan government.

37. This was a turning point and a major breakthrough in that the public position of the SSLM had always been secession of the Southern region from the rest of the Sudan.

38. Mading de Garang was charged in Malakal in the mid-1960s for collaborating with the Anya-Nya Army. Abel Alier who was in private practice at the time, defended him in court. Soon after the case was over, Mading de Garang left the Sudan.

39. This view was widely held by some foreign individuals who generously contributed to the education of Southern Sudanese refugee students and also made material contributions to the refugees settled in camps in Uganda. Some of them became self-styled advisers to the Southern Sudanese politicians in exile.

40. This was a strategy to persuade the SSLM negotiators at Addis Ababa that the Sudan government was genuine in what it was saying about resettlement of refugees and reconstruction of the region after a negotiated settlement.

41. These were: Natale O. Akolawin (who was at the time studying at Oxford University); Dr. Justin Yac (on medical postgraduate research in London); Dr. Francis M. Deng (Human Rights Officer, U.N. at the time), and Bona M. Ring (at the time a student in New York).

42. All the members of the Sudan Diplomatic Missions in Ethiopia, Uganda, Kenya, and Zaire were Northern Sudanese and were hated by the Southern exiles because they had been spying on their activities.

43. I talked to a number of Southerners from Equatoria province in London and I learned

that there were complaints against the way the preliminary talks were being conducted. On a closer examination of the facts, I concluded that there was resentment against the Dinka for allegedly dominating the discussions with the Sudan government.

44. Vice President Abel Alier had already successfully won the support of two members of Nimiery's inner Cabinet: Major General Mohammed el Baghir Ahmed and Dr. Gaafar Bakheit.

45. The emperor was represented by a certain Nabiy elu Kifle.

46. Canon Burgess Carr preferred to be referred to as a moderator, but he chaired the talks.

47. All references here are to *The Addis Ababa Agreement on the Problem of South Sudan.*

48. See chap. 4, art. 7 of the *Draft Organic Law to Organize Regional Self-Government in the Southern Provinces of the Democratic Republic of the Sudan.*

49. Ibid., art. 11, sec. ii, iii, xi.

50. Ibid., art. 2.

51. Ibid., art. 25, chap. 8.

52. Ibid., chaps. 5 and 6.

53. Ibid., art. 22.

54. The extension was for two weeks.

55. Particularly chap. 6, on the powers of the HEC versus the national President. It was thought that the national President was given too much control over both the regional President and the HEC.

56. President Nimiery decided to publicly ratify the Addis Ababa Agreement in his birthplace at Wad Nubawi in Omdurman, to a receptive audience.

57. When General Lagu went to Addis Ababa, no one among the politicians in East Africa was sure that he would ratify the peace accord. Many thought that he would press for reduction of the powers of the national President on the HEC before ratifying it. He did not.

58. Bowyer Bell, "The Sudan's African Policy Problems." Also see *Grass Curtain*, vol. 2, no. 3 (May 1972), pp. 8–9.

59. See the text of Resolution No. 6692/058//92 adopted by the Arab League in its 58th Ordinary Session held in Cairo between 9–13 September 1972.

60. President L. Senghor of Senegal in a congratulatory message to President Nimiery of the Sudan (Ministry of Information Bulletin, Sudan 1972).

61. *Sunday Nation* (Nairobi), 5 March 1972.

62. Maybe the "solution" of the African-Arab conflict in the Sudan underscores its uniqueness as a problem in postindependent Africa.

63. See text of the speech delivered by President Nimiery on March 3, 1972, at Wad Nubawi, Omdurman on the Southern problem (Khartoum), pp. 4–5.

64. Nimiery accused Amin of being an agent of imperialism and Zionism and urged Ugandans to overthrow him. Amin hit back that "there is no difference between the way the Sudanese government treats black Africans and Christians and the way the South Africans treat Africans. Both are barbarous and aggressive. Refugees from the Sudan are coming into Uganda in large numbers: some without an arm or with multiple injuries." Amin insisted that Uganda's involvement with the Southern Sudanese was purely humanitarian and he offered to pay the air fares of a Sudanese military reconnaissance mission and put his presidential helicopter at their disposal to ascertain that there were Sudanese guerrillas operating from Uganda. He claimed "if I want to help the Southern Sudanese . . . I would have done so directly and not through Israel." Amin has since then come out strongly in support of the Arabs in the Middle East War. After the Peace Settlement in the Sudan, President Nimiery stopped training Obote's supporters. See *Uganda Argus*, September 21 and 23, 1971, October 9, 1971, for exchanges between Amin and Nimiery.

65. When the negotiators disagreed on the proportion of troops to be stationed in the Southern region, they turned to Emperor Haile Selassie who suggested parity. The emperor's suggestion was accepted by both sides.

66. This is in no way to minimize the important role of the WCC in the resolution of the Sudan conflict. It had, after all, assumed that role as far back as 1965, four years before General Nimiery came to power. The point is that the WCC's role was made much easier by a number of factors mentioned here.

67. As it will be shown in chapter IX, the WCC played a significant role in relief and rehabilitation in the Southern Sudan after the peace agreement.

68. See the WCC's resolution on *Unity and Human Rights in Africa* adopted during the CCIA's meeting at Addis Ababa, Ethiopia, January 10–21, 1971.

69. Whether the WCC will play a similar mediating role in other conflicts in Africa such as those in Southern Africa, remains unclear. It may not find it easy to assume a mediating position because it is no longer an impartial observer of the confrontations between the white minority regimes and the African liberation movements: both the WCC and the AACC have identified themselves with the freedom fighters. In fact, support for the liberation movements, morally, financially, and materially, is unanimous among the membership of the AACC.

In August 1976, the WCC donated $560,000 to thirty-seven antiracist groups and to groups fighting racial discrimination. About $275,000 of that sum was given to black African liberation movements. *International Herald Tribune*, published with the *New York Times* and *Washington Post*, Paris, August 20, 1976.

Chapter IX

1. *The Addis Ababa Agreement on the Problem of South Sudan, 1972*. See Appendix VII, in Wai, ed., *The Southern Sudan* (1973). [Hereinafter referred to as *The Addis Ababa Agreement*.]

2. Tristram Betts, *The Southern Sudan: The Cease-Fire and After* (London: The Africa Publications Trust, 1974), p. 5.

3. Ibid., p. 4.

4. UNHCR (Geneva, October 1974), p. 5.

5. For details of contributions by the international agencies for repatriation, resettlement, relief, rehabilitation, and development in the Southern Sudan, see Betts, *The Cease-Fire and After*.

6. *The Addis Ababa Agreement*, "Protocols of Interim Arrangements," chap. 11, art. 2.

7. Since the peace agreement, there have been two minor incidents in Juba and Akobo (Upper Nile Province) involving the Anya-Nya in a confrontation with their own officer (in case of the Juba incident), and with a unit of the National Army (in case of the Akobo incident). The soldiers involved were court-martialed and sentenced accordingly. Since then no incident has occurred arising out of the planned integration of the two forces.

8. Abel Alier, speech on occasion of National United Day celebrations, Juba, March 2, 1973, p. 2 (mimeographed).

9. Many Southern Sudanese who were not actively in the services of the Anya-Nya Army turned up as Anya-Nya soldiers after the peace agreement so that they could be given jobs.

10. These officers included Major General Taffeng, who was once the figurehead of the Anya-Nya Army, and Major Ali Batala, who also served in the Anya-Nya forces. Both were officers in the Southern Corps.

11. *Report of the Joint Military Commission*, Khartoum, October 1972.

12. The Regional Ministers of the Provisional HEC included: Vice President Abel Alier (President of the HEC); Hilary P. Logali (Finance, Planning, and Natural Resources); Mading de Garang (Information, Culture, and Tourism); Ezibon Mondiri (Communications and Transport); Gamma Hassan (Agriculture and Animal Production); Dr. Toby Maduot (Health); Elia Lupe (Public Service and Labor); Joseph H. Oduho (Housing and Public Utilities); Michael Tawil (Rural Development and Cooperatives); Michael Duany (Cabinet Affairs); Samuel Aru (Regional Administration, Police and Prisons). Luigi Adwok (Education). Messrs. Alier, Logali, and Adwok were formerly members of the Southern Front; Oduho, Mondiri, and Lupe were veteran Southern Sudanese political exiles; Mading de Garang was at one time a Southern Front member and later SSLM representative in Europe based in London; Tawil was with the Anya-Nya Army; Gamma Hassan was not actively involved in the Southern Sudanese politics of liberation, and worked for an Italian multinational corporation; Samuel Aru and Toby Maduot (were former SANU members); Duany (was a student in the United States).

13. For details, see A. K. Pickering and G. W. Glentworth, *Development Administration and Training in the Sudan: Report of a Mission to the Sudan, March–June 1974* (Birmingham, England: Development Administration Group, Institute of Local Government Studies, University of Birmingham, 1974.

14. Ibid., p. 15. The Ministry of Local Government has been abolished.

15. Ibid., pp. 13–15.

16. *The Addis Ababa Agreement*; "Protocols on Interim Arrangements," art. 7.

17. For a detailed discussion of the elections and the evolution of a new political system in the Sudan, see Timothy C. Niblock, "A New Political System in the Sudan," *African Affairs*, vol. 73, no. 293 (October 1974).

18. The defeated Regional Ministers were: Michael Duany, Samuel Aru, Elia Lupe, Luigi Adwok, and Ezibon Mondiri. In the 1978 elections, all the above ministers, except for Elia Lupe, who died, were elected. General Lagu succeeded Abel Alier as President of the HEC.

19. *The Addis Ababa Agreement,* chap. 4, art. 19.

20. There were only four Southern Sudanese in Politbureau of the SSU: Abel Alier, Hilary P. Logali, Lawrence Wol Wol, and Joseph Lagu. The total number of the members of the Politbureau is about twenty, but the number kept changing frequently depending on the political fortunes of the members.

21. The following national departments of the state are the exclusive monopoly of the Northern Sudanese: Foreign Affairs; National Security Committee; Finance, Planning, Foreign Trade, and Higher Education.

22. Myron Weiner, "Political Integration and Political Development," *The Annals of the American Academy of Political and Social Science*, vol. 358, no. 2 (March 1965), pp. 52–64.

23. Ibid., p. 53.

24. Huntington, *Political Order in Changing Societies*, pp. 37–38.

25. This is the view expressed by Milton J. Esman, see his paper on "Management of Communal Conflict," (October 1972) (mimeograph). I am indebted to this article for some intellectual insights.

26. K. C. Wheare, *Federal Government* (New York, 1964). Wheare suggested the following six conditions as being necessary for a successful federation: (1) a sense of military insecurity and of the consequent need for a common defense; (2) a desire to be independent of foreign powers, for which union is a necessity; (3) a hope for economic advantage from the union; (4) some previous political association; (5) geographical neighborhood; and (6) similarity of political institutions.

27. For some comments and criticism of Wheare's model of federalism, consult A. H. Birch, "Approaches to the Study of Federalism," *Political Studies*, vol. 14, no. 1 (February 1966).

Also see Michael B. Stein, "Federal Political System of Federal Societies," *World Politics*, vol. 20, no. 4 (July 1968).

28. Birch, "Approaches to the Study of Federalism," p. 18. Also consult Carl Friedrich, "International Federalism in Theory and Practice," in *Systems of Integrating the International Community*, ed., Elmer Plischle (New York, 1964).

29. Ibid.

30. Riker, *Federalism, Origin, Operation Significance*, p. 11.

31. Ibid.

32. Ibid., p. 12.

33. For example, Mexico.

34. For example, the Soviet Union.

35. *The Federalist*, no. 10 (New York: Random House), p. 61. I have benefited, and indeed borrowed some ideas expressed on this page from the writings of Donald Rothchild. See particularly, D. Rothchild, "The limits of Federalism: An Examination of Political Institutional Transfer in Africa," *Journal of Modern African Studies,* Vol. 4, No. 3, November, 1960, pp. 275–293; "From Federalism to Neo-Federalism in East Africa," *Institute for Development Studies* (Nairobi: University College), Discussion paper No. 34, (December, 1960).

36. In February, 1980, the SSU Congress approved a policy of regionalism in the North—it could make the Sudan a federal state if implemented fully.

Chapter X

1. Parallels between Southern Sudan and Katanga were virtually nonexistent. There was no external interest pulling strings in Southern Sudan as did, for example, the Union Miniére in Zaire. Katanga had been a clear case of foreign agitation and not of genuine secession by the people of Katanga. Indeed, the people who spearheaded the secession of Katanga were predominantly Europeans—it was an abortive maneuver for the recapture of the natural resources of Zaire (Shaba I and II were different events from the attempted Katanga secession in that they were aimed at ultimately capturing power in Kinshasa).

On the other hand, the Southern Sudanese case was entirely different. There was absolutely no element of military intervention by the former metropolitan power in support of its cause. Also there was no significant selfish economic consideration whatsoever in the Southern Sudan's decision to secede. That is, the Southern Sudanese case was indigenously rooted and was not imposed by external actors to protect their interests.

2. Crawford Young, *Politics of Cultural Pluralism,* University of Wisconsin Press, 1976, p. 473.

3. Crawford Young, *The Politics of Cultural Pluralism* (Madison: University of Wisconsin Press, 1976), p. 503.

4. Louis B. Sohn, "The Role of the U.N. in Civil War," *American Society of International Law Proceedings* 57 (1963): pp. 208–215.

Bibliography

Books

Abbas, Mekki. *The Sudan Question*. London: Faber and Faber, 1952.

Abd-al-Rahim, Muddathir. *Imperialism and Nationalism in the Sudan*. Oxford: Oxford University Press, 1969.

———, ed. *Fourteen Documents on the Problem of the Southern Sudan*. New York: United Nations, 1965.

Albino, Oliver. *The Sudan: A Southern Viewpoint*. London: Oxford University Press, 1970.

Apter, David E. *Choice and the Politics of Allocation*. New Haven: Yale University Press, 1971.

———. *The Political Kingdom*. Princeton: Princeton University Press, 1967.

Apter, David E., and Eckstein, Harry, eds. *Comparative Politics*. New York: The Free Press of Glencoe, 1963.

Barbour, K. M. *The Republic of the Sudan: A Regional Geography*. London: University of London Press, 1961.

Beshir, Mohammed Omer. *The Southern Sudan: Background to Conflict*. London: C. Hurst, 1968.

———. *The Southern Sudan: From Conflict to Peace*. London: C. Hurst, 1975.

Betts, Tristram. *The Southern Sudan: The Cease-Fire and After*. London: The Africa Publications Trust, 1974.

Butt, Audrey. *The Nilotes of the Anglo-Egyptian Sudan and Uganda*. London: International African Institute, 1952.

Cash, W. W. *The Changing Sudan*. London: Church Missionary Society, 1930.

The Central Office of Information. *Basic Facts About the Southern Provinces of the Sudan*. Khartoum: The Central Office of Information, 1964.

Cobban, Alfred. *The Nation State and National Self-Determination*. New York: Thomas Y. Crowell, 1969.

Coleman, James S., and Rosberg, Carl G., eds. *Political Parties and National Integration in Tropical Africa*. Berkeley: University of California Press, 1970.

Collins, Robert O. *The Southern Sudan 1883–1898*. New Haven: Yale University Press, 1962.

———. *The Southern Sudan in Historical Perspective*. Tel Aviv: University of Tel Aviv, The Israel Press, 1975.

Deng, Francis M. *Dynamics of Identification: A Basis for National Integration in the Sudan*. Khartoum: Khartoum University Press, 1973.

Despres, Leo A. *Cultural Pluralism and Nationalist Politics in British Guiana*. Chicago: University of Chicago Press, 1967.

Deutsch, Karl W. *Nationalism and Social Communication*. Cambridge: The MIT Press, 1953.

———. *The Nerves of Government*. New York: The Free Press, 1963.

Deutsch, Karl W., and Foltz, W., eds. *Nation-Building*. New York: Atherton Press, 1966.

Diamond, Stanley, and Burke, Fred G., eds. *The Transformation of East Africa: Studies in Political Anthropology*. New York: Basic Books, 1966.

Doro, M. E., and Stultz, N. M., eds. *Governing in Black Africa: Perspectives on New States*. Englewood Cliffs, N.J.: Prentice-Hall, 1970.

Dotson, Floyd, and Dotson, Lillian O. *The Indian Minority in Zambia, Rhodesia, and Malawi*. New Haven: Yale University Press, 1968.

Duncan, J. S. R. *The Sudan: A Record of Achievement, 1898–1947*. Edinburgh: William Blackwood and Sons, 1952.

———. *The Sudan's Path to Independence*. Edinburgh: William Blackwood and Sons, 1957.

Dupuy, T. N., and Blanchard, C. W. *The Almanac of World Military Power*. Dunn Lorgin, Va.: T. N. Dupuy Associates, 1972.

Eckstein, Harry. *History and Theory*, vol. 4, no. 2. Middletown, Conn.: Wesleyan University Press, 1965.

———, ed. *Internal War*. London: The Free Press, 1963.

Eisenstadt, S. N. *Modernization: Protest and Change*. Englewood Cliffs, N.J.: Prentice-Hall, 1966.

Emerson, Rupert. *Self-Determination Revisited in the Era of Decolonization*. Occasional Papers in International Affairs. Cambridge: Center for International Affairs, Harvard University, 1964.

Fabian Society. *The Sudan: The Road Ahead*. London: Faber and Faber, 1947.

Fanon, Frantz. *The Wretched of the Earth*. New York: Grove Press, 1968.

Fey, H., ed. *A History of the Ecumenical Movement*. London: Oxford University Press, 1970, vol. 2.

Friedland, W. H., and Rosberg, Carl G., eds. *African Socialism*. Stanford, Calif.: Stanford University Press, 1967.

Furnival, J. S. *Colonial Policy and Practice*. Cambridge: Cambridge University Press, 1948.

Geertz, Clifford, ed. *Old Societies and New States*. New York: The Free Press, 1963.

Goodall, Norman. *Ecumenical Progress, 1961–1971*. London: Oxford University Press, 1972.

Graham, Hugh Davis, and Gurr, Ted Robert, eds. *Violence in America: Historical and Comparative Perspectives*. New York: Bantam, 1969.

Gray, Richard. *A History of the Southern Sudan, 1839–1889*. London: Oxford University Press, 1961.

Grundy, Kenneth W. *Guerrilla Struggle in Africa: An Analysis and Preview*. New York: Grossman Publishers, 1971.

Gurr, Ted Robert. *Why Men Rebel*. Princeton: Princeton University Press, 1970.

Hassan, Yusuf Fadl, ed. *Sudan in Africa*. Khartoum: Khartoum University Press, 1971.

Holt, P. M. *The Mahdist State in the Sudan, 1881–1899: A Study of Its Origins, Development, and Overthrow*. Oxford: Clarendon Press, 1970.

Huntington, Samuel P. *Political Order in Changing Societies*. New Haven: Yale University Press, 1968.

Ismael, T. Y. *The U. A. R. in Africa: Egypt's Policy Under Nasser*. Evanston, Ill.: Northwestern University Press, 1971.

Jackson, R. J., ed. *Issues in Comparative Politics*. New York: St. Martin's Press, 1971.

Keller, Suzanne. *Beyond the Ruling Class: Strategic Elites in Modern Society*. New York: Random House, 1963.

Kuper, Leo, and Smith, M. G., eds. *Pluralism in Africa*. Berkeley: University of California Press, 1969.

Lasswell, Harold. *Politics: Who Gets What, When, How*. New York: Meridian Books, 1960.

Leys, Colin. *Underdevelopment in Kenya: The Political Economy of Neo-Colonialism*. Berkeley: University of California Press, 1974.

Lipset, Seymour Martin. *Political Man*. New York: Anchor Books, 1963.

Low, D. Anthony, and Pratt, C. R., eds. *Buganda and British Overrule*. Oxford: Oxford University Press, 1960.

MacMichael, Harold. *A History of the Arabs in the Sudan*. New York: Barnes & Noble, 1967.

Mahgoub, Mohammed Ahmed. *Democracy on Trial*. London: Andre Deutsch, 1974.

Mazuri, Ali. *Cultural Engineering and Nation-Building in East Africa*. Evanston, Ill.: Northwestern University Press, 1972.

Middleton, John, and Tait, David. *Tribes Without Rulers: Studies in African Segmentary Systems*. London: Routledge and Kegan Paul, 1958.

Mill, John Stuart. *Representative Government* (1861). Reprint ed. New York: Dutton, 1962.

Mills, C. W. *The Power Elite*. New York: Oxford University Press, 1956.

Moore, John Norton, ed. *Laws and Civil War in the Modern World.* Baltimore, Md.: The Johns Hopkins University Press, 1974.

Nordlinger, Eric A. *Conflict Regulation in Divided Societies.* Occasional Papers in International Affairs, no. 29. Cambridge: Harvard University Press, 1972.

———, ed. *Politics and Society.* Englewood Cliffs, N.J.: Prentice-Hall, 1970.

Nye, Joseph P. *Pan-Africanism and East African Integration.* Cambridge: Harvard University Press, 1965.

Oduho, Joseph, and Deng, William. *The Problem of the Southern Sudan.* London: Oxford University Press, 1963.

Parsons, Talcott; Shils, Edward: Naegele, Kaspar D.; and Pitts, Jesse R., eds. *Theories of Society.* New York: The Free Press of Glencoe, 1961.

Plischle, Elmer, ed. *Systems of Integrating the International Community. Princeton: Princeton University Press, 1964.*

Riker, W. H. *Federalism, Origin, Operational Significance.* Boston: Little, Brown, 1964.

Rouse, R., and Neill, S. C., eds. *A History of the Ecumenical Movement.* Vol. 1. London: Oxford University Press, 1967.

Runciman, W. G. *Relative Deprivation and Social Justice.* Berkeley: University of California Press, 1966.

Said, Beshir Mohammed. *The Sudan: Crossroad of Africa.* Chester Springs, Pa.: Dufour Editions, 1965.

al-Sayid Baddur, Abdul Fattah Ibrahim. *Sudanese-Egyptian Relations: A Chronological and Analytical Study.* The Hague: Martinus Nijhoff, 1960.

Smith, M. G. *Plural Society in the British West Indies.* Berkeley: University of California Press, 1965.

Smock, A. *Ibo Politics: The Role of Ethnic Unions in Eastern Nigeria.* Cambridge: Harvard University Press, 1971.

Strachey, J., gen. ed. *Collected Papers.* Vol. 5. London: The Hogarth Press, 1932.

Toynbee, Arnold. *Between Niger and Nile.* London: Oxford University Press, 1965.

Van den Berghe, Pierre L. *South Africa: A Study in Conflict.* Middletown, Conn.: Wesleyan University Press, 1965.

Verona Fathers. *The Black Book of the Sudan.* Vatican City, Rome: Verona Fathers, 1965.

Vincent, R. J. *Nonintervention and International Order.* Princeton: Princeton University Press, 1974.

Von der Mehden, Fred R.; Anderson, Charles; and Young, Crawford. *Issues of Political Development.* Englewood Cliffs, N.J.: Prentice-Hall, 1967.

Wai, Dunstan M., ed. *Political Change and Political Participation in Africa.* Forthcoming.

——, ed. *The Southern Sudan: The Problem of National Integration.* London: Frank Cass, 1973.

Wheare, Kenneth C. *Federal Government.* London: Oxford University Press, 1951.

Wright, Q. M. *A Study of War.* Abridged by Louise Leonard. Chicago: The University of Chicago Press, 1969.

Young, Crawford. *The Politics of Cultural Pluralism.* Madison: The University of Wisconsin Press, 1976.

Zawodny, J. K., gen. ed. *Man and International Relations,* 2 vols. San Francisco: Chandler Publishing Company, 1966.

Articles and Reports

Abd-al-Rahim, Muddathir. "Arabism, Africanism, and Self-Identification in the Sudan." In *The Southern Sudan: The Problem of National Integration.* Edited by Dunstan M. Wai. London: Frank Cass, 1973.

——. "Introduction." In *Fourteen Documents on the Problem of the Southern Sudan.* Edited by Muddathir Abd-al-Rahim. New York: United Nations, 1965.

"The Addis Ababa Agreement on the Problem of South Sudan." Appendix 7. In *The Southern Sudan: The Problem of National Integration.* Edited by Dunstan M. Wai. London: Frank Cass, 1973.

Aguda, Oluwadare. "Arabism and Pan-Africanism in Sudanese Politics." *Journal of Modern African Studies*, vol. 11, no. 2 (1973).

——. "The State and the Economy in the Sudan." *Journal of Developing Areas*, vol. 7, no. 3 (April 1973).

Alier, Abel. "The Southern Sudan Question." In *The Southern Sudan: The Problem of National Integration.* Edited by Dunstan M. Wai. London: Frank Cass, 1973.

Ankrah, Kodwo. "In Pursuit of Peace in the Sudan." *Study Encounter,* vol. 8, no. 2 (1972).

Apter, David E. "Introduction to Non-Western Government and Politics." In *Comparative Politics.* Edited by David E. Apter and Harry Eckstein. New York: The Free Press of Glencoe, 1963.

Aron, Raymond. "Social Structure and the Ruling Class." *British Journal of Sociology*, vol. 1 (1950).

Barbour, K. M. "North and South in Sudan: A Study in Human Contrasts." *Annals of the Association of American Geographers*, vol. 54, no. 2 (June 1964).

——. "Tribal Administrative Framework." In K. M. Barbour. *The Republic of the Sudan: A Regional Geography.* London: University of London Press, 1961.

Bell, J. Bowyer. "The Conciliation of Insurgency: The Sudanese Experience." *Military Affairs*, vol. 39, no. 3 (October 1975).

———. "The Sudan's African Policy Problems and Prospects." *Africa Today,* vol. 20, no. 3 (Summer 1973).

Birch, A. H. "Approaches to the Study of Federalism." *Political Studies*, vol. 14, no. 1 (February 1966).

Bowett, D. W. "Self-Determination and Political Rights in the Developing Countries." American Society of International Law. *Proceedings of Sixtieth Annual Meeting, 28–30 April 1966.* Washington D.C.

Casanova, P. A. "Internal Colonialism and National Development." *Studies in Comparative International Development*, vol. 1, no. 4 (1965).

Collins, Robert O. "The Sudan: Link to the North." In *The Transformation of East Africa: Studies in Political Anthropology*. Edited by Stanley Diamond and Fred G. Burke. New York: Basic Books, 1966.

Davies, James D. "Toward a Theory of Revolution." *American Sociological Review*, vol. 27, no. 1 (February 1962).

Deutsch, Karl W. "External Involvement in Internal War." In *Internal War*. Edited by Harry Eckstein. London: The Free Press, 1963.

———. "The Growth of Nations: Some Recurrent Patterns of Political and Social Integration." *World Politics*, vol. 5 (January 1953).

Eckstein, Harry. "On the Causes of Internal Wars." In *Politics and Society*. Edited by Eric A. Nordlinger. Englewood Cliffs, N.J.: Prentice-Hall, 1970.

———. "Toward the Theoretical Study of Internal War." In *Internal War*. Edited by Harry Eckstein. London: The Free Press, 1963.

Esman, Milton J. "The Management of Communal Conflict." *Public Policy*, vol. 21 (Winter 1973).

Eysenck, H. J. "War and Aggressiveness: A Survey of Social Attitude Studies." In *Man and International Relations*, vol. 1. Edited by J. K. Zawodny. San Francisco: Chandler Publishing Company, 1966.

Feierabend, Ivo K.; Feirerabend, Rosalind L.; and Nesvold, Betty A. "Social Change and Political Violence: Cross-National Patterns." In *Violence in America: Historical and Comparative Perspectives*. Edited by Hugh Davis Graham and Ted Robert Gurr. New York: Bantam, 1969.

Friedrich, Carl. "International Federalism in Theory and Practice." In *Systems of Integrating the International Community*. Edited by Dunstan M. Wai. London: Frank Cass, 1973.

Garang, Joseph U. "On Economics and Regional Autonomy." In *The Southern Sudan: The Problem of National Integration*. Edited by Dunstan M. Wai. London: Frank Cass, 1973.

Geertz, Clifford. "The Integrative Revolution." In *Old Societies and New States*. Edited by Clifford Geertz. New York: The Free Press of Glencoe, 1963.

Gingyera-Pinycwa, A. G. G. "The Border Implications of the Sudan Civil War: Possibilities for Intervention." In *The Southern Sudan: The*

Problem of National Integration. Edited by Dunstan M. Wai. London: Frank Cass, 1973.

Gray, Richard. Introduction to *The Problem of the Southern Sudan*, by Joseph Oduho and William Deng. London: Oxford University Press, 1963.

Harlow, Vincent T. "Memorandum on the Projected Measures of Constitutional Reform in the Sudan." Appendix 2 in *Report of the Work of the Constitutional Amendment Commission*. Khartoum: McCorquedale, 1952.

Hassan, Yusaf Fadl. "External Islamic Influences and the Progress of Islamization in the Eastern Sudan Between the Fifteenth and Nineteenth Centuries." In *Sudan in Africa*. Edited by Yusuf Fadl Hassan. Khartoum: Khartoum University Press, 1971.

Hodgkin, T., and Morgenthau, Ruth Schachter. "Mali." In *Political Parties and National Integration in Tropical Africa*. Edited by James S. Coleman and Carl G. Rosberg. Berkeley: University of California Press, 1970.

Horowitz, Donald L. "Multiracial Politics in the New States." In *Issues in Comparative Politics*. Edited by R. J. Jackson. New York: St. Martin's Press, 1971.

Howell, John, and Hamid, Beshir. "Sudan and the Outside World." *African Affairs*, vol. 68, no. 273 (October 1969).

Huntington, Samuel P. "Civil Violence and the Process of Development." Adelphi Papers no. 83. London: The International Institute for Strategic Studies, 1972.

James, Wendy. "Social Assimilation and Changing Identity in the Southern Funj." In *Sudan in Africa*. Edited by Yusuf Fadl Hassan. Khartoum: Khartoum University Press, 1971.

Keesings Research Report 6. *Africa Independent: A Study of Political Development*. New York: Charles Scribner's Sons, 1972.

Kilner, Peter. "A Year of Military Rule in the Sudan." *The World Today* (November 1959).

Kilson, Martin L., Jr. "The Masses, the Elite, and Post-Colonial Politics in Africa." *Journal of Modern African Studies*, vol. 1 (1963).

Kirk-Greene, A. H. M. "The Genesis of the Nigerian Civil War and the Theory of Fear." *Scandinavian Institute of African Studies Research Report*, no. 277 (1975).

Krotki, Karal Jozef. "Political Statistics in the Sudan." In *Population of the Sudan: Report on the Sixth Annual Conference of the Philosophical Society of the Sudan, 1958. Sudan Notes and Records,* vol. 40 (1958).

Legum, Colin. Introduction to *The Sudan: Crossroad of Africa*, by Beshir Mohammed Said. Chester Springs, Va.: Dufour Editions, 1965.

Mazrui, Ali A. "The Monarchical Tendency in African Political Cultures." *British Journal of Sociology*, vol. 18, no. 3 (September 1967).

———. "Violent Contiguity and the Politics of Retribalization in Africa." *Journal of International Affairs*, vol. 23, no. 1 (1969).

Modelski, George. "The International Relations of Internal War." Research Monograph no. 11. Center of International Studies, Woodrow Wilson School of Public and International Affairs. Princeton: Princeton University Press, May 1961.

Morrison, Donald G., and Stevenson, Hugh. "Integration and Instability: Patterns of African Political Development." *American Political Science Review*, vol. 66, no. 3 (September 1972).

Niblock, Timothy C. "A New Political System in the Sudan." *African Affairs,* vol. 73, no. 293 (October 1974).

Nye, Joseph P. "Corruption and Political Development: A Cost-Benefit Analysis." *American Political Science Review*, vol. 11, no. 2 (June 1967).

Parsons, Talcott. "An Outline of the Social System." In *Theories of Society*. Edited by Talcott Parsons, Edward Shils, Kaspar D. Naegele, and Jesse R. Pitts. New York: The Free Press of Glencoe, 1961.

Pickering, A. K., and Glentworth, G. W. *Development Administration and Training in the Sudan: Report of a Mission to the Sudan, March–June 1974*. Birmingham, England: Development Administrative Group, Institute of Local Government Studies, University of Birmingham, 1974.

Pratt, Crawford R. "The Politics of Indirect Rule: Uganda, 1900–1955." In *Buganda and British Overrule*. Edited by D. Anthony Low and C. R. Pratt. Oxford: Oxford University Press, 1960.

Report of the Commission on Coordination Between the Central and Local Government. Khartoum, 1971.

Report of the Commission of Inquiry into the Disturbances in the Southern Sudan During August 1955. Khartoum: McCorquedale, 1956.

Report of the Joint Military Commission. Khartoum: Government Printing Press, October 1972.

Report of the Sudan Administration Conference. Governor's Palace, Khartoum, 23 April 1946.

Report of the Work of the Constitutional Amendment Commission. Khartoum: McCorquedale, 1952.

Rothchild, Donald. "Ethnicity and Conflict Resolution." *World Politics,* vol. 22, no. 4 (1970).

Rubin, Vera. "Social and Cultural Pluralism in the Caribbean." *Annals of the New York Academy of Sciences*, vol. 83, art. 5 (1960).

Russell, Peter, and McCall, Storrs. "Can Secession Be Justified? The Case of the Southern Sudan." In *The Southern Sudan: The Problem of National Integration*. Edited by Dunstan M. Wai. London: Frank Cass, 1973.

Sharma, B. S. "Elections in the Sudan During the Military Regime." *Parliamentary Affairs*, vol. 10, no. 3 (Summer 1967).

———. "Failure of 'Local Government Democracy' in the Sudan." *Political Studies*, vol. 15 (1967).

Sklar, Richard L. "Political Science and National Integration: A Radical Approach." *Journal of Modern African Studies*, vol. 5, no. 1 (May 1967).

Sohn, Louis B. "The Role of the U.N. in Civil War." *American Society of International Law Proceedings*, 57 (1963).

Southern Front Party. *Documents on the Southern Problem Compiled by the Southern Front Party*. Khartoum: Southern Front Party, 1965.

Stein, Michael B. "Federal Political System of Federal Societies." *World Politics*, vol. 20, no. 4 (July 1968).

Sudan Information News Agency. *Documents on the Round Table Conference on the Southern Sudan*. Khartoum: Sudan Information News Agency, 1965.

Toynbee, Arnold. "Interview." *Playboy*, 1965.

Van den Berghe, Pierre L. "Ethnicity: The African Experience." *International Social Science Journal*, vol. 23, no. 4 (April 1971).

Wai, Dunstan M. "Civilian-Military Regimes and the Crisis of Political Participation in the Sudan." In *Political Change and Political Participation in Africa*. Edited by Dunstan M. Wai. Forthcoming.

———. "Political Trends in the Sudan and the Future of the South." In *The Southern Sudan: The Problem of National Integration*. Edited by Dunstan M. Wai. London: Frank Cass, 1973.

Wallerstein, Immanuel. "Ethnicity and National Integration in West Africa." In *Governing in Black Africa: Perspectives on New States*. Edited by M. E. Doro and N. M. Stultz. Englewood Cliffs, N.J.: Prentice-Hall, 1970.

Weiner, Myron. "Political Integration and Political Development." *The Annals of the American Academy of Political and Social Science*, vol. 358, no. 2 (March 1965).

West, Richard. "The Accusing Face of Biafra." *Sunday Times* (London), 1 June 1969.

Wyld, J. W. A. "The Zande Scheme." *Sudan Notes and Records*, vol. 30 (1949).

Miscellaneous Sources

Alier, Abel. Speech on occasion of National United Day celebrations. Juba, 2 March 1973. (Mimeographed.)

el-Azhari, Sayed Ismael, President of the National Unionist Party. Address to the Round Table Conference on the Problem of the Southern Sudan. 16 March 1965.

Beshir, Mohammed Omer. "The Southern Sudan." Khartoum: Khartoum University Press, 1972. (Pamphlet.)

Deutsch, Karl W. "Peace, Research: The Need, the Problems, and the Prospects." John Hamilton Fulton Memorial Lecture. Middlebury College, Vt., 26 April 1972. (Mimeographed.)

Evans-Pritchard, E. Evans. "Ethnographic Survey of the Sudan." Oxford University. (Mimeographed.)

Government of Kenya. Sessional Paper no. 10. Nairobi: Government Printers, 1965.

Government of the Sudan. *The Missionary Societies Act*. Khartoum: Government Printing Office, 1962.

Grundy, Kenneth W. "Segmented Instability: An Exploration of the Problems of Comparative Analysis." (Unpublished paper.)

Jaden, Aggrey. Speech at Khartoum Conference on the Southern Sudan. Khartoum, March 1965. (Mimeographed.)

Khartoum, Ministry of Information and Culture. *Facts About the Sudan*. Khartoum, 1973.

Loiria, Angelo L. "Political Awakening in the Southern Sudan 1946–1955: Decolonization and the Problem of National Integration." Ph.D dissertation, University of California at Los Angeles, 1969.

Marquis of Reading. Interview. *East Africa and Rhodesia* (10 November 1955).

McLoughlin, P. M. "Economic Development and the Heritage of Slavery in the Sudan." (Mimeographed.)

Nyerere, J. K. "The Nigerian/Biafra Crisis." Memorandum. Dar es Salaam, 4 September 1969.

Sarkesian, Sam C. "The Southern Sudan: A Reassessment." Paper presented at the African Studies Association Annual Meeting. Philadelphia, Pa., 8–11 November 1972.

Sudan Government Gazette. No. 731 (1964).

U. S. Department of State. *U.S. Aid: Economic, Military, and Other, Prior to 1967, to the Republic of the Sudan*. Unclassified material, 1976.

Index

Abboud, Ibrahim, 75, 76, 80-83, 85-95, 97, 110, 139, 184-85
Abdallah, Mohammed Idris, 94
Abdullah, Bushra, 191
Abdullah, Mohammad Ahmed ibn, 30
Abdullah, Mohieddin Ahmed, 81, 82
Abdulla, Mohieddim al-Din, 185
Abdullahi, Khalifa, 31, 33
Abyssinia, 26
Acholis, 17, 130
Adam, Abdulla Mohammed, 188
Addis Ababa Agreement on the Problem of South Sudan, 11-12, 157-62, 165, 169, 172, 173, 174, 179
Adier, Job, 154
Advisory Council for the Southern Sudan, 42, 43
Adwok, Luigi, 74, 106
African-Arab schism, 15-25
 communal cleavages in, 15-24
 conclusion on, 24-25
 physical setting of, 15
African Medical Research Foundation International, 170
Agar, 17
Ahmed, Mohammed el Baghir, 154
Ajak, Luath, 43
Al-Abbas, 21
Algeria, 134, 137
Ali, Mohammad, 26, 27
Aliab Dinka, 33. *See also* Dinka
Alien Refugees Ordinance, 130
Alier, Abel, 118, 144-45, 146, 148, 149, 150, 152, 154-57, 160, 161, 163, 164, 171, 173, 174, 180
All African Council of Churches (AACC) 142-44, 149-58, 162, 165
Amarar, 22
Amin, Idi, 164
Anba el Sudan (Anab), 86
Anglican Church, 143
Anglo-Egyptian Agreement of 1953, 47, 99
Anglo-Egyptian rule, 47, 99
 Condominium regime, 33, 44-47, 69, 182-83
 imperialism of, 33-35, 64-68
Animal domestication, 18
Ankrah, Kodwo, 154
Ansar Insurrection, 188
Ansar Sect, 30, 48, 50, 74, 115, 121, 149, 188
Anti-Imperialist Front Party, 62-64, 73
Anuak, 17
 resistance of, 33
Anya-Nya forces, 91, 92, 93, 96, 109-12, 114, 118, 120, 132, 136-40, 143, 145, 146, 149, 150, 151, 153, 155, 157, 159, 160, 162, 163, 164, 170, 171, 179-80, 184
Arab culture:
 and ethnic groups, 21-24
 language, 23, 41, 89, 92
 as prejudice, 52
 and slave trade, 28, 29
 and Sudan, 19-20, 23
Arab League, 126, 127, 132-35, 161, 165
Ashigga Party, 48
Assistant District Commissioner (ADC), 58, 59, 60
Assistant Provisional Commissioner (APC), 172
Association of Southern Intellectuals, 163
Atta, Hashim el-, 189
Australia, 176
Avungara clans, 19
 and administration, 60
 and slave trade, 29
Azande, 17, 60
 economy of, 19
 language of, 62
 resistance of, 33, 62
Azanian Liberation Front (ALF), 111, 112
Azhari, Ismael el-, 50, 51, 55-56, 69, 72, 73, 75, 76, 82, 108, 117-20

Badri, Ibrahim Yusif, 48
Baggara Arabs, 21, 48

Bagu, Henry, 157
Bahr el Ghazal province, 17, 112, 113
Baka, 17
Baker, Samuel, 28
Bakheit, Gaafar Ali, 152
Bakr and political parties, 48
Banda, Kamuzu, 138
Bangasu, 60
Bar Association, 72, 117
Bari, 17
  language of, 35
  resistance of, 33
Barta, 22
Barum, 22
Bedeiriya tribes, 21
Beigo, 22
Beir, 17
Beja, 21, 22, 116
  and Arabs, 23
  political demands of, 74–75
Belgium, 33, 34, 51
Beni Amer, 22
Beni Rashid, 21
Benja Congress, 108
Berti, 22
Beshir, Hassan, 186
Biafra, 5, 7, 126, 133, 135, 139, 140, 162, 165
Birch, A.H., 176
Biri, 17
Bisharin, 22
Boma Murle, 17
Bongo, 17
Bor, 17
Bor Belanda, 17
Botswana, 129
Boxall Company, 89
Britain:
  Advisory Council, 37–38
  appraised, 51–52
  and Egypt occupation, 33-35, 44–47, 64–68, 182–83
  imperial regime of, 1
  and regional autonomy-decolonization, 41–47
  resistance to imperialism from, 33-36
  and self-determination, 1-2, 68–69, 70
  and Southern Sudan, 9, 29-30, 35–41
  and Sudan War, 136, 139
British East Africa, 35, 67
British Royal Air Force, 65, 136
Burundi, 129
Butt, Audrey, 17
Bwogo, Samuel, 154

Cameroons, 8, 128, 129
Canada, federalism in, 176
Caritas Catholic International Charity Organization, 138
Carr, Canon Burgess, 154, 157
Catholics, 143. *See also* Christianity
  and Arab hegemony, 87
  and Sudan, 138
  in Uganda, 132
Central African Republic, 129, 170
Central Sudan Parliament, 100
Chadians, Moslem, 7, 128, 132, 137, 161
China and Sudan War, 137
Christianity. *See also* Catholics
  and African elite, 19
  and Arab military hegemony, 85
  and Islam, 36, 86–89, 96, 117
  missionaries of, 34, 36
Church Missionary Society, 143
Cic, 17
Civil Service Administration, 187
Collins, Robert O., 30, 86, 89, 93–94, 114
Colonial interregnum in Sudan:
  Anglo-Egyptian imperial occupation, 33–35
  and decolonization-self-government preparation, 41–47
  and elections-transfer of power, 47–51
  pax Britannica appraised, 51–52
  Southern policy, 35–41
    abandonment of, 39–41
Colonial Southern Policy, 35
Commission of Inquiry Report, 78–79
Communist Front, 62. *See also* Sudan Communist Party
Communist Party. *See* Sudan Communist Party
Communist Party Dissolution Act of 1965, 116
Condominium Agreement, 33, 44–47, 69, 182–83
Congo, 33, 131, 132, 135
Constituent Assembly, 71, 97, 108, 116, 117, 118
Constitutions:
  ALF, 111
  Amendment Commission, 45
  Federal, rejected, 70–72
  Interim, 97, 106, 116
  Islamic, 118–19
  Transitional, 70
Council of Ministers, 81, 88, 100
Culture and colonialism, 35–36
Czechoslovakia, 135

Dafallah, El Nazir, 98, 99
Dahomey, 129
Daju, 22
Dangala Arabs, 20, 21
Darfur, 22, 108
Declaration of Independence, Sudanese, 68–70
Declaration of Regional Autonomy for the Southern Provinces, 147
Defense of the Sudan Act of 1958, 87

Dembo, Shatt, 17
Democratic Republic of the Sudan, 15
Democratic Unionist Party (DUP), 120
Deng, Francis, 18
Deng, Santino, 114
Deng, William, 90, 91, 92, 98, 99, 100, 111, 115, 120
Department of Religious Affairs, 85-86
Dhol, Camillo, 113
Didinga, 17
Din, Mohieddin al-, 185
Dinka, 17, 157
  cultural traits of, 18
  language of, 35
  political power of, 19, 113
  resistance of, 33, 34
  and slave trade, 29
  and Turks, 31
District Commissioner (DC), 58
Diu, Buth, 55, 114-15
Dogale, Paulino, 87
Domjiro, 17
Dongolaw, 31

Education:
  Islamic, compulsory, 90
  and language, 38, 41
Effendi courtesy title, 41
Egypt, 76, 133, 134, 147, 163, 181, 188
  and Anglo occupation, 33-35, 44-47, 64-68, 182-83
  and British negotiations, 44
  and Condominium agreement, 44-47, 182-83
  and ideology, 116
  and Nile Valley, 51
  and self-determination, 69, 70
  Sudan ambitions of, 26-32, 38, 40, 74
  and Sudanese parties, 50-52
  and Sudan War, 136, 137
Election Law of 1973, 172
Elections, 179-80
  and transfer of power, 47-51
El Fatah, 132
Elites:
  and authenticity, 2-3
  and cultural conflict, 5, 9
Equatoria Corps, 184
Equatoria Projects Board (EPB), 63
Equatoria region, 59-62, 66, 109, 112, 113, 114, 157
Eritrean Liberation Front (ELF), 132
Eritreans, 7, 128, 132, 135, 137, 157. *See also* Ethiopia
Ethiopia, 132, 136, 151, 153, 154, 156, 160, 161, 170. *See also* Eritreans
Ethnicity, 17-20
  and civil ties, 4
  and colonial policy, 35
  consciousness of, 4
  and culture, 21-24
  and elections, 50-51
  and elites, 2-3
  and liberation movement, 110-11
  and religion, 118-19
Exogamy, 18

Fabian Colonial Bureau of London, 40
Factionalization in African politics, 3
Federalism, future of, 174-79
Ferguson, Vere, 34
Feroge, 17
Fertit (Mandala), 17
Five-Year Development Plan, 147
France, 33, 51
Free Officers Organization, 187
Frustration and aggression, 6
Fulani, 5
Fur, 22, 23, 116

Gabon, 129
Gambia, 129
Garang, Franco, 74
Garang, Joseph, 144-45, 146, 148, 149, 152, 163
Garang, Mading de, 149, 151, 153-57
Gatkwoth, Peter, 149, 156
Gellaba, 43
Gessi, Romolo, 29
Gezira, 21
Giirdit, Chief, 31
Gima, 21
Gimr, 22
Gordon Memorial College, 41, 46
Gray, Richard, 28
Gubid, 22
Guhayna Arabs, 21
Guinea, 129

Habaniya, 21
Hadendowa, 22
  and political parties, 48
Hadi, Iman el-, 115, 117, 119, 120, 121, 148, 188
Hadramut, 21
Haj, Magboul el-Amin el-, 81
Halawin, 21
Hamadallah, Farouk Osman, 187, 189
Hamar, 21
Harlow, Vincent, 45
Hassan, Khalid, 186, 187
Hassaniya, 21
Hausa, 5
Hawara, 21
Heiban, 22
Helm, Knox, 67, 69
High Executive Council (HEC), 158, 159, 169-74, 180
Hindi, Sharif Hussain el-, 191
House of Representatives:

failure of, 72–77
and independence, 68–70
representativeness of, 49–50
Humr, 21
Huntington, 175
Husaynat, 21

Ibo, 5
Ideology and national interest, 9, 116
Idris, Abdel Rahman, 191
Independence Resolution of 1955, 99, 100
Inflation, 75, 187
Ingessana tribes, 22, 23
Institutional approach and federalism, 176
International Agency for Cooperation in Development, 170
International Convention on Refugees, 130
International Organization for Rural Development (IORD), 170
International Red Cross, 68, 138
International University Exchange Fund, 170
Islam, 23, 184
and Arab military hegemony, 85–90, 95–96
British policy on, 41
and Christianity, 36, 86–89, 96, 117
and culture, 20
Democratic Republic of, 73
Institutes of, 86–87
and law, 19
and slave trade, 29
and Southern Sudan, 36
Islamic Charter Front, 99, 108, 115, 116, 190. *See also* Moslem Brotherhood
Ismailite tribes, 20–21
Israel:
and Southern Sudan, 139
and Uganda, 164
Ivory trade, 27, 28

Jaal, Ibrahim, 21
Ja'aliyin Arabs, 20, 21
Jaden, Aggrey, 16, 92, 98, 99, 111, 112, 113
Jamala, 21
Jatala, 22
Jellaba, 21
Jiye, 17
Joint Military Commission, 171
Juba, 63, 67, 82, 99
Conference, 42, 43, 44, 57, 58
Juhani, Abdullah al-, 21
Jur (Jo Luv), 17

Kababish, 21, 48
Kadugli, 22
Kakwa, 17
Katanga, 162
Kawahla, 21
Kawka, 130
Keiga-Girru, 22
Kenya, 66, 113, 129, 136, 143, 153, 154, 160
Khalid, Mansour, 157, 161
Khalifa, el Katim el, 98, 99, 105, 106
Khalil, Abdullah Bey, 73, 75, 76, 77, 81, 82, 184, 185
Khartoum Round Table Conference, 98, 107, 109, 110, 111
Khartoum University, 94, 98, 190, 191
Khatmiyya, 48, 50, 74, 76, 84, 115
Khatmiyyah tariga, 49
Kinshasa, 132
Kitchener, General, 33
Koalib, 22
Kordofan, 26
Korobat, 21
Kosti affair, 72–73
Krotki, Karal J., 49
Kuru, 17
Kurqusawi, Karamallah, 31
Kuze, Elia, 59–64, 77
Kwanai, George, 111

Lagu, Joseph, 114, 149, 153, 155, 156, 160, 161, 171
Lake Albert Dam, 39
Lake Victoria, 15
Lango, 17
Language, 17, 35, 62
and colonialism, 35–36
and culture, 23, 41, 89, 92
in education, 38, 41
and government advancement, 89
and military, 92
recognition, 35
Lappanya, Chief, 43
Latim, Alexander, 131
Latuko, 17
Legislative Assembly Ordinance of 1948 44, 45
Legum, Colin, 16
Leopold of Belgium, 33
Lesotho, 129
Liberal Party, 49, 55–58, 60, 62, 65, 67, 71, 73, 74, 114
Libya, 134, 147, 163, 188, 190, 191
Logit, 17
Lohure, Saturnino, 74, 90, 91, 92, 112, 132
Lokoya, 17
Lolik Lado, Chief, 43
Luce, 66
Lugbara, 130
Luluba, 17
Lupe, Elia, 111
Lwoke, Benjamin, 55

McLoughlin, Peter, 37
MacMichael, Harold, 20, 35
Madi, 17, 130
language of, 35
Madison, James, 177

Maghrib, 20
Mahdi, Sadiq el-, 115, 117–21, 143, 191
Mahdi, Sayed Saliq el, 24
Mahdi, Sayeid al-, 48, 49, 50
Mahdi family, 39
Mahdists, 30–33, 48, 75, 86, 148
Mahdiyyah religious brotherhood, 108
Mahgoub, Abdel Khaliq, 82, 115, 117, 118, 119
Mahgoub, Mohammed Ahmed, 69, 70, 72, 82, 108, 109, 110, 119, 120
Majok, Philemon, 114, 115
Makerere University, 41, 145, 146
Malakal, 63
Malawi, 138
Manasir, 21
Mansur, Az-Zubair Rahman, 29
Marshall Plan, 171
Masalit, 22
Mayen, Gordon M., 113
Mayom, Elijah, 74
May Revolutionary Council, 144
Mboro, Clement, 105, 106, 111
Measures of Constitutional Reforms in the Sudan, 45
Mecca, pilgrimage to, 23
Mesiriya, 21
Messellimiya, 21
Middleton, John, 18
Military, 65, 80–96, 136
  Abboud and Southern Sudan, 85–93
  and civilian coup, 93–95
  conclusion on, 95–96
  future of, 171–74
  government structure/divisions within, 80–82
  legitimacy in, 82–84
Ministry of Education, 86, 97
Ministry of Southern Affairs, 46
Mirghani, Sayeid Ali al-, 49
Mirifab, 21
Miscengenation, racial, 20
Missionary Societies Act of 1962, 87–88, 143
Modelski, George, 126
Modernization process, 175
Mondira, Ezibon, 105, 111
Moru, 17, 35
Moruland, 113
Moslem Brotherhood, 98, 186, 189, 191. *See also* Islamic Charter Front
Mula, Elisapana, 154
Mundari, 17
Mundo, 17
Murle Group, 17

Nasr, Hassan Beshir, 75, 76, 81, 94, 185
Nasser, 116, 134
National Assembly, 186
National Constitutional Committee, 70–71
National Front Party (NFP), 48–49, 94, 190, 191
National identity, 4
Nationalism in Third World, 37
National Unionist Party (NUP), 48, 50, 51, 56–57, 62, 65, 98, 99, 108, 115, 116, 117, 119, 120
  and independence, 68, 71, 73
  and military, 81, 83–84
  and parliamentary failures, 75, 76
  and Umma Party, 110
Nawai, Abdel Rahman Shahi, 191
Ndogo, 17
  language of, 35
Negroid peoples of Southern Sudan, 35
  and Arabs, 8
  customs of, 35–36
  ethnic schisms in, 17–20
  and prejudice, 52
Nequib, Mohammed, 46
Netherlands, 136, 170
Ngok, 17
Niger, 129
Nigeria, 4, 5, 6, 126, 135
Niilus, Leopoldo, 154
Nile Provisional Government (NPG), 113, 114, 145
Nile Valley, 1
  economic significance of, 51
  unity movement for, 46
Nile Waters Agreement, 84
Nilo-Hamitic group, 17–19
  cultural traits of, 17–19
Nilotes, 17, 18
Nimiery, Gaafar Mohammed el-, 121, 135, 144–49, 154, 155, 160–65, 169, 171, 173, 174, 180, 187–91
Northern Camel Corps, 67
Northern Sudan, 8, 16, 126
  administrators in, 57–62
  Anglo-Egyptian occupation of, 33–35
  Arab culture in, 19–24
  Army, 65, 136
  chronology on, 184–91
  conclusions on, 181–83, 192
  and decolonization, 41–47
  elections in, 47–51
  failure of, 169–80
  Graduate Congress, 38
  military dictatorship in, 80–96
  Ottoman hegemony in, 26
  and secessionist movement, 9, 10, 11
  and Southern Sudan, 36–41, 43–44, 64–68, 78–79, 109–10
  and Sudanization, 55–57, 68–72
  and Turko-Egyptian forces, 31–32
Norway, 138, 170
Norwegian Refugee Council, 170
Nuba, 15, 22, 23, 75, 116

Nuba Independents, 108
Nubians, 21, 22, 23, 26
Nuer, 17
language of, 35
political power in, 19
resistance of, 33, 34
and slave trade, 29
Nur, Babiker el, 187, 189
Nyaka, Chief, 60
Nyangwara, 17
Nyepo, 17
Nyerere, Julius K., 133
Nzara riots, 62–64

Obote, Milton, 130–33, 164
October Revolution, 95
Oduhu, Joseph, 90, 91, 92, 111, 112, 132
Organization of African Unity (OAU), 10, 90, 102, 125, 127–28, 133, 138, 141, 152, 157, 161, 165
Othman, Hasan Hussain, 191
Owen, Richard, 40, 42

Pakistan and Sudan War, 136
Palmer, Jr., Joseph, 135
Pari, 17
Parliament, Sudanese, 47, 121
failures of, 72–77
and independence, 68–70
Pasha, Ismail, 28, 29
Passports and Permits Ordinance of 1922, 34
Paysama, Stanislaus, 55, 114
Peace Commission, 101
Pedak, Philip, 92
Peoples Democratic Party, 48, 71, 73–76, 81, 84, 99, 107, 108, 115, 118, 120
People's Local Government, 172
People's Regional Assembly, 158, 159, 173
Plebiscite, 104, 118
Pluralism, cultural, 3–8
Pojulu, 17
Political parties, 47–51
Precolonial period, 26–32
conclusion on, 32
and Mahidiyyah and South, 30–32
and Turks, 26–30
Professional Front, 99
Province Authority, 88
Provisional Commissioners, 172
Provisional High Executive Council, 169, 170

Qursh tribes, 21

Racial consciousness, 4. *See also* Ethnicity
Rahim, Abdal Rahman Abdal el-, 73
Rai el Amm, 86
Railway Workers' Union, 48
Rashaida, 21
Reading, Marquis of, 68
Realist School and federalism, 176–77
Regional Executive Council, 101
Regional Government, 104
Regional Police and Prison forces, 171
Reizeigat, 21
Religion. *See* Catholics; Christianity; Islam; World Council of Churches
Renzi, Basia, Chief, 58
Resettlement, Relief, and Rehabilitation Commission, 170
Reth, power of, 19
Riker, 176–77
Riots, Nzaran, 62–64
Robertson, James W., 39, 40, 43
Roman Catholic Church. *See* Catholics
Round Table Conference, 115, 117–18
Rubatab, 21
Rufa, 21
Rume, Marko, 90, 91
Rwanda, 129

Saad, Mohammed Nour, 191
Salam, Mohammed al-Sayyid, 73
Salim, 27, 29
Sarkesian, Sam C., 110
Saudi Arabia, 134, 181
Secession, political, defined, 3
Selassie, Haile, 132, 157, 165
Seleim, 21
Self-determination, 68–69, 70, 128, 129
and British policy, 1–2
and communal conflict, 7–8
rights of, 103, 118
and violence, 8
Self-Government Statute, 45, 47
Senate, failure of, 72–77
Senegal, 129
Senghor, 161
Sennar, 26
Sere, 17
Shaiqiya, 21
Sheikh, role of, 22
Shenan, Mohammed, 189
Shenan, Abdal-Kalhim, 185
Shenan, Abdal Rahim, 81, 82, 189
Shibly, Amin el, 117
Shilluk, 17, 19, 33, 35
Shilluk Luo (Dembo, Shatt), 17
Shukriya, 21
Simba rebels, 110
Six-Day War, 139
Slave trade, 26–29, 34, 36–37
Smith, M.G., 3
Socialist Republican Party, 48
Sokoto Empire, 5–6
South African National Union (SANU), 90, 98, 99, 100, 111, 115, 118, 120
Southern Equatorial Corps, 136
Southern Front Party, 99, 100, 118, 145, 157
Southern House of Parliament, 100
Southern Liberation Movement, 171

Southern Negroid Africans, 5
Southern Party, 49, 55. *See also* Liberal Party
Southern Political Association, 49
Southern Provinces Regional Self-Government Act of 1972, 160, 169
Southern Sudan, 8–11, 30–32, 97–122
  administrators in, 57–62
  Arab hegemony in, 21, 80–96
  and Britain, 9, 29–30, 35–41
  chronology on, 184–91
  coalition government in, 109–10
  and colonial policy, 35–41
  conclusions on, 122, 181–83, 192
  decolonization in, 41–47
  elections in, 47–51
  ethnicity in, 16–20
  external aid for, 136–40
  future of, 169–80
  geographical sectors of, 15, 17, 27
  Khartoum Conference on, 88–105
  liberation movement of, 110–15
  Mahdist period in, 31
  and Northern Sudan, 36, 43–44, 64–68, 78–79, 109–10
  and independent African countries, 129
  political change in, 1–12
  politicians' failure in, 115–21
  regional autonomy for, 144–49
  religious rivalry in, 36
  resistance to imperialism, 33–35
  seccessionist movement of, 130, 132
  slave trade in, 27–28
  and Sudanization, 55–57, 68–72
  transitional government for, 97–98, 105–108
  and Turko-Egyptian forces, 30, 31–32
Southern Sudanese Corps, 64–68, 91, 184
Southern Sudan Intellectuals Association, 147
Southern Sudan Liberation Movement (SSLM), 114, 149, 151, 152, 163, 164, 165
Southern Sudan Provisional Government (SSPG), 112, 113, 114
Southern Youth and Students Organization, 147
Soviet Union, 148, 163
  and Sudan War, 134–39
Steiner, Rolf, 138
Stereotypes, cultural, 4
Stigand, Chancery, 34
Strike, labor, 94
Student Executive Committee, 87
Sudan Administrative Conference, 39–41, 42, 44
Sudan African Closed Districts National Union (SACDNU), 90, 91–92
Sudan African Liberation Front (SALF), 111
Sudan Bar Association, 72, 117
Sudan Communist Party (SCP), 48, 73, 84, 94, 99, 108, 115–17, 135, 144, 148, 149, 188–89
Sudan Council of Churches, 150, 151, 154
Sudanese Nationalist Movement, 47–48
Sudan Federation of Trade Unions, 48
Sudanization Committee report, 55–57
Sudan Penal Code, 60
Sudan Socialist Party (SSP), 117
Sudan Socialist Union (SSU), 172, 173, 179
Sudan Unity Party, 114
Sudan War, 134–37, 139, 140
Suez Canal, 51, 139
Suleiman, 29
Supreme Council of the Armed Forces, 70, 81, 95
Switzerland, 136, 176
Syria, 163

Ta'aisha, 21
Taffeng, Emidio, 113
Tait, David, 18
Talodi, 22
Tama, 22
Tanzania, 133, 164
Tegali, 22
Teis-um-Danab, 22
Tembura Rural Council, 58, 59
Temein, 22
Tenants and Workers Party Front, 108
Tete, Chief, 43
Third World nationalism, 37
Titherington, 29
Togoland, 8, 128, 129
Tom, Mohammed Mahmoud el-, 191
Tombalbye, 137
Toposa (Topotha), 17, 19
Toynbee, Arnold, 24
Trade and colonial policy, 34–35
Tripoli Agreement, 147
Tumtum, 22
Tunisia, 129
Turabi, Hassan el-, 115
Turkey, 26–32

Uduk, 22
Uganda, 90, 91, 112, 129–33, 136, 153, 160, 164, 170
Uganda Parliamentary Opposition Party, 131, 132
Umma Opposition Party, 48, 50, 68, 71–76, 81, 83, 98, 99, 108, 110, 115–18, 120, 121, 190
Unionist Party, 48
United National Front, 84, 95, 97, 105, 107
United Nations, 141
  Development Program, 171
  High Commission for Refugees (UNHCR), 170–71
  Security Council, 126
  and Sudanese unification, 68–69

Universal Declaration on Human Rights, 102
Unity of the Nile Valley Party, 48
Upper Nile region, 112–13

Values:
and communal cleavages, 16
conflict in, 4–5
preservation of, 4
Violence:
psychological factors in, 6–7
and self-determination, 8

Wahab, Ahmed Abdah al-, 75, 76, 81, 185
Wau, 63
Weiner, Myron, 174
West, Richard, 129
West Germany and Sudan War, 136
Wheare, K.S., 176
White Nile, 29
Wol, Ambrose, 105
Wol Wol, Lawrence, 149, 153–57
Women, status of in Arab culture, 21–22
Workers' Syndicates Union, 73
World Bank, 171
World Council of Churches (WCC), 10, 138, 141–66, 170
and AACC, 142–44
and Addis Ababa Agreement, 157–62
Commission on the Churches of International Affairs, 143, 149–58, 162, 165
and Nimiery regime, 144–49, 154

Yambio District, 63
Yassin, Sayyid Ahmad Mohammad, 93
Yemen, 21
Yoruba, 5
Yugoslavia and Sudan War, 135, 136

Zaghawa, 22
Zaire, 131, 136, 137, 153, 156, 160, 170
Zande, 35
Zandeland, 62–64, 113
Zaroug, Sayed Mubarak, 82
Zarrug, Hassan al-Tahir, 73
Zebaydiya Arabs, 21
Zeribas network, 27
Zubair, 29